Birds of Texas

Number Fourteen:
The W. L. Moody, Jr., Natural History Series

A FIELD GUIDE

John H. Rappole and Gene W. Blacklock

Texas A&M University Press
College Station

BIRDS
of TEXAS

Library of Congress Cataloging-in-Publication Data

Rappole, John H.
  Birds of Texas : a field guide / John H. Rappole and Gene W. Blacklock. — 1st ed.
    p.   cm. — (The W.L. Moody, Jr., natural history series : no. 14)
  Includes bibliographical references (p.   ) and index.
  ISBN 0-89096-544-7. — ISBN 0-89096-545-5 (pbk.)
  1. Birds—Texas.   2. Birds—Texas—Identification.   I. Blacklock, Gene W.   II. Title.   III. Series.
QL684.T4R365   1994
598.29764—dc20   93-8448
                                                                           CIP

Dedicated with love and respect to
Francesca Goodell Rappole, Albertus Whitney Rappole,
Van R. Blacklock, and Eva L. Blacklock

Contents

ILLUSTRATIONS

PREFACE

Why? Why should you own a field guide to Texas birds? Aren't the numerous national guides enough? Yes, they are enough; more than sufficient if your goal is to log as many birds as possible from across the continent in as short a time as possible. However, if you want to develop some sense of what a particular bird is about within a relatively confined geographical area, the state guide is essential.

The purpose of a state guide is to give those necessary and particularly satisfying bits of information about a bird that make birding such a popular pastime. National guides don't have the space to tell you whether a Buff-breasted Sandpiper is likely to be on a stubble sorghum field in Kleberg County in August or not. Using a national guide, you'll be lucky to find mention of Texas, and for a migrant like the Buff-breasted, it won't help if you do, because there is little or no information on transient timing or migration routes. How could there be? Such information would require several volumes.

As a matter of fact, you *are* likely to see a small flock of Buffbreasts on a Kleberg County stubble field in late summer, and that raises a second important point about a state guide. Ludlow Griscom, renowned ornithologist and professional birdwatcher from the American Museum in New York, made a special trip to southern Texas in order to prove once and for all that Connie Hagar's Buff-breasted Sandpiper reports from Rockport were erroneous. Mrs. Hagar told him when to come and, when he arrived, took him out and showed the doyen of American birding more of that species than he had previously seen in his entire life. The point being that, no matter how good you are, you can only tell so much about a place by inference. Eventually you actually have to go there. With this guide, we save you some trouble by providing a handy summary of what is already known about Texas birds. The guide includes all of the information on plumage, voice, and behavior needed to identify the bird, while giving specific data on where and when the bird is likely to be found in the state, and in what kinds of habitats.

National guides are good. Some of them are very good, particularly for the novice who dreams of finding Phainopeplas in Buffalo. They have everything— serving as a stimulus to find strange birds or visit exotic places. But once in one of those exotic places, you need more precise information; a Baedeker to direct you to the right sections of it at the right times; or, alternatively, to indicate what to look for right where you are now.

The state guide can also serve to satisfy a more refined taste. The seasoned birder comes to recognize the singular beauties of a choice habitat, a habitat containing its own special set of inhabitants. Texas has many such choice habitats — obvious ones like the desert canyons of Big Bend and subtropical riparian areas of Santa Ana, and less obvious ones like Lost Maples State Park, the Audubon sabal palm grove, and Kleberg County stubble fields. With a key to time and place, you can find them. That is what this guide is all about.

ACKNOWLEDGMENTS

We thank Noel Parsons, editor-in-chief of Texas A&M University Press, for first suggesting that we undertake this project. Alan Tipton and Carol Altman provided help with computer graphics and word processing software. Greg W. Lasley was extremely helpful in providing up-to-date information on the status of species officially recognized by the Texas Bird Records Committee. Keith Arnold reviewed and made useful comments on two versions of the manuscript. Volunteers Sharon Bartels, Doris Harmonson, Doris Granberry, Lonnie Selby, Louis Cluiss, and Carolyn Wood assisted with careful review of many of the range maps.

We especially thank the director, Dr. Sam Beasom, and trustees of the Caesar Kleberg Wildlife Research Institute, and the director, Dr. Jim Teer, and trustees of the Welder Wildlife Foundation for providing funds toward the purchase of photos. Without their interest and assistance the work would not have been possible.

Several of the most outstanding wildlife photographers in North America donated slides for this venture, including Dr. W. A. Paff, Dr. Vernon E. Groves, and Dr. David W. Parmelee. Barth Schorre supplied 150 of his superb photos of small passerines. It was his donation that proved a major impetus toward initiation of the work. Roy Garrett was the artist of the seven drawings comparing various birds.

Finally, we thank Bonnie Rappole, who gave invaluable encouragement and support throughout the long history of the project.

BIRDS OF TEXAS

INTRODUCTION

The state of Texas encompasses 267,338 square miles of seacoast, forest, swamp, prairie, chaparral, mountains, and desert. Well over six hundred species of birds have been recorded from the state, and surely there are many others that visit on occasion, and are yet to be discovered. Of those recorded, 576 species have been officially accepted as part of the state's avifauna by the Texas Bird Records Committee (G. W. Lasley, *pers. comm.*), more species than in any other state in the Union. The rest are hypothetical — that is, they may be the result of "an undigested bit of beef" (Dickens 1843:22) or some more potent hallucinogen, or they may actually have been here.

Each species account begins with the species' common name in capital letters followed by the Latin name in italics. Nomenclature follows the sixth edition of the American Ornithologists' Union *Check-list of North American Birds* (1983) and supplements. The size of the bird is given in parentheses — L = length in inches: W = wingspread in inches. A description of the adult male breeding plumage follows. Other plumages are described where necessary. In most cases, the juvenile plumage (immediate postfledging period) is not described since an adult is usually in attendance. Immature (First Basic, that is, first winter after hatching), female, and other plumages are described when they differ significantly from that of the breeding male. The plumage description necessarily involves the use of a few arcane morphological terms. These areas of the bird are shown in figure 1. The book includes photographs of almost every species described, exceptions being birds recorded in Texas only hypothetically or accidentally. We feel that, while photos can be misleading in terms of plumage coloration, they capture an essence of the way the bird carries itself that is peculiar to that particular species, a quality that is very difficult to capture in a painting. In addition, photos often place the bird in a fairly typical environment.

Habits — This category was included only when we felt that some peculiarity of the bird's behavior would be useful in identifying the species, for example that it hangs upside down while foraging, or flicks its tail.

Voice — This section consists of a phonetic rendering of the call, which is normally given by both sexes at any time during the year, and, where appropriate, a description of the song, which is often given only by the male during the breeding season. More or less "typical" calls and songs are described based on field notes, recordings, or, where necessary, descriptions in the literature (author credited). It should be remembered that songs vary not only from one region

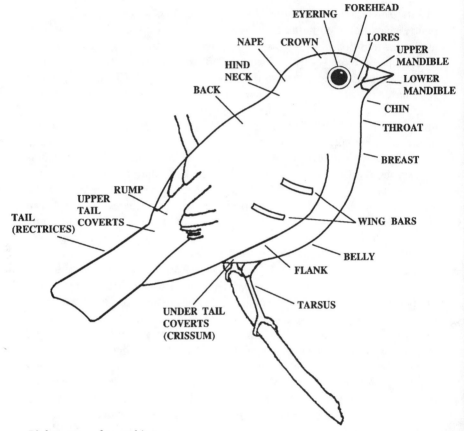

Bird parts as referenced in text

to the next but from one individual to the next. Also, one person's interpretation of what a call sounds like will differ from another's. To some people "chip" is "ship" or "tschip" or "slip."

Similar species—This category is omitted unless there is a bird that is very similar in size, pattern, and coloration. A person who can confuse a Yellow-breasted Chat with a Yellow-throated Vireo needs more experience in the field, not more help from the guide.

Habitat—We describe those habitats most often used by the bird in Texas and on its North American breeding grounds. No attempt is made to describe tropical habitats used by birds except in special cases, such as accidentals from the tropics. Transients are found in a variety of habitats in which they would not normally forage. We make no attempt to catalog all such habitats. A discussion of major Texas habitat types, their appearance, characteristics, and location in the state is provided below.

Texas—Here we address the abundance and principal time and place of occurrence for the bird in the state. The counties and major biogeographic divisions to which we refer are shown in figures 2 and 3. Normally only regular (common, uncommon, rare) occurrences of the bird within the state are noted, unless only a few records exist for the species anywhere in Texas. As an example, the Bay-breasted Warbler is a common spring transient in the eastern third and casual in the west. We note only the eastern status. All species that have been recorded as breeding in the state are marked with an asterisk (*) following a statement of their residency status.

The meanings of the abundance categories used are as follows:

Common—Ubiquitous in specified habitat; high probability of finding several individuals in a day.

Uncommon—Present in specified habitat; high probability of finding a few individuals in a day.

Rare—Scarce in specified habitat, with only a few records per season; low probability of finding the bird.

Casual—A few records per decade.

Accidental—Not expected to recur.

For more detailed distributional information see Oberholser (1974) and Texas Ornithological Society (1984) for statewide summaries, Rappole and Blacklock (1985) for the central coast, Pulich (1988) for the Dallas region, Seyffert (1985) for breeding birds in the Panhandle, and Wauer (1973) for the Big Bend. There are 256 counties, Anderson to Zavala, and each is outlined on the range maps.

Range—Total (world) range of the bird is provided in abbreviated form, based on information from the A.O.U. *Check-list,* sixth edition (1983), plus supplements. Throughout this book, "Middle America" refers to Mexico, Guatemala, Belize, El Salvador, Honduras, Costa Rica, Nicaragua, and Panama. "Central America" refers to the same region minus Mexico.

Texas counties (courtesy Texas Department of Transportation)

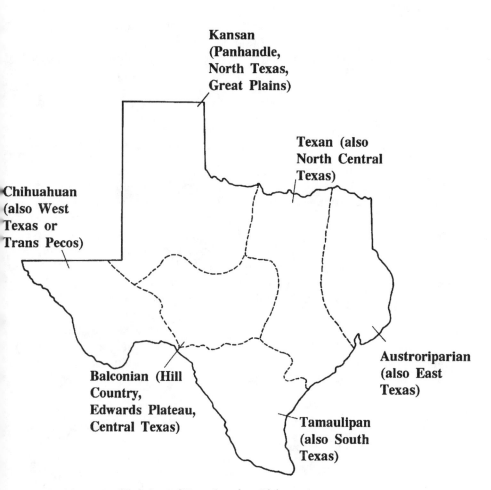

Kansan (Panhandle, North Texas, Great Plains)

Texan (also North Central Texas)

Chihuahuan (also West Texas or Trans Pecos)

Balconian (Hill Country, Edwards Plateau, Central Texas)

Austroriparian (also East Texas)

Tamaulipan (also South Texas)

Major biogeographic regions of Texas (based on Blair 1950)

Physiographic Regions

Texas is divided into four major physiographic regions: the coastal plain, central lowland, great plain, and basin and range. The coastal plain is a largely flat and featureless expanse in terms of topography, though there are some low, rolling hills in the western portions of the province. The Balcones Escarpment separates the coastal plain from the Edwards Plateau of Central Texas. This southern portion of the Great Plain Province is an ancient uplift. The central lowland is an area of low rolling plains, separated from the high plains by an uplift that runs along the eastern side of the Panhandle. The mountains of Texas are located in the basin and range region west of the Pecos River (that is, the Trans-Pecos), the highest of which is Guadalupe Peak (8,751 feet).

Texas Habitats

Texans are notorious for their "national" pride in things Texan. With regard to habitats, they have a strong case. There are dozens if not hundreds of significant habitats in the state, each with its own set of plant and animal species. We depict and discuss a few, simply as an illustration of the experiences that are available.

Birdwatching aficionados know that observing a wide variety of birds requires visiting a large number of different habitats; indeed this is a major allure of the pastime (Science? Sport? Hobby?). With a car in good condition, and a month or two to spare, you can chalk up quite a few distinctive Texas habitats and the birds that live in them. Oberholser (1974) goes into some detail on the climate, physiography, ecology, and location of Texas habitats. Kutac (1982) provides excellent, specific information on some of the best birding spots, and the birds that you can find at each. The regional bird books also provide information of this type (Wauer 1973, Rappole and Blacklock 1985, Pulich 1988).

Chihuahuan Desert
Cactus, yucca, and creosote bush dominate the landscape in the Chihuahuan Desert. This habitat is found mainly in the Trans-Pecos region of West Texas, but elements extend well into the Edwards Plateau and South Texas plains, where Hebbronville (Jim Hogg County) is justly famous as the easternmost locality for creosote bush on the continent. Characteristic birds include the Phainopepla, Elf Owl, Scott's Oriole, and Crissal Thrasher.

Montane Forest
Pinyon, juniper, and oak cover the lower elevations, with Douglas fir and ponderosa pine higher up. The mountains of the Trans-Pecos form the southeastern end of the Rocky Mountains, and contain isolated populations of birds typical

of the Rockies, including Steller's Jay, Acorn Woodpecker, and Mountain Chickadee, along with one species all their own, the rare Colima Warbler. Wauer's (1973) *Birds of the Big Bend National Park and Vicinity* provides a fine introduction to the region.

Thorn Forest

The northern half of the Tamaulipan Biotic Province covers South Texas from the Balcones Escarpment, just north of San Antonio, to the Mexican border. This region extends well into Mexico, nearly to the state of Veracruz. It is semiarid country dominated by dense stands of mesquite, spiny hackberry, lime prickly ash, brazil, and ebony. Larry McMurtry provides a not-too-flattering description of this country in his book, *Lonesome Dove*. But the avifauna is rich and varied, including mixtures of arid, mesic, and tropical species. Typical birds are the Long-billed Thrasher, Kiskadee, Olive Sparrow, Brown-crested Flycatcher, Hooded Oriole, Groove-billed Ani, and Pauraque.

Prairie

Vast areas of Texas were once prairie; several different kinds of prairie, from the high, shortgrass prairie of the staked plains in the northwestern Panhandle to the mid- and tallgrass prairies of north-central Texas and the coastal plain. Few native pieces remain, and those species apparently dependent on relatively natural prairie, like the Greater and Lesser Prairie-Chickens, have almost disappeared. However, many prairie species are able to survive in the pastures and croplands that have replaced the native grasslands: Dickcissel, Burrowing Owl, Scissor-tailed Flycatcher, White-tailed Hawk, Swainson's Hawk, Long billed Curlew, and Sandhill Crane.

Eastern Hardwoods

Trees and other plants characteristic of the moist bottomlands of the eastern United States are found in East Texas and south and west to the San Antonio and Guadalupe river systems. American elm, sycamore, green ash, box elder, and sweet gum communities harbor birds of the eastern deciduous forest biome: Pileated Woodpecker, Hairy Woodpecker, White-breasted Nuthatch, Carolina Chickadee, Chuck-will's-widow, and Kentucky Warbler.

Southern Bayous

Most people do not associate the backwater swamps typical of the coastal plain in the southeastern United States with Texas, but a portion of that habitat is found in East Texas, with plant and animal species typical of this environment extending as far south and west as Calhoun County. The cypress bays and canebrakes are home to Prothonotary and Swainson's warblers, Wood Ducks, and Fish Crows, and formerly harbored Ivory-billed Woodpeckers.

Piney Woods

Most of the longleaf pine, oak, and palmetto habitat once characteristic of the upland areas of the eastern Texas coastal plain has been converted to pine planta- tion or cropland, and portions of its avifauna have become scarce as a result. Some representative species of this habitat are: Bachman's Sparrow, Pine Warbler, Brown- headed Nuthatch, Red-cockaded Woodpecker, Wild Turkey, and Summer Tanager.

Cedar Brakes

The caves, canyons, springs, juniper-covered hills, and scrub oak thickets of the Ed- wards Plateau constitute the figurative as well as literal heart of Texas. Luckenbach is here, and the LBJ Ranch. Michener (1985:497), in his book, *Texas,* described the area as a land of "low, wooded hills of the most enchanting variety, graced by ex- quisite valleys hiding streamlets." It is pretty country, dominated by oak and juniper in the uplands and many of the riparian plant species typical of eastern North America in the lowlands, and it has some interesting birds: Canyon Wren, Scrub Jay, Zone-tailed Hawk, Green Kingfisher, and Cave Swallow, along with a couple of endangered specialities, the Golden-cheeked Warbler, and the Black- capped Vireo.

Gulf Coast

The richest birding area in North America north of the tropics is here. Connie Hagar put together her spectacular list mostly based on sightings in and around the little resort town of Rockport in Aransas County on the central coast. Mc- Cracken (1986) relates the exploits of Mrs. Hagar, and in the process provides an excellent review of what the Texas Gulf Coast has to offer in the way of birds. We also made an attempt to document the birds of this region in *Birds of the Texas Coastal Bend* (Rappole and Blacklock 1985). Some of the birds characteristic of the Texas coast are: Reddish Egret, Whooping Crane, American White Pelican, Soo- ty Tern, and Magnificent Frigatebird.

Subtropical Riparian

This habitat was never very extensive in Texas, and is practically gone now, with only a few remnant stands along the immediate banks of the Lower Rio Grande and elsewhere in the delta region of Hidalgo and Cameron counties. The Montezuma cypress that was once a part of this community exists in only a few patches, and the native sabal palm is all but extirpated as well. Tall ebonies, brazil, cedar elm, and sugar hackberry dominate the remaining forest in places like Santa Ana, Bentsen State Park, and Falcon Dam. The bird life is probably missing many of the tropical components that it once had, but a few remain: Chachalaca, Red-billed Pigeon, Altamira Oriole, White-tipped Dove, Ringed Kingfisher, and Brown Jay. Yellow- headed and Red-crowned parrots and the Green Parakeet may be reestablishing populations in some areas of the region.

ACCOUNTS OF SPECIES

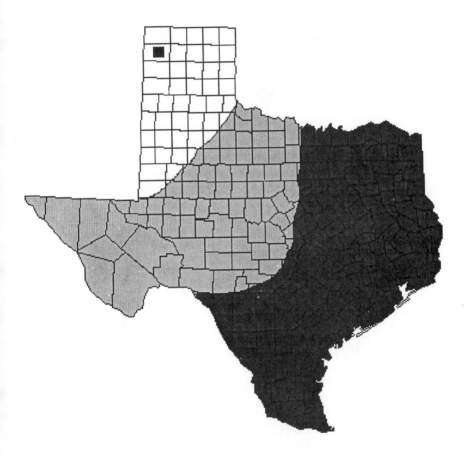

■ Common – Uncommon

▨ Rare – Casual

▣ Accidental

Order Gaviiformes
Family Gaviidae
Loons

Mallard-sized waterbirds with tapered body and chisel-shaped bill. Legs set far back for swimming and diving. Awkward on land, they require a considerable distance of flapping and running on water to become airborne. In flight, rapid wing beats, humpbacked silhouette, and feet extending beyond tail are characteristic.

1. Red-Throated Loon

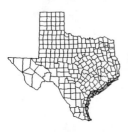

Gavia stellata (L— 25 W— 42)
Black mottled with gray on back; gray, rounded head; gray neck striped with white on nape; rufous throat; red eye; white below with barring on flanks; relatively thin, slightly upturned bill. *Winter:* Black back with indistinct white spots; head grayish with some white below eye; throat and underparts white. *Similar species:* White spotting on black back and thin, upturned bill separate this bird from other winter loons. *Habitat:* Marine, bays, lakes. *Texas:* Casual winter visitor (Nov.–Mar.) mainly along coast; has occurred in summer. *Range:* Breeds in high arctic; winters in coastal temperate and boreal regions of northern hemisphere.

2. Arctic Loon

Gavia arctica (L— 24 W— 39)
Similar to Pacific Loon, but with dark green (not purple) throat. *Winter:* See Pacific Loon. *Similar species:* Nearly identical to Pacific Loon. *Habitat:* Marine, bays, estuaries. *Texas:* Hypothetical—along coast and at large inland lakes. *Range:* Breeds in northern Eurasia; winters in central and southern Eurasia.

3. Pacific Loon

Gavia pacifica (L— 24 W— 39)
Black back with barred white patches; head gray; purple throat with white streaking on neck; white below with black streaks on flanks; red eye; slim, pointed bill. *Winter:* Gray back, nape, and crown; white throat and cheek with dark gray edging; often shows a grayish line across upper throat. *Similar species:* Winter Common Loon usually has a partial white collar, but lacks gray edging to throat and gray line across upper throat. *Habitat:* Marine, bays, estuaries, large lakes. *Texas:* Casual winter visitor (Nov.–Mar.) mainly along coast, and at large, inland lakes; has occurred in summer. *Range:* Breeds in high arctic; winters along boreal and temperate coasts of northern hemisphere, primarily along west coast of North America.

4. Common Loon

Gavia immer (L— 31 W— 54)
Checked black and white on back; black head with a white streaked collar; white below with black streaking on breast and flanks; thick, heavy bill; red eye. *Winter:* Dark gray above; white below; dark gray crown and nape; white face and throat with a partial collar of white around neck. *Similar species:* See Pacific Loon. *Habitat:* Marine, bays, lakes. *Texas:* Uncommon to rare transient (Oct.–Nov., Mar.–Apr.) on large lakes nearly throughout; uncommon winter resident along coast, scarcer inland. *Range:* Breeds in Alaska, Canada, and northern U.S.; winters in coastal North America and on large lakes inland south to Baja California, Sonora, and South Texas.

5. Yellow-billed Loon

Gavia adamsii (L— 34 W— 56)
The Yellow-billed Loon is considered to be conspecific with the Common Loon by some authors. The two species (subspecies?) are very similar, but the Common Loon has a dark bill (not yellow). *Winter:* See Common Loon. *Similar species:* The winter Yellow-billed Loon generally has a paler bill, brownish back, and paler head than the Common Loon. It also often shows a dark ear patch lacking in the Common Loon. *Habitat:* Lakes, seacoasts. *Texas:* Accidental—Lubbock Co. *Range:* Breeds in circumpolar arctic regions; winters in northern coastal regions mainly along west coast in North America south to California.

Order Podicipediformes
Family Podicipedidae
Grebes

Loon-like birds the size of a small to medium-sized duck; chisel-shaped bill and lobed toes are distinctive. Seldom seen in flight though most species are migratory.

6. Least Grebe

Tachybaptus dominicus (L—10 W—14)
Dark above; rusty flanks; white undertail coverts; golden eye; thin, pointed bill. *Winter:* Shows whitish throat. *Voice:* "Peep"; also a chatter. *Similar species:* Larger Pied-billed Grebe has thick bill and dark eye. *Habitat:* Ponds, ditches. *Texas:* Uncommon resident* in South Texas. *Range:* South Texas to northern Argentina; West Indies.

7. Pied-billed Grebe

Podilymbus podiceps (L—13 W—22)
Grayish-brown body; pale bill with dark black ring; black throat; dark brown eye with white eyering. *Winter:* Whitish throat; lacks black ring on bill. *Voice:* A cuckoo-like "hoooo hoo hoo hoo hoo kow kow kow." *Similar species:* See Least Grebe. *Habitat:* Ponds, lakes, swales, marshes, estuaries, bays. *Texas:* Common resident* in eastern half; uncommon to rare in west. *Range:* Breeds across most of western hemisphere from central Canada to southern Argentina; West Indies; winters in temperate and tropical portions of breeding range.

8. Horned Grebe

Podiceps auritus (L—14 W—23)
Dark back; rusty neck and sides; whitish breast; black head with buffy orange ear patch and eyebrow; red eye. *Winter:* Upper half of head dark with white spot in front of eye; cheek, throat, and breast white; nape and back dark. *Similar species:* Winter Eared Grebe has gray cheek and neck (not white) with white spot on neck; lacks preorbital white spot. *Habitat:* Lakes, ponds, estuaries. *Texas:* Locally common to rare winter resident (Nov.–Mar.), mainly in eastern quarter. *Range:* Breeds in boreal and northern temperate regions; winters coastally in boreal and temperate regions of northern hemisphere.

9. Red-necked Grebe

Podiceps grisegena (L— 20 W— 32)
A large, long-necked grebe; dark back and upper half of head; rusty neck; white lower half of head and chin; dark brown eye; rusty breast; yellowish lower mandible. *Winter:* Dark back, posterior portion of neck and crown; white chin and partial collar; grayish white anterior portion of neck, breast and belly. *Voice:* Crow-like "aaahh"s; also high-pitched squeaks. *Similar species:* Long neck, light-colored bill, and dark brown eye are distinctive. *Habitat:* Lakes, ponds, estuaries. *Texas:* Casual winter visitor (Oct.–Mar.), mainly along coast. *Range:* Breeds locally in boreal and northern temperate areas; winters along temperate and boreal coasts of northern hemisphere.

10. Eared Grebe

Podiceps nigricollis (L—12 W— 22)
Dark back; black neck and rusty sides; whitish breast; black head with buffy orange ear tufts; red eye. *Winter:* Dark gray throughout except white chin and ear patch, whitish on breast and throat. *Voice:* "Kip kip kip kuweep kuweep," etc. *Similar species:* See Horned Grebe. *Habitat:* Marshes, lakes, ponds, estuaries, marine. *Texas:* Common to uncommon winter resident (Nov.–Mar.) nearly throughout; casual summer resident* east of Trans-Pecos. *Range:* Breeds locally in southern boreal, temperate, and tropical regions of the world; mainly western in North America.

11. Western Grebe

Aechmophorus occidentalis (L— 25 W— 34)
A very large, long-necked grebe; dark gray above, white below; front half of neck and chin are white; back half of neck, face, and crown are dark gray; red eye; long, pointed, yellow-green bill. *Voice:* Two-note courtship call (single note in the similar Clark's Grebe). *Similar species:* Clark's Grebe, long considered a light color phase of the Western Grebe, has cheeks, lores, and superciliary stripe white, not black as in Western Grebe; fall and winter birds can be difficult to separate. *Habitat:* Lakes, marshes, bays. *Texas:* Casual winter visitor (Nov.–Mar.) mainly in western half; details of the status of Western versus Clark's Grebe in Texas are not well known. *Range:* Breeds in central and southwestern Canada and western half of U.S. south to western Mexico; winters mainly along Pacific Coast from southwestern Canada

to southern Mexico. Western Grebe is more common in northern and eastern portions of the range, replaced by Clark's Grebe south and west.

12. Clark's Grebe

Aechmophorus clarkii (L— 25 W— 34)
Very similar to Western Grebe but lighter in color; bill yellow-orange; superciliary stripe, lores, and cheek white. *Voice:* Single note courtship call. *Similar species:* See Western Grebe. *Habitat:* Lakes, marshes, bays. *Texas:* See Western Grebe. *Range:* See Western Grebe.

Order Procellariiformes
Family Diomedeidae
Albatrosses

Large seabird with exceptionally long, narrow wings, relatively short tail, heavy, hooked bill, and tubed nasal passages.

13. Yellow-nosed Albatross

Diomedea chlororhynchos (L— 32 W— 78)
Back and upper wings dark; body and underwings white; tail black; dark bill with yellowish nose tube. *Habitat:* Spends most of its life on the wing at sea. *Similar species:* Almost completely white wing linings, yellow nose tube, and bluish legs separate this from other albatrosses. *Habitat:* Pelagic. *Texas:* Accidental—Willacy Co., Cameron Co. *Range:* Tropical and southern temperate seas of the world.

Family Procellariidae
Shearwaters

Dove-sized seabirds with long, narrow wings, short legs and tail, tubed nose, and hooked bill; rapid fluttering flight with frequent glides.

14. Cory's Shearwater

Calonectris diomedea (L—18 W—44)
Plump, large-bodied shearwater; gray-brown above; brownish head; pale throat; white below; white wing linings with dark tips; pale bill. *Similar species:* Greater Shearwater has contrasting sharp black cap and white throat; also has black (not pale) bill, white rump, and black smudge on belly. *Habitat:* Pelagic. *Texas:* Casual along coast but probably uncommon to rare in open Gulf. *Range:* Mainly temperate and tropical areas of Atlantic Ocean, Caribbean and Mediterranean seas, and Gulf of Mexico.

15. Greater Shear-water

Puffinus gravis (L—19 W—44)
Plump; dark gray above; white below with dark belly smudge; contrasting dark cap and white throat; white collar, base of tail, and wing linings; black bill; pinkish legs. *Similar species:* See Cory's Shearwater. *Habitat:* Pelagic. *Texas:* Accidental—Galveston Co.; probably casual in Gulf. *Range:* Atlantic Ocean.

16. Sooty Shearwater

Puffinus griseus (L—19 W—42)
Entirely dark gray except for paler wing linings; dark bill and legs. *Similar species:* Nearly identical to the Short-tailed Shearwater (unreported from western Gulf) which usually lacks pale wing linings. *Habitat:* Pelagic. *Texas:* Casual in summer (Apr.–July) along coast; probably rare in Gulf. *Range:* Oceans of the world.

17. Manx Shearwater

Puffinus puffinus (L—14 W—33)
A small shearwater; black above; white below with white wing linings and undertail coverts; black bill; pink legs. *Similar species:* Audubon's Shearwater has dark primary linings and undertail coverts. *Habitat:* Pelagic. *Texas:* Casual along coast. *Range:* Atlantic Ocean, Caribbean and Mediterranean seas.

18. Audubon's Shear-water

Puffinus lherminieri (L—12 W—27)
Black above, white below; primaries and undertail co-verts dark below; pale legs contrast with dark under-tail coverts. *Similar species:* See Manx Shearwater. *Habitat:* Pelagic. *Texas:* Casual along coast; probably uncommon in most seasons in open Gulf. *Range:* Warm temperate and tropical seas of the world.

Family Hydrobatidae
Storm-Petrels

Dark, swallow-like seabirds that feed by hopping and skipping over the waves.

19. Wilson's Storm-Petrel

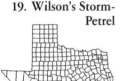

Oceanites oceanicus (L—7 W—16)
Dark gray with white rump and undertail coverts; whitish stripe runs diagonally on secondaries of upper wing; square tail; feet extend beyond tail. *Habits:* Skims and flutters over water surface, often dabbling feet in water. *Similar species:* Dabbling behavior is distinctive. Leach's Storm-Petrel has slightly forked tail; feet do not extend beyond tail in either Leach's or Band-rumped. *Habitat:* Pelagic. *Texas:* Casual along coast, probably rare in Gulf. *Range:* Atlantic, Indian, and southern Pacific oceans.

20. Leach's Storm-Petrel

Oceanodroma leucorhoa (L—8 W—19)
Dark gray; white rump with dark central stripe; slightly forked tail. *Habits:* flight is erratic, low over water. *Similar species:* See Wilson's Storm-Petrel; Band-rumped Storm-Petrel has square (not forked) tail and lacks dark central stripe through rump. *Habitat:* Pelagic. *Texas:* Casual along coast. *Range:* Atlantic and Pacific oceans.

21. Band-rumped Storm-Petrel

Oceanodroma castro (L—9 W—18)
Dark gray; white rump; square tail. *Habits:* Flight is shearwater-like with alternate flapping and gliding. *Similar species:* See Leach's and Wilson's storm-petrels. *Habitat:* Pelagic. *Texas:* Casual along coast, probably rare in open Gulf. *Range:* Tropical and warm temperate portions of Atlantic and Pacific oceans, Caribbean Sea.

Order Pelecaniformes
Family Phaethontidae
Tropicbirds

Graceful, long-tailed, narrow-winged, white seabirds of tropical oceans.

22. White-tailed Tropicbird

Phaethon lepturus (L— 28 W— 36)
White with black patch running diagonally on wing from wrist; black on primaries; black around eye; extremely long central tail feathers (streamers); yellow bill. *Immature:* white with black barring on back and head; no streamers. *Similar species:* Yellow bill separates this from other tropicbird species; terns have forked tails— tropicbird tail is wedge-shaped, even when lacking streamers. *Habitat:* Pelagic. *Texas:* Hypothetical, several sightings along coast. *Range:* Tropical seas.

23. Red-billed Tropicbird

Phaethon aethereus (L— 40 W— 44)
White mottled with black above; white below; black primaries; extremely long white tail streamers; red bill. *Immature:* White with black barring on back; black collar; orange or yellow bill; no streamers. *Similar species:* Immature White-tailed Tropicbird has a dark cap (white in immature Red-billed Tropicbird). *Habitat:* Pelagic. *Texas:* Accidental— Harris Co., Zapata Co. *Range: Tropical seas.*

Family Sulidae
Boobies and Gannets

Boobies and gannets are large, heavy-bodied seabirds with long, cone-shaped bills, narrow, tapered wings, and webbed feet. They dive for prey from considerable heights.

24. Masked Booby

Sula dactylatra (L— 32 W— 63)
White body; wings white with black primaries and secondaries; black wedge-shaped tail with elongated central feathers; orangish bill; dark legs; bare skin at base of bill and around eyes is dark. *Immature:* Brown mottled with white on wings and lower back; brown head; white breast and belly; wings patterned white and dark brown from below. *Similar species:* The combination of dark head, white upper back, and yellow bill separate the immature from other young boobies. *Habitat:* Pelagic. *Texas:* Rare summer resident (Mar.–Sept.) along coast; uncommon in open Gulf. *Range:* Tropical seas.

25. Blue-footed Booby

Sula nebouxii (L— 32 W— 62)
Brown lower back and wings; white patch on upper back; white head streaked with brown; white breast and belly; legs blue; bill steely gray; bare skin on face is dark. *Immature:* Similar to adult but more brownish on head and underparts. *Similar species:* Bright blue feet are diagnostic in adult; immature Masked Booby has yellowish (not bluish) bill. *Habitat:* Pelagic. *Texas:* Accidental— Cameron Co. *Range:* Mainly in eastern Pacific Ocean.

26. Brown Booby

Sula leucogaster (L— 29 W— 48)
Brown back, wings and hood; yellowish bill and legs; white at base of wing lining extending in a wedge toward wing tip; bare skin on face is bluish; western birds have whitish heads. *Immature:* Similar in pattern to adult but with brownish-white rather than white underparts. *Similar species:* Immature Masked Booby has mostly white wing linings (dark in immature Brown Booby) and yellowish (not bluish) bill. *Habitat:* Pelagic. *Texas:* Casual along coast (Mar.–Sept.), probably rare in open Gulf. *Range:* Tropical western Atlantic and eastern Pacific oceans.

27. Red-footed Booby

Sula sula (L— 29 W— 60)
Brown body; white rump, undertail coverts, and tail; bluish bill; red legs; pinkish skin at base of bill. *White Phase:* White with black primaries and secondaries; black carpal patch. *Immature:* Dark throughout with bluish bill and dark feet. *Similar species:* This is the only red-footed booby, whether in white or brown phase. Immatures lack the wing lining patterns of other boobies. *Habitat:* Pelagic. *Texas:* Accidental — 53 miles off Galveston in open Gulf; and lost specimen from Aransas Co. *Range:* Tropical western Atlantic, Pacific, and Indian oceans.

28. Northern Gannet

Morus bassanus (L— 38 W— 75)
Largest of the boobies; entirely white except for black primaries; rusty wash on head; bill bluish; feet dark. *Immature:* Brown except for whitish belly and white spots on upper wing and back; bluish bill; *Habits:* Occasionally visible with a spotting scope from barrier islands as they dive for fish in the open Gulf. *Voice:* A series of crow-like "caw"s. *Similar species:* Immature gannets lack white wing lining patterns of other boobies, and have a whitish belly (which immature Red-footed Booby lacks). *Habitat:* Pelagic. *Texas:* Uncommon to rare immediately offshore in winter (Nov.– Mar.). *Range:* North Atlantic Ocean, Gulf of Mexico, Mediterranean Sea.

Family Pelecanidae
Pelicans

Extremely large, heavy-bodied waterbirds with long bill and gular pouch.

29. American White Pelican

Pelecanus erythrorhynchos (L— 62 W—105)
White body; black primaries and secondaries; enormous orange bill and gular pouch; often with a horn-like growth on upper mandible (breeding); orange-yellow feet. *Habits:* Does not dive for fish like Brown Pelican. Forages by dipping for prey, often in groups. *Voice:* Various coughs and croaks. *Similar species:* Immature Brown Pelicans can appear a dusty brownish-white but the American White Pelican is bright white

in all plumages. *Habitat:* Estuaries, lakes, bays. *Texas:* Common transient (Apr.–May, Aug.–Oct.) in eastern third, rare in west; common winter resident along coast; summer resident*– single breeding colony in Nueces Co., uncommon to rare elsewhere in summer along central and lower coast. *Range:* Breeds locally in central and western Canada south through western half of U.S.; winters along Pacific Coast from California to Nicaragua, and from Florida around the Gulf of Mexico to Yucatán.

30. Brown Pelican

Pelecanus occidentalis (L— 48 W— 78)
Grayish above; brownish below with dark chestnut nape and neck; whitish head tinged with yellow; enormous bill and gular pouch. *Immature:* Entirely brownish-gray. *Habits:* Dives from a considerable height to catch fish. *Voice:* Occasional croaks. *Similar species:* See American White Pelican. *Habitat:* Marine. *Texas:* Nearly extirpated in 1950s and 1960s but now uncommon and increasing permanent residents* along coast. *Range:* Coastal western hemisphere from North Carolina to eastern Brazil, including West Indies in the east and California to southern Chile in the West.

Family Phalacrocoracidae
Cormorants

Dark waterbirds the size of a small goose with tapered body, long, hooked bill, small gular pouch, and webbed feet. They generally fly in small flocks with necks extended.

31. Double-crested Cormorant

Phalacrocorax auritus (L— 32 W— 51)
Entirely iridescent black; whitish or dark ear tufts during breeding season; gular pouch of bare orange skin. *Immature:* buffy head and neck. *Habits:* Forages by swimming low in water and diving for long periods. Sits on snags and posts with wings spread to dry. *Voice:* Various croaks. *Similar species:* The smaller, more delicate Olivaceous Cormorant has a relatively longer tail; it also has a yellowish gular pouch with a greenish or brownish tinge that ends in a point on the cheek; the gular pouch of the Double-

crested is orange-yellow and has a rounded edge. The gular pouch is edged with white feathers in adult Olivaceous, but not in the Double-crested. *Habitat:* Estuaries, marine, lakes, ponds. *Texas:* Common transient (Oct.–Nov., Mar.–Apr.) in eastern third, rare in west; common winter resident along coast and locally inland on large lakes; casual summer resident* along southeast coast and in north-central Texas. *Range:* Breeds locally across central and southern Canada and the northern and central U.S., along both coasts from Arkansas to southern Mexico and Newfoundland to East Texas, and in Cuba; winters in coastal breeding range to South Texas, Greater Antilles, Yucatán Peninsula, and Belize.

32. Olivaceous Cormorant

Phalacrocorax olivaceus (L— 26 W— 42)
Entirely black with an iridescent green tinge; gular pouch is yellowish tinged with greenish or brownish, edged in white feathers. *Immature:* Brownish; darker brown on back, wings, and tail. *Voice:* An occasional croak. *Similar species:* See Double-crested Cormorant. *Habitat:* Rivers, ponds, lakes. *Texas:* Uncommon resident* along coastal plain. *Range:* Resident in lowlands from Texas and northwestern Mexico south to southern South America, Cuba.

33. Red-legged Cormorant

Phalacrocorax gaimardi (L— 28 W— 42)
Grayish throughout; white patch on side of neck; white plumes behind eye (breeding); gray eye; yellow bill; orange gular sac; legs and feet red. *Immature:* Brownish; white neck patches; red feet. *Habitat:* Coastal regions. *Texas:* Hypothetical—Galveston Co. *Range:* South America from Peru to central Chile.

Family Anhingidae
Anhingas

Dark waterbirds similar to cormorants but with serpentine neck, long, pointed bill, and long, wedge-shaped tail.

34. Anhinga

Anhinga anhinga (L—35 W—45)
Snake-like neck and long triangular tail with terminal buffy band; long, sharp, yellow-orange bill; black body with iridescent green sheen; mottled white on shoulders and upper wing coverts. *Female and immature:* Light buff head, neck, and breast; lack white wing spotting. *Habits:* Often forages with only the sinuous neck and head protruding above water. Sits with wings spread to dry. *Voice:* A series of metallic "kaakk"s, some reminiscent of a cicada. *Similar species:* Cormorants have hooked rather than stiletto-shaped bill; tail is shorter than that of Anhinga and lacks terminal buffy band. *Habitat:* Rivers, lakes, ponds. *Texas:* Uncommon summer resident* (Mar.–Oct.) in eastern third and South Texas; uncommon in winter along coast; sometimes seen in large kettles during migration. *Range:* Breeds from southeastern U.S. south through lowlands to southern Brazil, Cuba; winters throughout breeding range except inland in Gulf states.

Family Fregatidae
Frigatebirds

Dark, long-winged, fork-tailed seabirds of tropical waters.

35. Magnificent Frigatebird

Fregata magnificens (L—40 W—90)
Black body; red, bare-skinned throat; extremely long, narrow wings and long, forked tail; long, hooked beak. *Female:* White breast and belly, black throat. *Immature:* Variable—white on head and underparts. *Habits:* Uses superior flying skill to rob gulls and terns of fish. *Habitat:* Coastal marine. *Texas:* Uncommon summer resident (May–Sept.) along immediate coast, rare in winter, has bred*; increased sightings occur after hurricanes. *Range:* Tropical and subtropical coasts and islands of western hemisphere, also Cape Verde Islands off West Africa.

Order Ciconiiformes
Family Ardeidae
Herons, Egrets, and Bitterns

Long-billed, long-necked, long-legged wading birds.

36. American Bittern

Botaurus lentiginosus (L— 26 W— 39)
A chunky, relatively short-legged heron; buffy brown above and below streaked with white and brown on throat, neck, and breast; dark brown streak on side of neck; white chin; greenish-yellow bill and legs; yellow eyes. *Habits:* A very secretive bird; often, rather than fly when approached, it will "freeze" with its neck extended in an attempt to blend into the reeds and rushes of the marsh. *Voice:* A deep "goonk glunk-a-lunk," like blowing on an empty bottle. *Similar species:* Could be mistaken for an immature night heron in flight, but dark brown primaries and secondaries contrast with light brown back and upper wing coverts; night herons lack prominent dark streak on side of neck. *Habitat:* Marshes. *Texas:* Uncommon transient (Apr.–May, Sept.–Oct.); rare to casual summer resident*; common winter resident along coast, rare to casual elsewhere. *Range:* Breeds from central and southern Canada south to southern U.S. and central Mexico; winters southern U.S. to southern Mexico and Cuba.

37. Least Bittern

Ixobrychus exilis (L—14 W—17)
A very small heron; dark brown with white streaking on back; tan wings, head, and neck; dark brown crown; white chin and throat streaked with tan; white belly; yellowish legs and bill; yellow eyes; extended wings are half tan (basally) and half dark brown. *Habits:* Like the American Bittern, this bird will often "freeze" with neck extended when approached. *Voice:* A rapid, whistled "coo-co-co-co-coo." *Similar species:* Immature Green-backed Heron is heavily streaked below and lacks buff shoulders. *Habitat:* Marshes. *Texas:* Common (along coast) to uncommon summer resident* (May–Aug.) in eastern third of state; rare to casual in west. *Range:* Breeds in eastern half of U.S. and southeastern Canada, locally in western U.S., south through lowlands to southern Brazil, West Indies; winters through breeding range from southern U.S. southward.

38. Great Blue Heron

Ardea herodias (L— 48 W— 72)
A very large heron; slate gray above and on neck; white crown bordered with black stripes that extend as plumes (breeding); white chin and throat streaked with black; gray breast and back plumes; white below streaked with chestnut; chestnut thighs; orange-yellow bill; dark legs. *Immature:* Dark cap; brownish-gray back; buffy neck. *White phase:* Entirely white with yellow bill and legs. *Voice:* A low "krarrrk." *Habitat:* Bays, estuaries, rivers, lakes, marshes. *Texas:* Common permanent resident* in eastern half, uncommon to rare in west. *Range:* Breeds from central and southern Canada south to coastal Colombia and Venezuela, West Indies; winters southern U.S. southward through breeding range.

39. Great Egret

Casmerodius albus (L— 39 W— 57)
Entirely white, with shaggy plumes on breast in breeding season; long, yellow bill; long, dark legs that extend well beyond tail in flight. *Voice:* Various "krrank"s and "krronk"s. *Similar species:* White phase of Great Blue has yellow legs (not dark); Snowy Egret has black bill and yellow feet; immature Little Blue Heron has two-tone bill (dark tip, pale base), pale legs, and usually some gray smudging on white plumage; white phase Reddish Egret has dark or two-tone bill (dark tip, pinkish base) and dark legs; Cattle Egret is half the size; has short, thick, yellow bill and yellowish legs that barely extend beyond tail in flight. *Habitat:* Estuaries, bays, marshes, rivers, lakes, ponds. *Texas:* Common permanent resident* along coast; locally common summer resident* (Mar.–July) in eastern third; rare to casual in west. *Range:* Breeds in temperate and tropical regions of the world; winters mainly in subtropical and tropical portions of breeding range.

40. Snowy Egret

Egretta thula (L— 23 W— 45)
Small, entirely white heron; black legs with yellow feet; black bill; yellow lores; white plumes off neck and breast (breeding). *Immature:* Has yellow line up back of leg. *Habits:* Occasionally arches wings to form a canopy while foraging; also puts foot forward and shakes it on substrate. *Voice:* A crow-like "caaah." *Similar species:* See Great Egret. *Habitat:* Bays, estuaries, ponds, marshes. *Texas:* Common perma-

nent resident* along coast; uncommon summer resident* in eastern third, rare in west. *Range:* Breeds locally across U.S. and extreme southern Canada south in lowlands to southern South America, West Indies; winters from coastal southern U.S. southward through breeding range.

41. Little Blue Heron

Egretta caerulea (L—23 W—39)
A smallish heron; dark blue body; maroon neck and head; two-tone bill, black at tip, pale gray or greenish at base; plumes on neck, breast and head; dark legs. *Winter:* Mainly navy blue on neck with maroon tinge; no plumes. *Immature:* Almost entirely white in first year with some gray smudging; greenish legs; two-tone bill; more smudging in second year. *Voice:* Pig-like squawks. *Similar species:* See Great Egret. *Habitat:* Mainly inland marshes, lakes, ponds. *Texas:* Uncommon permanent resident* along coast; uncommon summer resident* in eastern third, rare to casual in west. *Range:* Breeds along coastal plain of eastern U.S. from Maine to Texas south through lowlands to Peru and southern Brazil, West Indies; winters from southern U.S. south through breeding range.

42. Tricolored Heron

Egretta tricolor (L—26 W—36)
Slate blue body; red eye; greenish lores; rusty chin; white central stripe down neck streaked with dark blue; maroon on breast; white belly and thighs; buffy plumes on back (breeding). *Immature:* Rusty and slate above, whitish below. *Voice:* Crow-like "krraww," repeated. *Similar species:* Similar pattern to the much-larger Great Blue Heron but note white (not chestnut) thighs, and lack of black on head. *Habitat:* Bays, estuaries, lakes, ponds. *Texas:* Common permanent resident* along coast; rare summer straggler in eastern third. *Range:* Breeds in coastal plain of eastern U.S. from Maine to Texas, south through coastal lowlands to Peru and northern Brazil, West Indies; winters from Gulf states south through breeding range.

43. Reddish Egret

Egretta rufescens (L— 29 W— 39)
A medium-sized heron; slate blue body; pinkish-beige head, neck and breast with shaggy plumes; two-tone bill, pink at base and black at tip; bluish lores; dark legs; nonbreeding plumage is duller with shorter plumes. *White phase:* Entirely white with two-tone bill; dark legs. *Immature:* (Both phases) bill entirely dark. *Habits:* Peculiar feeding behavior involving arching of wings over head ("canopy") and various runs and lurches in somewhat tipsy fashion. *Voice:* "Krraaah." *Similar species:* See Great Egret. *Habitat:* Shallow tidal pools. *Texas:* Common permanent resident* along central and lower coast; uncommon along upper coast. *Range:* Breeds locally along coast in Florida and Gulf states, both coasts of Mexico, and Greater Antilles; winters through breeding range to Lesser Antilles and coastal Venezuela.

44. Cattle Egret

Bubulcus ibis (L— 20 W— 36)
A small, entirely white heron; yellow-orange bill and legs; buff coloration and plumes on crest, breast and back (breeding). *Immature:* Like adult but lacks buff coloration, and legs are dark. *Similar species:* See Great Egret. *Habitat:* The Cattle Egret is not an aquatic species, though it occasionally nests on bay islands. It prefers savanna and grasslands where it feeds on insects. *Texas:* Common permanent resident* along coast; common to uncommon summer resident* (Apr.–Sept.) in eastern third; rare in west. *Range:* Formerly strictly an Old World species, the Cattle Egret appeared in South America in the late 1800s and has expanded steadily northward, reaching Texas in 1955. Current distribution includes most temperate and tropical regions of the world. Northern populations are migratory.

45. Green-backed Heron

Butorides striatus (L— 19 W— 28)
A small, dark heron; olive back; black cap; chestnut neck; white throat with chestnut striping; yellow eye and lores; white malar stripe; grayish belly; greenish legs; bill dark above, yellowish below. *Immature:* Heavily streaked below. *Habits:* Forages in a very slow, deliberate manner. *Voice:* A loud "kyoook." *Similar species:* Least Bittern is buffy, not dark, and has two-tone wings; wings of Green-backed Heron are uni-

formly dark in flight. *Habitat:* Streams, rivers, lakes, marshes. *Texas:* Common to uncommon summer resident* (Mar.–Oct.) in eastern half; uncommon to rare in Edwards Plateau and Trans-Pecos; rare to casual in north-central Texas and Panhandle; rare winter resident along coast. *Range:* Breeds from southern Canada south to northern Argentina (absent from drier plains and deserts), West Indies; winters from southern U.S. through breeding range.

46. Black-crowned Night-Heron

Nycticorax nycticorax (L— 26 W— 45)
A rather squat heron; black on back and crown with long, trailing white plumes (breeding); gray wings; pale gray breast and belly; white forehead, cheek and chin; red eye; dark beak; pale legs. *Immature:* Dark brown above, heavily streaked with white; whitish below streaked with brown; red eye; bluish lores; pale legs. *Habits:* Nocturnal. *Voice:* "Kwark." *Similar species:* Immature Yellow-crowned Night-Heron has longer legs that extend well beyond end of tail in flight — Blackcrown's barely reach beyond end of tail; also the Yellowcrown is finely spotted (not streaked) on back. *Habitat:* Bays, lakes, marshes. *Texas:* Common permanent resident* along coast; uncommon to rare summer resident* (Apr.–Oct.) elsewhere; rare to casual inland in winter. *Range:* Breeds locally in temperate and tropical regions of the world; withdraws from seasonally cold portions of breeding range in winter.

47. Yellow-crowned Night-Heron

Nyctanassa violacea (L— 24 W— 42)
Gray body, streaked with black above and on wings; black head with white cheek patch and creamy crown and plumes (breeding); red eye; dark bill; pale legs. *Immature:* Dark brown above, finely spotted with white; whitish below streaked with brown; dark bill; yellow legs; red eye. *Habits:* Mostly nocturnal. *Voice:* "Aaak." *Similar species:* See Black-crowned Night-Heron. *Habitat:* Wetlands. *Texas:* Uncommon to rare transient (Mar.–May, Aug.–Oct.) throughout; uncommon summer resident* in eastern third south to the Guadalupe River; uncommon winter resident along central and lower coast, rare to casual inland. *Range:* Southeastern U.S. south in coastal regions to Peru and southern Brazil, West Indies; winters from coastal Gulf states south through breeding range.

Family Threskiornithidae
Ibises and Spoonbills

Ibises are small to medium-sized, heron-like birds with long, decurved bills.

48. White Ibis

Eudocimus albus (L— 25 W— 39)
Entirely white with long, pink, decurved bill; pink facial skin; yellow eye; pink legs. *Immature:* Brown above; white below; neck and head mottled brown and whitish; pinkish bill and legs. *Voice:* Various "aaaah"s and "aaaww"s. *Similar species:* Immature Glossy and White-faced ibises have dark bills, legs and underparts. *Habitat:* Bays, rivers, estuaries. *Texas:* Common transient (Mar.–May, Aug.–Oct.) along coastal plain; uncommon summer resident* mainly on the upper coast, rare in winter. *Range:* Coastal southeastern U.S. south to French Guiana and Peru, West Indies; withdraws from northern portions in winter.

49. Scarlet Ibis

Eudocimus ruber (L— 23 W— 37)
Entirely red except black wingtips. *Immature:* Brown above; white below; neck and head mottled brown and whitish; pinkish bill and legs. *Similar species:* Immature is virtually indistinguishable from immature White Ibis in the field. *Habitat:* Coastal marshes and swamps. *Texas:* Hypothetical—Chambers, Galveston, Cameron cos. *Range:* Eastern South America from Venezuela to northeastern Brazil.

50. Glossy Ibis

Plegadis falcinellus (L— 22 W— 36)
Body entirely dark purplish-brown with green sheen on wings and back; bare dark skin on face, edged with bluish skin (breeding); dark bill; dark legs; brown eyes. *Immature:* Brownish throughout with white streaking on head and neck; dark bill and legs. *Similar species:* See White-faced Ibis. *Habitat:* Bays, marshes, lakes, ponds. *Texas:* Casual—Upper coast. *Range:* Breeds along coast of eastern U.S. from Maine to Louisiana south through West Indies to northern Venezuela, and in Old World temperate and tropical regions; withdraws from colder portions of breeding range in winter.

51. White-faced Ibis

Plegadis chihi (L— 22 W— 36)
Body entirely dark purplish brown with green sheen on wings and back; bare pinkish skin on face, edged with white feathers (present only briefly during height of breeding); pale bill; pinkish legs; red eyes. *Immature:* Brownish throughout with white streaking on head and neck; dark bill and legs. *Voice:* "Kruk." *Similar species:* Glossy Ibis has dark (not pinkish) loral skin, dark (not reddish) legs, and brown (not red) eyes; immatures of these species are indistinguishable in the field. *Habitat:* Bays, marshes, lakes, ponds. *Texas:* Common transient (Mar.–May, Aug.–Oct.) along coastal plain, rare inland in eastern third; uncommon summer resident* along coast; uncommon to rare in winter along coast. *Range:* Breeds locally in western U.S., from South Texas through Mexico and along Pacific Coast to El Salvador, and locally in northern and south-central South America; winters from southwestern U.S. south through breeding range.

52. Roseate Spoonbill

Ajaia ajaja (L— 30 W— 51)
A medium-sized, heron-bodied bird with long, spatulate bill; pink body and legs; white neck and breast; dark nape; bald crown of greenish skin; bright red shoulder patch. *Immature:* Whitish body with pinkish wings. *Habits:* Forages by swishing bill back and forth through water, capturing invertebrates. *Voice:* "Rraaaak-ak-ak-ak," etc. *Habitat:* Bays, estuaries, lakes, ponds. *Texas:* Common summer resident* (Mar.–Oct.) along coast; uncommon to casual inland in eastern half; uncommon in winter along coast. *Range:* Coastal areas of Gulf states south through coastal regions to northern Argentina, West Indies; partially withdraws from northern portions of breeding range in winter.

Family Ciconiidae
Storks

Tall, long-legged, heavy-billed, long-necked wading birds.

53. Jabiru

Jabiru mycteria (L—53 W—93)
A very tall bird with a huge black bill like a cudgel; white body; naked black head and neck; red throat; black legs. *Immature:* grayish-brown including feathered head and neck. *Voice:* Clacks mandibles. *Habitat:* Coastal marshes. *Texas:* Casual along coast. *Range:* Locally from southern Mexico to northern Argentina.

54. Wood Stork

Mycteria americana (L—41 W—66) **Endangered**
A large, white-bodied bird with long, heavy, bill, down-turned toward the tip; black primaries and secondaries; naked, black-skinned head and neck; pale legs with pinkish feet. *Immature:* Patterned like adult but with grayish feathering on neck and head; yellowish bill. *Habitat:* Coastal marshes, bays, prairies, lakes. *Texas:* Common summer resident along coastal plain (July–Sept.), rare to casual at large inland lakes; may have bred formerly. Current populations are composed of postbreeding transients, apparently from southern Mexico. *Range:* Georgia, Florida and Gulf states south in coastal regions to central Argentina, West Indies.

Order Phoenicopteriformes
Family Phoenicopteridae
Flamingos

Colorful, stork-like birds with large bent bills.

55. Greater Flamingo

Phoenicopterus ruber (L—45 W—63)
A large, long-legged, long-necked, pink bird with heavy, right-angled bill; black primaries and secondaries; legs pink; bill pink tipped with black. *Immature:* Similar to adult but paler. *Habits:* Swishes bill through water to strain invertebrate prey. *Habitat:* Coastal marshes. *Texas:* Casual visitor to central and lower coast. *Range:* Resident locally in tropical and subtropical areas of the world, mainly in Caribbean region of New World.

Order Anseriformes
Family Anatidae
Ducks, Geese, and Swans

Heavy-bodied waterbirds with short legs, webbed feet, and broad, flat bills. Johnsgard (1979) and Hines (1985), provide in-depth identification information for members of this group.

56. Fulvous Whistling-Duck

Dendrocygna bicolor (L— 20 W— 36)
A long-necked, long-legged duck; body a rich, tawny buff; mottled black and tan on back; dark streak running from crown down nape to back; whitish streaking on throat; white on flanks; gray bill and legs; dark wings; dark tail with white base. *Habits:* Mainly a grazer in flooded fields. *Voice:* A shrill, whistled "ker-chee." *Similar species:* Black-bellied Whistling-Duck has black belly, orange bill, and extensive white in wings visible in flying bird. *Habitat:* Lakes, marshes, grasslands. *Texas:* Common transient (Mar.–May, Aug.–Oct.) along coastal plain; uncommon summer resident* along central and lower coast, rare on upper coast; rare in winter along central and lower coast. *Range:* Breeds locally from southern California, Arizona, Texas, Louisiana, and Florida south in coastal regions to Peru and central Argentina, West Indies; also in Old World from East Africa, Madagascar, and India.

57. Black-bellied Whistling-Duck

Dendrocygna autumnalis (L— 21 W— 36)
A long-necked, long-legged duck; neck and breast a rich, tawny buff; black belly; gray head with brown crown; dark streak running from crown down nape to back; red-orange bill and legs; dark wings with broad white stripe; dark tail. *Voice:* A shrill, whistled "per-chee-chee-chee." *Similar species:* See Fulvous Whistling-Duck. *Habitat:* Lakes, marshes, grasslands, croplands. *Texas:* Common summer resident* (Apr.–Oct.) in South Texas coastal plain, rare to casual in central portions of state and along upper coast; rare in winter along central and lower coastal prairies. *Range:* Breeds from South Texas and northwestern Mexico south in lowlands to Peru and southern Brazil.

58. Tundra Swan

Cygnus columbianus (L— 52 W— 81)
Very large, entirely white bird; rounded head; black bill, often with yellow, preorbital spot. *Immature:* Brownish-gray with orangish bill. *Voice:* A mellow "hoonk," repeated. *Similar species:* The larger Trumpeter Swan has an angular, wedge-shaped rather than rounded head; Trumpeter also has orange base of lower mandible and lacks yellow eye spot; immature Tundra Swans have orangish bill with black tip while immature Trumpeter has black base of orange bill. *Habitat:* Lakes, bays. *Texas:* Rare to casual winter visitor (Dec.–Feb.) throughout. *Range:* Breeds in arctic regions of northern hemisphere; winters in coastal boreal and northern temperate areas.

59. Trumpeter Swan

Cygnus buccinator (L— 59 W— 87)
Very large, entirely white bird; black bill with orange base of lower mandible. *Immature:* Brownish-gray with orangish bill, black at base. *Voice:* A loud, bugling, low-pitched note followed by two or three notes on a higher pitch. *Similar species:* See Tundra Swan. *Habitat:* Lakes, ponds, marshes. *Texas:* Formerly a winter visitor to eastern half; current status is hypothetical, based on recent sightings from Starr and Washington cos. *Range:* Much reduced from former years. Breeds locally in Alaska, western Canada, and northwestern U.S.; winters in northwestern U.S. and western Canada, particularly along coast.

60. Greater White-fronted Goose

Anser albifrons (L— 28 W— 57)
Grayish-brown body; barred with buff on back; speckled with black on breast and belly; white lower belly and undertail coverts; pinkish bill with white feathering at base, edged in black; orange legs; in flight white rump and gray wings are key. *Immature:* Lacks white feathering at base of bill and speckling on breast and belly; pale legs and bill. *Voice:* A tremulous, high-pitched, "ho-ho-honk." *Similar species:* Other dark geese of the region have white heads or chin straps clearly visible in flight. *Habitat:* Lakes, marshes, grasslands, croplands. *Texas:* Common to uncommon winter resident (Nov.–Feb.) on coastal plain; uncommon to rare transient in eastern half, rare to casual in west. *Range:* Breeds in arctic regions; winters in temperate regions of northern hemisphere.

61. Snow Goose

Chen caerulescens (L—28 W—57)
A medium-sized white goose with black primaries; red bill with dark line bordering mandibles; red legs. *Immature:* Patterned like adult but with gray bill and legs and grayish wash on back. *Blue phase:* Dark gray body with white head, neck, and belly; red legs and bill. *Immature:* Dark brownish-gray throughout with white chin and belly; dark legs and bill. *Voice:* A shrill, high-pitched, "honk." *Similar species:* The immature Greater White-fronted Goose has no white on chin and has pale legs and bill (not dark as in blue phase immature); see Ross' Goose. *Habitat:* Lakes, marshes, grasslands, croplands. *Texas:* Common transient (Oct.–Nov., Feb.–Mar.) across eastern half; common winter resident along coastal plain; rare to casual in west. *Range:* Breeds in Canadian arctic; winters in the west along Pacific Coast from southwestern Canada to central Mexico, and in the east from Chesapeake Bay through southeastern U.S. to northeastern Mexico, also eastern Asia.

62. Ross' Goose

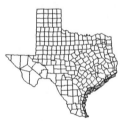

Chen rossii (L—23 W—48)
A small white goose with black primaries; red bill and legs. *Immature:* Patterned like adult but with grayish wash on back. *Blue phase:* Dark gray body with white head and belly; red legs and bill. *Voice:* Soft "kek-kek." *Similar species:* White phase Snow Goose has dark line on mandible edges ("grin patch") which Ross' lacks; Snow Goose bill is longer than head while Ross' is shorter. *Habitat:* Lakes, marshes, grasslands, croplands. *Texas:* Rare in winter along coast (Nov.–Mar.). *Range:* Breeds in high arctic of central Canada; winters mainly in California.

63. Emperor Goose

Chen canagica (L—26 W—53)
A dark, medium-sized goose; gray body barred with black and white; black throat and neck; white head and nape; pink bill; yellow legs. *Immature:* Entirely grayish barred with white. *Voice:* "Keek, keek," etc. *Habitat:* Reefs, rocky beaches, tundra ponds and lakes. *Texas:* Hypothetical—Aransas Co. *Range:* Breeds in arctic of western Alaska and eastern Siberia; winters in Aleutians.

64. Brant

Branta bernicla (L—24 W—39)
A small goose; dark above, barred with brown; white upper tail coverts nearly obscure dark tail; white below with gray barred flanks; black breast, neck, and head with white bars on side of throat; dark bill and legs. *Immature:* Lacks barring on throat. *Habits:* Feeds by dabbling for sea grasses in shallows of bays and estuaries. *Voice:* A rolling, guttural "krrrronk." *Similar species:* Black breast contrasting with white belly, and white upper tail coverts are distinctive even in flight. *Habitat:* Bay shores, estuaries. *Texas:* Casual winter visitor along coast. *Range:* Breeds in high arctic; winters along northern coasts of northern hemisphere.

65. Barnacle Goose

Branta leucopsis (L—25 W—51)
A small goose; gray above barred with black and white; white below; white rump and undertail coverts frame the black tail; black breast and neck; white head with black line from bill to eye. *Similar species:* Brant has black head. *Habitat:* Feeds in marshes and grasslands near coast. *Texas:* Hypothetical—Aransas Co. *Range:* Breeds on islands of Greenland and Barents seas; winters in coastal northern Europe.

66. Canada Goose

Branta canadensis (L—26 to 48 W—54 to 84)
Subspecies of this goose vary considerably in size; grayish brown above; grayish below; black neck and head with white chin strap; white rump, belly, and undertail coverts; black tail. *Habits:* These geese often fly in large Vs. *Voice:* A medium or high-pitched, squeaky "honk", given at different pitches by different flock members. *Similar species:* The Brant has black across breast and lacks white chin strap. *Habitat:* Lakes, estuaries, grasslands, croplands. *Texas:* Common transient (Nov., Mar.) across eastern half of state; uncommon to rare in west; common winter resident along coastal plain, scarcer inland. *Range:* Breeds across northern half of North America; winters from northern U.S. south to northern Mexico, further north along coasts; also introduced in various Old World localities.

67. Muscovy Duck

Cairina moschata (L— 25 to 30 W— 50 to 55)
A large, iridescent, black duck; broad white patches on upper wing; wing linings white; red knobs at base of bill. *Female:* Duller; smaller; often lacks bill knobs. *Habitat:* Tropical rivers and swamps; nests mainly in tree cavities. *Texas:* Uncommon to rare permanent resident (*?) along Rio Grande near Falcon Lake (Zapata Co.). *Range:* Lowlands of northern Mexico south through Middle and South America to northern Argentina.

68. Wood Duck

Aix sponsa (L— 19 W— 29)
Green head and crest streaked with white; red eye, face plate, and bill; white throat; purplish breast; iridescent dark bluish back; beige belly with white flank stripes. *Female:* Deep iridescent blue on back; brownish flanks; grayish belly; brownish-gray head and crest; white eyering and postorbital stripe; white chin. *Voice:* A high, whistling "aweek aweek aweek," etc. *Similar species:* The shrill flight call, relatively short neck, large head, and long square tail are distinctive for the birds in flight. *Habitat:* Mainly rivers and swamps. *Texas:* Uncommon summer resident* in eastern third south to San Antonio River; rare to casual further south and west; uncommon winter resident in eastern half, rare to casual in west. *Range:* Breeds across southeastern Canada and eastern half of U.S., and in west from southwestern Canada to southern California, also Cuba and Bahamas; winters in southeastern U.S. south to northeastern Mexico, and California south to northwestern Mexico.

69. Green-winged Teal

Anas crecca (L— 15 W— 24)
A small, fast-flying duck; chestnut head with broad iridescent green stripe above and behind eye; gray body; beige breast with black spots; white bar on side of breast; white tail; black rump and undertail coverts. *Female:* Mottled brown and white above and below; whitish undertail coverts; green speculum. *Voice:* A high-pitched "teet" or a nasal "kik quiik kik kik." *Similar species:* Female Green-winged Teal has smaller bill than other teal and white (not spotted) undertail coverts; female Blue-winged Teal often shows some light blue on wing, has yellowish (not grayish) legs; female Cinnamon Teal is a dark rusty

brown, rather than the grayish brown of Bluewing and buffy brown of the Greenwing. *Habitat:* Lakes, estuaries, marshes, ponds. *Texas:* Common winter resident (Nov.–Mar.) nearly throughout, scarcer in Trans-Pecos; rare summer resident* in Panhandle. *Range:* Breeds in boreal and arctic areas; winters in temperate and subtropical regions of northern hemisphere.

70. American Black Duck

Anas rubripes (L— 23 W— 36)
A large duck; dark brown body, mottled with light brown; violet speculum; reddish legs; yellowish or greenish bill; light brown head and neck finely streaked with dark brown. *Voice:* A relatively high-pitched "quack," repeated. *Similar species:* Mottled Duck has buffy, unstreaked chin and throat; female Mallard has a white tail (dark brown in Mottled and Black ducks). *Habitat:* Rivers, lakes, ponds, estuaries. *Texas:* Rare winter visitor in eastern third south to Matagorda Co. *Range:* Breeds across notheastern North America south to North Carolina; winters eastern U.S. south to northern portions of Gulf states.

71. Mottled Duck

Anas fulvigula (L— 22 W— 35)
A large duck; dark brown body, mottled with light brown; violet speculum; reddish legs; yellowish or greenish bill; light brown head and neck finely streaked with dark brown. *Habits:* Often in pairs. *Voice:* A nasal "quack" or series of "quack"s. *Similar species:* See Black Duck. *Habitat:* Ponds, lakes, bays. *Texas:* Common permanent resident* along coastal plain. *Range:* Resident in Florida and coastal plain of Gulf states to northeastern Mexico.

72. Mallard

Anas platyrhynchos (L— 23 W— 36)
A large duck; iridescent green head; yellow bill; white collar; rusty breast; gray scapulars and belly; brownish back; purple speculum; black rump and undertail coverts; curling black feathers at tail; white tail. *Female:* Brown body mottled with buff; orange bill marked with black; white outer tail feathers; blue speculum. *Voice:* A nasal "quack" (male) or series of "quack"s (female). *Similar species:* See Black Duck. *Habitat:* Ponds, lakes, marshes, estuaries, bays. *Texas:*

Northern Pintail

Green-winged Teal

Mallard

Blue-winged Teal

American Black Duck

Cinnamon Teal

Mottled Duck

Wood Duck

Gadwall

Black-bellied Whistling-Duck

Northern Shoveler

Fulvous Whistling-Duck

American Wigeon

Canvasback

Bufflehead

Ruddy

Redhead

Hooded Merganser

Common Goldeneye

Oldsquaw

Greater Scaup

Red-breasted Merganser

Lesser Scaup

Ring-necked Duck

Common Merganser

Female ducks in flight

Common to uncommon winter resident (Oct.–Mar.); rare summer resident* over most of state except south and west. The Mexican Duck (*A. p. diazi*), considered a southwestern form of the Mallard, is a rare permanent resident* in the Trans-Pecos and east along the Rio Grande to Starr Co. *Range:* Breeds across boreal and temperate regions of the northern hemisphere; winters in temperate and subtropical regions.

73. White-cheeked Pintail

Anas bahamensis (L—17 W—27)
Body grayish-brown mottled with dark brown; long, pointed, buffy tail; whitish cheek, chin, and throat; green speculum; bluish-gray bill with reddish spot at base. *Voice:* "Quack." *Habitat:* Ponds, lagoons. *Texas:* Accidental—Cameron Co. *Range:* West Indies and coastal South America to central Argentina.

74. Northern Pintail

Anas acuta (L—26 W—36)
A long-necked, long-tailed duck; gray back and sides; brown head; white neck, breast and belly; black rump, undertail coverts, and tail with extremely long central feathers; speculum iridescent brown. *Female:* Brownish mottled with dark brown throughout; grayish bill; pointed tail. *Voice:* A high-pitched "quip" (male); a series of "quack"s (female). *Similar species:* Female resembles other female dabblers but shape (long neck and relatively long, pointed tail) is distinctive. *Habitat:* Flooded fields, swales, shallow ponds, bays. *Texas:* Common winter resident (Sept.–Apr.) throughout; rare summer resident* in Panhandle. *Range:* Breeds in arctic, boreal, and temperate grasslands and tundra; winters in temperate, subtropical and tropical areas of northern hemisphere.

75. Garganey

Anas querquedula (L—16 W—25)
A small duck; chestnut head and breast; broad white eyestripe, extending down side of neck; mottled gray-brown above; gray upper wing coverts; green speculum bordered in white; black and white scapulars and flanks. *Female:* Mottled brown and white above; whitish below; dark postorbital line bordered in buffy white; white lores; gray-brown upper wing coverts; green speculum bordered in white. *Voice:* "The voice of the male is a mechanical wooden rattling note, like

that of a fishing reel. The female has an infrequent, weak, quacking voice" (Johnsgard 1979:120). *Similar species:* Females have a more distinct postorbital line bordered in whitish than other female teal, but in general females cannot be safely identified in the field. *Habitat:* Lakes, ponds, swales. *Texas:* Accidental — Kleberg Co. *Range:* Breeds in northern Eurasia; winters in central and southern Eurasia, Africa, East Indies, Australia.

76. Blue-winged Teal

Anas discors (L—16 W—25)
A small duck; brown mottled with dark brown above; tan marked with spots below; light blue patch on wing; green speculum; dark gray head with white crescent at base of bill. *Female:* Mottled brown and dark brown above and below; tan undertail coverts spotted with brown; yellowish legs. *Voice:* A high-pitched "eeeee" (male); a series of soft "quack"s (female). *Similar species:* See Green-winged Teal. *Habitat:* Lakes, estuaries, marshes, ponds. *Texas:* Common to uncommon winter resident (Aug.–May) throughout except desert regions where rare or absent; uncommon summer resident* in Panhandle, rare and irregular elsewhere. *Range:* Breeds across boreal and temperate North America south to central U.S.; winters in southern U.S. to northern South America, West Indies.

77. Cinnamon Teal

Anas cyanoptera (L—16 W—25)
Dark chestnut head and underparts; red eye; dark brown and chestnut on back; light blue on wing; green speculum; black undertail coverts. *Female:* Mottled brown and dark brown above and below; tan undertail coverts spotted with brown; yellowish legs. *Voice:* A low "quack." *Similar species:* See Green-winged Teal. *Habitat:* Lakes, marshes, estuaries, ponds. *Texas:* Common to uncommon transient (Sept.–Oct., Apr.–May) through all but northeastern quarter where rare; uncommon winter resident along coast; rare summer resident* in Panhandle. *Range:* Breeds from southwestern Canada south through western U.S. to northwest Mexico; winters in southwestern U.S. south locally through Central and South America; some South American populations resident.

78. Northern Shoveler

Anas clypeata (L—19 W—31)
Medium-sized duck with large, spatulate bill; green head; golden eye; black back; rusty sides; white breast and belly; black rump and undertail coverts; blue patch on wing; green speculum. *Female:* Mottled brown and dark brown above and below; brown eye; orange "lips" on dark bill. *Voice:* A low, hoarse "kuk kuk." *Similar species:* The heavy, flattened bill is distinctive. *Habitat:* Lakes, estuaries, bays, ponds. *Texas:* Common winter resident (Sept.–May) throughout; rare (Panhandle) to casual summer resident.* *Range:* Breeds across boreal and northern temperate regions (mainly in western North America); winters along temperate coasts south to subtropics and tropics of northern hemisphere.

79. Gadwall

Anas strepera (L—20 W—34)
A dapper, medium-sized duck; gray above; scalloped gray, black, and white on breast and flanks; brownish head; white belly; black hindquarters; chestnut, black, and white patches on wing. *Female:* Brown body mottled with buff and dark brown; orange bill marked with black; white wing patch, which, when visible, is distinctive. *Voice:* A nasal "ack." *Similar species:* Female Mallard has mottled (not white) belly, white tail, and lacks white patch on wing. *Habitat:* Lakes, estuaries, ponds, bays. *Texas:* Common winter resident throughout (Nov.–Apr.); rare summer resident* in Panhandle. *Range:* Breeds in boreal and northern temperate steppe regions; winters in temperate and northern tropical areas of northern hemisphere.

80. Eurasian Wigeon

Anas penelope (L—19 W—32)
Medium-sized duck; gray above and on flanks; pinkish breast; chestnut head with creamy forehead and crown; white belly; black hindquarters; white and black patches on wing; green speculum. *Female:* Brown body mottled with buff and dark brown; grayish bill; black wing patch; green speculum. *Similar species:* Female American Wigeon has white axillaries visible in flight (gray in female Eurasian Wigeon), also has a brownish head (paler in American, contrasting with brown back). *Habitat:* Marshes, lakes. *Texas:* Casual winter visitor along coast and at large,

inland lakes. *Range:* Breeds in northern Eurasia; winters in temperate and subtropical Eurasia, but also occurs regularly along coasts in North America.

81. American Wigeon

Anas americana (L—19 W—33)
Medium-sized duck; gray above; purplish-brown on breast and flanks; white crown and forehead; broad, iridescent green stripe through and past eye; densely mottled black and white on cheek, chin and throat; pale blue bill with black tip; white belly; black hindquarters; green speculum. *Female:* Brown body mottled with buff and dark brown; grayish bill; black wing patch; green speculum. *Voice:* A wheezy "whip" or "wheep." *Similar species:* See Eurasian Wigeon. *Habitat:* Lakes, estuaries, bays, ponds. *Texas:* Common winter resident (Nov.–Mar.) throughout; rare in summer in Panhandle. *Range:* Breeds in Alaska, Canada, and northern U.S.; winters along Atlantic and Pacific coasts, and inland from southern U.S. to northwest Colombia, West Indies.

82. Canvasback

Aythya valisineria (L—21 W—33)
A medium-sized, heavy-bodied duck with steeply sloping forehead; rusty head; red eye; black breast; gray back and belly; black hindquarters. *Female:* Grayish body, brownish neck and head. *Voice:* A gabbling "kup kup kup," etc. *Similar species:* The sloping forehead is distinctive for both sexes; female Redhead has bluish bill with black tip (Canvasback is all black); also Canvasback female shows contrast between brown head and gray body that is lacking in the all-brown female Redhead. *Habitat:* Lakes, bays. *Texas:* Uncommon winter resident (Nov.–Feb.) throughout. *Range:* Breeds across northwestern North America south to California and Iowa; winters locally from southern Canada south through U.S. to southern Mexico.

83. Redhead

Aythya americana (L— 20 W— 33)
Rusty head; red eye; bluish bill with white ring and black tip; black breast; gray back and belly; dark brown hindquarters. *Female:* Brownish throughout; bluish bill with black tip. *Voice:* A soft, catlike "yow," repeated. *Similar species:* See Canvasback. *Habitat:* Bays, lakes, ponds. *Texas:* Common transient throughout (Oct.–Nov., Mar.–Apr.); common winter resident along coast, especially lower coast, scarcer inland; uncommon summer resident* in Panhandle. *Range:* Breeds in western Canada and northwestern U.S., locally in Great Lakes regions; winters in central and southern U.S. south to Guatemala; also Greater Antilles.

84. Ring-necked Duck

Aythya collaris (L— 17 W— 28)
A smallish duck with characteristically pointed (not rounded) head; black back, breast, and hindquarters; dark head with iridescent purple sheen; gray flanks with white bar edging breast; golden eye; white feather edging at base of bill; white band across dark bill. *Female:* Brown body and head; white eyering; bill with whitish band. *Voice:* "Caah," repeated. *Similar species:* Scaup have rounded heads; male scaup have light (not dark) backs; female scaup have distinct white face patch at base of bill. *Habitat:* Lakes, ponds. *Texas:* Uncommon winter resident (Nov.–Feb.) throughout. *Range:* Breeds across central and southern Canada, northern U.S.; winters along both U.S. coasts, southern U.S. south to Panama, West Indies.

85. Greater Scaup

Aythya marila (L— 19 W— 31)
Rounded head; back gray mottled with black; black breast and hindquarters; dark head with iridescent green sheen; gray flanks; golden eye; bluish bill with dark tip. *Female:* Brown body and head; white patch at base of bill; bill bluish-gray. *Voice:* A soft cooing, or rapid, whistled "week week week" (male); a guttural "caah" (female). *Similar species:* Male Lesser Scaup has purple sheen on a more pointed head; Lesser Scaup has white band on secondaries, Greater Scaup has white band on primaries and secondaries (both sexes, visible only in flight). *Habitat:* Bays, lakes. *Texas:* Rare winter resident (Nov.–Feb.) along upper and central coast and inland on large lakes in

eastern third. *Range:* Breeds in Old and New World arctic; winters along temperate and northern coasts and large lakes in northern hemisphere.

86. Lesser Scaup

Aythya affinis (L—17 W—28)
A smallish duck; gray back; black breast and hind-quarters; dark head with iridescent purple sheen (sometimes greenish); gray flanks; golden eye; bluish bill with dark tip. *Female:* Brown body and head; white patch at base of bill; bill grayish. *Voice:* A soft "wheeooo" or single whistled "weew" (male); a weak "caah" (female). *Similar species:* See Greater Scaup. *Habitat:* Bays, lakes. *Texas:* Common winter resident (Nov.–Feb.) throughout. *Range:* Breeds in Alaska, western and central Canada, and northern U.S.; winters in coastal and central inland U.S. south to northern South America, West Indies.

87. King Eider

Somateria spectabilis (L—22 W—36)
A large duck with distinct orange protuberance (frontal shield) from forehead (male); pale blue crown and nape; blood orange bill; beige cheek and chin; white neck and breast; black back and sides; white crissum; black hindquarters. *Female:* Entirely brown mottled with dark brown; dark brown markings are wedge-shaped on sides; feathering on side of bill extends nearly to midpoint of upper mandible. *Similar species:* Female Common Eider has barring rather than wedging on sides. *Voice:* Various "cooo"s and "crok"s. *Habitat:* Coastal waters. *Texas:* Hypothetical—Aransas Co. *Range:* Breeds in Old and New World high arctic; winters along northern coasts, south to Alaska and New York in U.S.

88. Harlequin Duck

Histrionicus histrionicus (L—17 W—21)
Dark gray head with white, black, and chestnut markings; dark gray back, neck, and breast with white collar and breast bar; chestnut flanks and belly. *Female:* Brown with whitish belly; white patches on ear, forehead, and base of bill. *Voice:* Various squeaks, whistles, and trills. *Habitat:* Rocky coasts. *Texas:* Hypothetical—Aransas Co. *Range:* Breeds in northwestern North America from Alaska to Idaho, in the northeast south to Quebec, also Iceland, Greenland,

and Siberia; winters mainly along northern coasts, south to California and New York in U.S.

89. Oldsquaw

Clangula hyemalis (L—19 W—29)
Dark head with white face; dark neck and breast; gray and brown on back; dark wings; white belly and undertail coverts; black, extremely long, pointed central tail feathers. *Female and winter male:* White head with dark brown cheek patch and crown; white neck; grayish-brown breast; white belly and undertail coverts; short, sharply pointed tail. *Voice:* "Ah ah ah-ah-ee-ah." *Similar species:* Combination of white head and all dark wings is distinctive, as is the call. *Habitat:* Marine, bays, large lakes. *Texas:* Rare winter visitor along coast. *Range:* Breeds in high arctic of Old and New World; winters mainly along north coasts of northern hemisphere, in U.S. south to California and South Carolina.

90. Black Scoter

Melanitta nigra (L—19 W—33)
Entirely black with orange knob at base of bill. *Female:* Dark brown with whitish cheek and throat contrasting with dark crown and nape. *Immature:* Patterned similarly to female but with whitish belly. *Voice:* a rattle-like "quack." *Similar species:* Female White-winged Scoter has feathering almost to nostrils on bill (lacking on Black and Surf scoters); Surf Scoter female has grayish bill and distinct white pre- and postorbital patches on otherwise brown head. *Habitat:* Marine, bays, lakes. *Texas:* Rare winter visitor (Nov.–Apr.) along coast. *Range:* Breeds locally in tundra regions of Eurasia and North America; winters in northern and temperate coastal waters of northern hemisphere, south to California and South Carolina in U.S.

91. Surf Scoter

Melanitta perspicillata (L—19 W—34)
Black with white patches on nape and forehead; orange bill with bull's-eye on side (white circle, black center); white eye. *Female:* Entirely brown with white patches in front of and behind eye; dark bill. *Voice:* A guttural croak. *Similar species:* See Black Scoter. *Habitat:* Marine, bays, lakes. *Texas:* Rare winter visitor along coast. *Range:* Breeds in northern North America

south to central Canada; winters mainly along coasts from Alaska to northwestern Mexico, and Nova Scotia to Florida; also Great Lakes.

92. White-winged Scoter

Melanitta fusca (L— 22 W— 39)
Black with white eye and wing patches; dark bill with black knob at base and orange tip. *Female:* Entirely dark brown (sometimes with whitish pre- and postorbital patches); bill dark orange with black markings; feathering on bill extends nearly to nostrils; white secondaries sometimes visible on swimming bird. *Voice:* A plaintive whistle or low growl. *Similar species:* See Black Scoter. *Habitat:* Bays, lakes. *Texas:* Rare winter visitor over most of Texas except southwestern sections where absent. *Range:* Breeds in bogs, ponds, and lakes in boreal and arctic regions of Old and New World; winters mainly along northern coasts, south to northwestern Mexico and South Carolina in North America.

93. Common Goldeneye

Bucephala clangula (L— 18 W— 30)
Iridescent green head (sometimes purplish); golden eye; white patch at base of bill; black back and hindquarters; white breast, sides and belly; black and white scapulars; white wing patch visible in flight. *Female:* Gray body; brown head; golden eye; gray bill yellowish at tip (mostly yellow in some birds). *Voice:* A high-pitched, nasal "eeh." *Similar species:* Bill of Common Goldeneye appears to be nearly as long as head while that of the Barrow's Goldeneye appears to be half the length of the head; Barrow's show less white in wing than Common; male Barrow's Goldeneye has purplish sheen on head and crescent-shaped preorbital patch; most female Barrow's have an orange bill (gray or mostly gray in most female Common Goldeneyes). *Habitat:* Bays, lakes. *Texas:* Uncommon winter resident along coast (Nov.–Apr.), uncommon to rare inland. *Range:* Breeds across boreal and northern temperate regions of Old and New World; winters along northern coasts south to temperate and subtropical regions of the northern hemisphere.

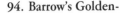

94. Barrow's Golden-eye

Bucephala islandica (L—18 W—29)
Iridescent purple head (sometimes greenish); white crescent-shaped patch at base of bill; golden eye; black back and hindquarters; white breast, belly, and sides; black and white scapulars. *Female:* Gray body; brown head; golden eye; orange bill (partially gray in some birds). *Voice:* "Eck eck eck," etc. *Similar species:* See Common Goldeneye. *Habitat:* Coastal waters, lakes. *Texas:* Casual winter visitor (Nov.–Apr.), mainly along coast. *Range:* Breeds locally in northwestern U.S. and Canada, northeastern Canada, Greenland, and Iceland; winters in coastal North America (Alaska to California and Nova Scotia to New York).

95. Bufflehead

Bucephala albeola (L—14 W—23)
A small, plump, short-billed duck; head white from top of crown to nape, the rest iridescent purple; black back; white breast, belly, and sides; gray bill; pink legs. *Female and immature:* Dark back; grayish-white below; dark head with large white patch extending below and behind eye. *Voice:* A weak, nasal "eeh." *Similar species:* The male Hooded Merganser also has white back of crown and nape but the white is edged in black; this merganser has a thin, pointed bill, rusty sides, and golden eye (dark in Bufflehead). *Habitat:* Bays, lakes, estuaries. *Texas:* Common winter resident (Nov.–Feb.) throughout. *Range:* Breeds across Canada and extreme northern U.S.; winters from subarctic along both coasts of North America, and inland from central U.S. south to central Mexico.

96. Hooded Mer-ganser

Lophodytes cucullatus (L—18 W—26)
Head with white crest from top of crown to nape broadly edged in black, the rest black; golden eye; black back and tail; white breast with prominent black bar; rusty sides; black bill. *Female and immature male:* Body brownish; head a pale orange with dusky crown; pale orange crest off back of crown and nape; upper mandible dark; lower mandible orangish. *Voice:* A trilled "crrroooo" (male); low grunt (female). *Similar species:* Other female mergansers have dark russet heads, bright orange bills, and grayish bodies. *Habitat:* Ponds, lakes, estuaries, bays. *Texas:* Common winter resident (Dec.–Apr.) in eastern third, uncommon to rare in west. *Range:* Breeds

across central and southern Canada and northern
U.S., further south in Rockies and Appalachians;
winters mainly along coasts from southern Canada to
northern Mexico, West Indies.

**97. Common Mer-
ganser**

Mergus merganser (L—25 W—36)
Iridescent green head; red-orange bill; black back;
gray rump and tail; white breast, sides, and belly. *Female and immature male:* Rufous, crested head;
white chin; rufous throat and neck ending abruptly at
white breast; gray back and sides; orange bill. *Voice:*
A low "uu-eek-wa" (male); a harsh "karr" (female).
Similar species: The female Red-breasted Merganser
has a white wing patch (absent in Common Merganser), and a whitish neck and throat with no abrupt
line between rufous neck and throat. *Habitat:* Lakes,
rivers, bays. *Texas:* Uncommon winter resident (Nov.-
Mar.) in Panhandle, rare elsewhere in northern half
and rare to casual in south. *Range:* Breeds in Old and
New World subarctic and boreal regions, and south in
mountains into temperate areas; winters from northern coasts south and inland through temperate and
subtropical zones of the northern hemisphere.

**98. Red-breasted
Merganser**

Mergus serrator (L—22 W—32)
Iridescent green, crested head; red-orange bill; white
collar; buffy breast streaked with brown; gray back,
rump, and tail; black shoulder with white chevrons;
white scapulars; grayish sides. *Female and immature
male:* Rufous, crested head; white chin and throat;
gray back and sides; white wing patch. *Voice:* "Eeoww"
(male); a harsh "karr" (female). *Similar species:* See
Common Merganser. *Habitat:* Bays, lakes, marine.
Texas: Common winter resident (Dec.-Mar.) along
coast, rare to casual inland. *Range:* Breeds in arctic
and boreal regions of Old and New World; winters
mainly along coasts in southern boreal and temperate
areas.

99. Ruddy Duck

Oxyura jamaicensis (L—15 W—23)
A small duck; chestnut body; stiff, black tail held at a 45-degree angle; black cap; white cheek; blue bill. *Winter:* Grayish-brown body; dark cap; white cheek. *Female:* Mottled grayish and white body; stiff, black tail; dark cap and dark line below eye. *Voice:* A staccato, cicada-like "tsk-tsk-tsk-tsk quark." *Similar species:* Female and winter male Masked Ducks have dark cap, a dark line through the eye, and a third dark line below the eye. *Habitat:* Lakes, ponds, bays. *Texas:* Common winter resident (Dec.–Mar.) throughout; rare summer resident.* *Range:* Breeds locally from northern Canada through the U.S. to central Mexico, West Indies, and South America; winters in coastal and southern U.S. south to Nicaragua and elsewhere in tropical breeding range.

100. Masked Duck

Oxyura dominica (L—14 W—22)
Rusty brown body with black head; back with dark spots edged in gold; blue bill; stiff tail. *Female and winter male:* Mottled brown body; buffy head with dark cap, dark line through eye and dark line below eye; back with dark spots edged in gold. *Voice:* "Curee curoo" repeated; a low "ooo ooo ooo"; a low chuckle. *Similar species:* See Ruddy Duck. *Habitat:* Ponds, lakes. *Texas:* Rare to casual resident* along coastal plain. *Range:* Lowlands of northern Mexico south to northern Argentina, West Indies.

Order Falconiformes
Family Cathartidae
Vultures

Large, black, diurnal raptors with long, hooked bills and featherless heads. They forage mostly from the air for carrion.

101. Black Vulture

Coragyps atratus (L—26 W—57)
Entirely black with naked, black-skinned head; primaries silvery from below. *Habits:* Black Vultures do not normally soar; they alternate flapping and gliding, usually at low levels. *Similar species:* Turkey Vultures soar, seldom flapping, and normally hold their wings at an angle while Black Vultures keep

their wings flat during glides; Black Vultures have silvery primaries while Turkey Vultures have silvery primaries and secondaries. *Habitat:* Savanna, thorn forest, second growth. *Texas:* Common resident* of eastern half. *Range:* Breeds from eastern (New Jersey) and southwestern (Arizona) U.S. south to central Argentina; winters from southern U.S. south through breeding range.

102. Turkey Vulture

Cathartes aura (L—26 W—69)
Black with naked, red-skinned head; relatively long tail; silvery flight feathers (outlining black wing lining). *Immature:* Black head. *Habits:* Soars for long periods with wings held at an angle above horizontal. *Similar species:* See Black Vulture. *Habitat:* Nearly ubiquitous except in extensive agricultural areas. *Texas:* Common summer resident*; common winter resident in southeast quarter, uncommon to rare or absent elsewhere. *Range:* Breeds from southern Canada south to southern South America, Bahamas and Cuba; winters from southern U.S. south through breeding range.

Family Accipitridae
Hawks, Kites, and Eagles

A diverse assemblage of diurnal raptors, all of which have strongly hooked bills and powerful talons. Clark and Wheeler (1987) and Dunne et al. (1988) provide identification guides for advanced students of this difficult group.

103. Osprey

Pandion haliaetus (L—23 W—63)
Dark brown above; white below often with dark streaking (females); white crown with ragged crest from back of head; broad dark line extending behind yellow eye; white chin and cheek; extended wings are white finely barred with brown with prominent dark patches at wrist. *Habits:* Feeds mainly on fish snatched from water surface. *Voice:* A shrill "kew," repeated. *Habitat:* Estuaries, lakes, rivers, bays. *Texas:* Uncommon transient (Sept.–Nov., Mar.–May) in eastern third, scarcer in west; rare in winter in eastern third; may have bred. *Range:* Breeds in boreal,

temperate, and some tropical localities of Old and New World, particularly along coasts; winters mainly in tropical and subtropical zones.

104. Hook-billed Kite

Chondrohierax uncinatus (L—16 W—32)
Gray above; heavily barred with rusty brown below; heavy, hooked bill; dark tail with two broad whitish bars; in flight, wings appear short and rounded, tail appears long and narrow. *Dark phase:* Entirely dark brown with broad, whitish tail bar. *Female:* Brown above, barred rusty below with rusty collar; dark tail with two pale bars. *Immature:* Brown above; buffy below with brown spotting; barred tail. *Habits:* Feeds on snails. *Habitat:* Swamps; riparian forest. *Texas:* Rare to casual resident in Starr and Hidalgo cos. *Range:* Northern Mexico to southern South America, Cuba.

105. American Swallow-tailed Kite

Elanoides forficatus (L—23 W—48)
White body and head; black back, wings and long, deeply forked tail; in flight note swallow tail and white wing linings outlined by black flight feathers. *Habits:* Primarily insectivorous. *Voice:* A high-pitched, squeaky "whee ki-we ki-we ki-we," etc. *Habitat:* Riparian forest, woodlands, prairies. *Texas:* Rare transient along coast (Sept., Apr.). *Range:* Formerly bred across eastern U.S., but now U.S. populations are rare and local in Louisiana, South Carolina, and Georgia, with good numbers remaining only in Florida; breeds from U.S. south to Argentina; winters mainly in South America.

106. Black-shouldered Kite

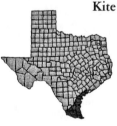
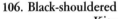

Elanus caeruleus (L—16 W—42)
Gray above; white below; red eyes and yellow legs; black shoulders; in flight note white tail and silvery wings with black wrist mark. *Immature:* Rusty wash on back, head and breast. *Habits:* Often hovers while foraging. *Voice:* A shrill "kee kee kee," etc. *Habitat:* Prairie, savanna, thorn forest. *Texas:* Common winter resident (Nov.–Mar.), uncommon summer resident* along central and lower coastal plain. *Range:* Resident from Oregon, California, Oklahoma and Louisiana south to central Argentina; also in Old World tropics and subtropics.

107. Snail Kite

Rostrhamus sociabilis (L—17 W—39)
Entirely dark brown with white rump and base of tail; red lores and cere (base of upper mandible); red eyes; red-orange legs; long, hooked bill. *Female and immature:* Dark brown and rusty above; variably streaked buff and brown below with buffy throat and eyebrow. *Habits:* Feeds mainly on *Pomacea* snails. *Voice:* A low, nasal, frog-like "ah-ah-ah-ah-ah-ah-ah-ah." *Habitat:* Fresh water wetlands. *Texas:* Accidental—Jim Wells Co.; sight records—Cameron Co. *Range:* Resident in Florida, Cuba, southern Mexico to central Argentina.

108. Mississippi Kite

Ictinia mississippiensis (L—15 W—35)
Dark gray above; pale gray below with black primaries and tail; red eye; orange-yellow legs; gray cere; in flight note pointed wings, uniform gray underparts and dark, slightly forked tail. *Immature:* Streaked rusty below; barred tail; red or yellow eye. *Habitat:* Riparian and oak woodlands; deciduous forest and swamps; savanna. *Texas:* Uncommon summer resident* in Panhandle and north-central Texas, rare in East Texas south to the Guadalupe River; uncommon transient nearly throughout except in Trans-Pecos where rare to casual. *Range:* Breeds in southern U.S.; winters in central South America.

109. Bald Eagle

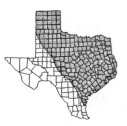

Haliaeetus leucocephalus (L—35 W—84) **Endangered**
Huge size; dark brown body; white head and tail; yellow beak and legs. *Immature:* Entirely brown with whitish wing linings and base of tail. *Habits:* Feeds primarily on fish. *Voice:* A descending "keee chip-chip-chip-chip." *Similar species:* Immature Golden Eagle has well-defined white (not whitish) base of tail and white wing patches at base of primaries; also has golden head. *Habitat:* Lakes, rivers, estuaries. *Texas:* Rare winter resident (Oct.–Mar.) in northern and eastern portions; occasional concentrations can be seen at lakes in northeast and north-central Texas; rare summer resident* in north and east; formerly common. *Range:* Breeds across Canada and northern U.S., south along coasts to Florida, California, and Texas; winters throughout breeding range from southern Canada southward, particularly along the coasts and at larger inland lakes.

110. Northern Harrier

Circus cyaneus (L—19 W—42)
A slim, long-tailed, long-winged hawk; gray above; pale below with dark spots; white rump; yellow eye and cere; long, yellow legs. *Female:* Streaked dark brown and tan above; whitish below heavily streaked with brown; yellow eyes; pale yellowish cere; yellow legs; barred tail; white rump. *Habits:* Flies low over open areas, usually within a few feet of the ground, alternately flapping and gliding; wings at an angle during glides; often hovers just above the ground. *Voice:* A rapid, descending "cheek-cheek-cheek-cheek-cheek." *Similar species:* Similar haunts and habits as Short-eared Owl but white rump is distinctive; Harris' Hawk has white rump but is usually dark below (except immature) and is mainly a sit-and-wait predator in thorn forest—doesn't flap and glide or hover. *Habitat:* Marshes, prairies, estuaries, savanna. *Texas:* Common winter resident (Sept.–Mar.) nearly throughout; rare to casual in summer.* *Range:* Breeds across boreal and temperate regions of northern hemisphere; winters in temperate and tropical zones.

111. Sharp-shinned Hawk

Accipiter striatus (L—12 W—24)
Slate gray above; barred rusty and white below; gray crown with rusty face; red eye; yellow cere; barred tail; long, yellow legs; as in other accipiters, the female is much larger than the male. *Immature:* Brown above; streaked brown and white on head, breast, and belly. *Habits:* Flight is characterized by a series of rapid wing beats followed by a short, flat-winged glide. *Voice:* A rapid, high-pitched "kew-ki-ki-ki-ki-ki-ki," etc. *Similar species:* The calls of the three similar species of accipiters are different; also, Sharpshin has a squared tail (slightly rounded in the larger Cooper's Hawk). *Habitat:* Forests. *Texas:* Common to uncommon winter resident (Oct.–May) throughout except Panhandle where scarce; has bred.* *Range:* Breeds from subarctic Alaska and Canada to northern Argentina (except prairie regions and most of southern U.S.), also in Greater Antilles; winters from northern coastal regions and southern Canada south through breeding range.

112. Cooper's Hawk

Accipiter cooperii (L—18 W—32)
Slate gray above; barred rusty and white below; gray crown with rusty face; red eye; yellow cere; barred tail; long, yellow legs. *Immature:* Brown above; streaked brown and white on head, breast, and belly. *Voice:* A wheezy "peeew," repeated. *Similar species:* See Sharp-shinned Hawk. Adult Northern Goshawk is barred gray and white below, and has a prominent white eyebrow; immature Goshawk closely resembles immature Cooper's but has white eyebrow. *Habitat:* Forests. *Texas:* Uncommon to rare winter resident (Oct.–May) throughout except Panhandle where rare; rare summer resident.* *Range:* Breeds from southern Canada to northern Mexico; winters from northern U.S. to Honduras.

113. Northern Goshawk

Accipiter gentilis (L—23 W—39)
Slate gray above; barred gray and white below; gray crown with prominent white eyebrow; dark patch behind eye; red eye; yellow cere; unevenly barred tail; long, yellow legs. *Immature:* Brown above; streaked brown and white on head, breast, and belly; white eyebrow; uneven tail barring. *Voice:* "Tew tew tew tew tew tew," etc. *Similar species:* See Cooper's Hawk. *Habitat:* Forests. *Texas:* Rare winter visitor (Nov.–Mar.) to Trans-Pecos and Panhandle. *Range:* Breeds in boreal regions of northern hemisphere, south in mountains to temperate and tropical zones; winters in breeding range and irregularly southward and in lowlands.

114. Crane Hawk

Geranospiza caerulescens (L—19 W—32)
Black; long tail; two white bars; long, orange legs; red eye; in flight note that extremely long legs extend nearly to tip of long tail. *Immature:* Grayish streaking on head; buffy barring on belly. *Habitat:* Lowland riparian forest, swamps, wet woodlands. *Texas:* Accidental—Hidalgo Co. *Range:* Northern Mexico to northern Argentina.

115. Common Black-Hawk

Buteogallus anthracinus (L— 21 W— 48)
Black; black tail with broad white bar and thin, white terminal band; yellow cere and legs; in flight note the single white bar and white at base of primaries. *Immature:* Brown above; streaked brown and white on head, breast, and belly; prominent dark malar stripe (from base of bill); several sinuous bars on tail; buffy wing linings. *Voice:* A distinctive "keeeeeeeee" first rising in pitch, then trailing off, repeated — often given in flight. *Similar species:* Zone-tailed Hawk has three white tail bands plus terminal strip, and shows whitish primaries and secondaries in flight. *Habitat:* Riparian forest, woodlands, second growth, swamps. *Texas:* Rare summer resident*in Jeff Davis Co. *Range:* Breeds in lowlands from southwestern U.S. to northern South America; Cuba.

116. Harris' Hawk

Parabuteo unicinctus (L— 21 W— 45)
Dark brown; chestnut shoulders and thighs; yellow cere and legs; dark tail with broad white band at base and narrow white terminal strip; brown eyes. *Immature:* Dark below variably streaked with buff and white; in flight — wing linings and flight feathers are whitish finely barred with brown, but chestnut shows at wrist; tail whitish finely barred with brown. *Habits:* Mainly a "sit-and-wait" predator, often seen perched on telephone poles, fence posts and dead snags. *Voice:* A short, dry scream. *Similar species:* Northern Harrier has white rump but is long-winged, long-tailed, and much paler (Harris' Hawk usually appears black in flight, not brownish or grayish). *Habitat:* Thorn forest, arid scrub. *Texas:* Common resident* in South, Central, and West Texas. *Range:* Resident from southwestern U.S. to central Argentina.

117. Gray Hawk

Buteo nitidus (L—17 W— 35)
Gray above; whitish below finely barred with gray; white undertail coverts; yellow legs and cere; brown eyes; in flight — wings are whitish finely checked with gray, black-tipped; tail is barred gray and white. *Immature:* Brown above; buffy with dark markings below; head streaked with brown. *Voice:* "A plaintive *cree-eer*" (Peterson and Chalif 1973:33). *Similar species:* Immature Broad-winged and Roadside hawks are similar to the larger, paler immature Gray Hawk.

Habitat: Riparian forest, open woodlands; pastures with scattered trees and hedgerows. *Texas:* Rare to casual resident in Lower Rio Grande Valley; has bred.* *Range:* Southern Arizona and Texas south to northern Argentina.

118. Roadside Hawk

Buteo magnirostris (L—14 W—30)
Grayish-brown above, and on head and upper breast ("bib"); whitish throat streaked with brown; lower breast and belly barred rusty and white; tail dark with four broad, pale bars; yellow eyes, cere, and legs. *Immature:* Brown above; streaked brown and white on throat and breast; irregularly barred on belly. *Habits:* Largely a "sit-and-wait" predator, often seen sitting on posts and snags. *Voice:* A hoarse, high-pitched whistle. *Similar species:* Adult Broadwing has dark (not yellow) eyes, and is evenly barred with rust below (no "bib" effect). *Habitat:* Savanna, grasslands, agricultural areas, pastures, roadsides. *Texas:* Casual— Lower Rio Grande Valley. *Range:* Northern Mexico to northern Argentina.

119. Red-shouldered Hawk

Buteo lineatus (L—19 W—39)
Mottled dark brown and white above with rusty shoulders, head and upper breast; barred rusty below; tail dark with four narrow, whitish bars; brown eye; pale yellowish cere; yellow legs; in flight note brown and white barring on flight feathers, pale white patch at base of primaries ("window"), and rusty wing linings. *Immature:* Brown mottled with white above; buff streaked with brown on breast, barred on belly; rusty shoulders. *Voice:* A strident "ki-cheek ki-cheek ki-cheek keeew," etc. *Similar species:* Immature is similar to other immature buteos but usually shows rusty shoulders; wing "window." *Habitat:* Riparian forest, woodlands, swamps. *Texas:* Common to rare permanent resident* in eastern third and Central Texas. *Range:* Breeds in southeastern Canada and eastern U.S. south to central Mexico, also California; winters from central U.S. south through breeding range.

Red-shouldered

Broad-winged

Zone-tailed

White-tailed

Hawks in flight. *Left:* immature, *right:* adult

120. Broad-winged Hawk

Buteo platypterus (L—16 W—35)
Dark brown above; barred rusty and white below; dark tail with two white bands equal in width to dark bands; brown eye; yellowish cere; yellow legs; in flight note whitish flight feathers with black tips; buffy wing linings. *Immature:* Brown above; streaked brown and white below; tail narrowly barred with brown and white. *Habits:* Seen in Texas as an abundant transient, often in kettles of hundreds of birds. *Voice:* A high-pitched "ki-cheeeee." *Similar species:* See Roadside and Red-shouldered hawks. *Habitat:* Forests, but seen in migration kettles over any habitat. *Texas:* Common to uncommon transient (Mar.–Apr., Sept.–Oct.) in eastern third; rare summer resident* in eastern quarter. *Range:* Breeds across southern Canada from Alberta eastward, eastern half of U.S. south to Texas and Florida; winters from southern Mexico to southern Brazil; resident in West Indies.

121. Short-tailed Hawk

Buteo brachyurus (L—15 W—35)
Dark brown above; white below; dark brown head with white at base of beak; yellow cere and legs; chestnut patch on side of breast; finely barred tail with broad, dark subterminal band. *Dark phase:* Dark brown throughout; whitish forehead; in flight—wing linings are dark, flight feathers are light, barred with dark brown; tail as in light phase. *Immature, light phase:* Mottled brown above; buffy white below with sparse brown streaking; tail finely barred. *Immature, dark phase:* Dark brown mottled with buff above and below; finely barred tail. *Habitat:* Savanna, open woodlands. *Texas:* Hypothetical—Aransas and Hidalgo cos. *Range:* Resident, southern Florida, northern Mexico to northern Argentina.

122. Swainson's Hawk

Buteo swainsoni (L—20 W—50)
Brown above; reddish-brown breast; buffy belly with sparse brown streaking on flanks; whitish chin and cere; yellowish legs; in flight note dark flight feathers, whitish wing linings; barred tail with broad, dark subterminal band. *Dark phase:* Entirely dark brown; tail as in light phase, usually paler toward base. *Immature, light phase:* Dark above; mottled white and brown below; often with white forehead and dark patches on breast. *Habits:* Soars with wings slightly

angled above the horizontal. *Voice:* A shrill, descending "keeeeeeee." *Habitat:* Prairies, savanna, thorn forest, desert scrub. *Texas:* Common transient (Apr., Sept.) throughout except eastern quarter where rare; common to uncommon summer resident* in western half. *Range:* Breeds in deserts and Great Plains of western North America from Alaska and Canada south to northwestern Mexico; winters in southern South America.

123. White-tailed Hawk

Buteo albicaudatus (L— 24 W— 48)
Gray above with rusty shoulders; white below; white tail with broad, black, subterminal band; gray head with white at base of beak; yellow cere and legs; brown eye; in flight the tail is distinctive. *Immature:* Largely dark, some whitish streaking below; shows some rust on shoulders; brownish to whitish, finely barred tail. *Voice:* "Ki-lu ki-lu ki-lu," etc. *Habitat:* Savanna, prairie, thorn forest, pastures. *Texas:* Common to uncommon resident* of South Texas, mainly along coastal plain. *Range:* South Texas and northwestern Mexico south to central Argentina.

124. Zone-tailed Hawk

Buteo albonotatus (L— 20 W— 52)
Black; white lores; yellow cere and legs; black tail with two broad white bands; in flight note Turkey Vulture–like wing pattern of dark wing linings and whitish flight feathers. *Immature:* Flecked with white below. *Habits:* Soars like a Turkey Vulture with wings slightly angled. *Voice:* "A slurred, two-noted high-pitched whistle" (Edwards 1972:32). *Similar species:* Turkey Vulture does not have banded tail. *Habitat:* Arid scrub, pine-oak woodland. *Texas:* Rare to casual summer resident* in mountains of Trans-Pecos and western portions of Edwards Plateau. *Range:* Southwestern U.S. to southern Brazil.

125. Red-tailed Hawk

Buteo jamaicensis (L— 22 W— 53)
A large hawk, extremely variable in plumage; most common adult plumage is mottled brown and white above; white below with speckling across belly; rusty tail (appears whitish from below); in flight, dark forewing lining contrasts with generally light underwing. *Immature:* Mottled brown and white above; streaked

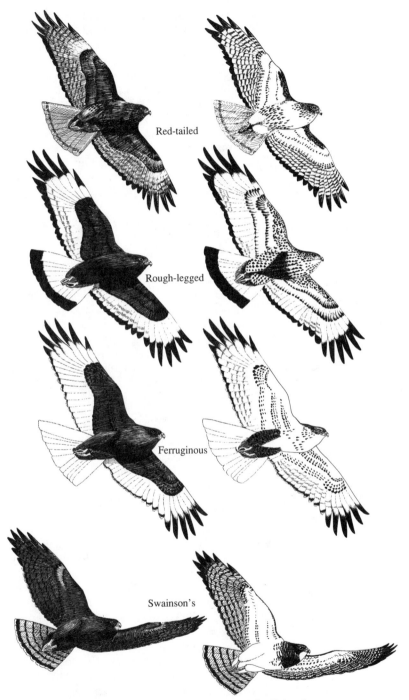

Red-tailed

Rough-legged

Ferruginous

Swainson's

Hawks in flight. *Left:* dark phase, *right:* light phase

brown and white below; brown tail finely barred with grayish-white. *Light phase* (Krider's): Much paler; pale orange tail. *Dark phase* (Harlan's): Dark throughout with some white speckling; dark tail, whitish at base, darker at tip with rusty wash. *Voice:* A hoarse, drawn out, screech, "ke-aaaaaaaah." *Similar species:* Rusty tail is distinctive for adults. *Habitat:* Open woodlands, thorn forest, savanna. *Texas:* Common winter resident (Oct.–Mar.) throughout; uncommon to rare summer resident.* *Range:* Breeds from subarctic of Alaska and Canada to Panama; winters from northern U.S. south through breeding range; resident in West Indies.

126. Ferruginous Hawk

Buteo regalis (L—23 W—55)
A large, pale buteo; rusty above; dark wings; whitish head streaked with rufous; breast and belly speckled with rust; rusty thighs; yellow cere and legs; whitish tail with pale orange terminal band; in flight note entirely white underparts except black wing tips and rusty thighs. *Dark phase:* Entirely dark brown except for whitish tail and flight feathers. *Immature:* Like adult but thighs whitish. *Voice:* A dry scream. *Similar species:* The whitish tail, lacking a dark band, separates this from other buteos. *Habitat:* Prairies, savanna, desert. *Texas:* Rare resident* in northern Panhandle; rare winter resident (Nov.–Feb.) nearly throughout except East Texas, uncommon along central and lower coast. *Range:* Breeds from southwestern Canada south to southwestern U.S.; winters from central and southern portions of breeding range south to central Mexico.

127. Rough-legged Hawk

Buteo lagopus (L—22 W—51)
A large hawk with legs feathered all the way to the toes; mottled brown and white above; buffy with brown streaks on breast; dark brown belly; white tail with dark subterminal band. *Dark phase:* Entirely dark except whitish flight feathers and tail with broad, dark, subterminal band. *Immature:* Similar to adult—whitish or finely barred tail with broad, dark, subterminal band; base of primaries show white from above in flight. *Habits:* Flies low over open areas, often hovering. *Voice:* A cat-like "keeeeew," dropping in pitch. *Similar species:* Northern Harrier forages in

similar fashion, but has a white rump (not tail), is much smaller and slimmer, and lacks dark band contrasting with buffy breast. *Habitat:* Open areas. *Texas:* Uncommon winter resident (Oct.–Feb.) in Panhandle, rare to casual further south. *Range:* Breeds in arctic and subarctic regions of Old and New World; winters mainly in temperate zone.

128. Golden Eagle

Aquila chrysaetos (L—34 W—71)
Huge; dark brown with golden wash on head and shaggy neck; legs feathered to feet; appears entirely dark in flight. *Immature:* Dark brown with white patch at base of primaries and basal half of tail white. *Voice:* A rapid series of nasal chips. *Similar species:* See Bald Eagle. *Habitat:* Open areas. *Texas:* Rare summer resident* in western third (where hunted as a sheep predator); uncommon to rare winter resident (Oct.–Mar.) in western two-thirds. *Range:* Breeds primarily in open and mountainous regions of boreal and temperate zones in northern hemisphere; winters in central and southern portions of breeding range.

Family Falconidae
Caracaras and Falcons

With the exception of the caracara, the falcons are sleek birds with pointed wings and long, square tails.

129. Crested Caracara

Polyborus plancus (L—23 W—50)
Black body; black, crested crown; white face and neck; white breast barred with black; red cere and eyering; bluish bill; long, yellow legs; in flight note white patches on basal half of primaries and white (actually finely barred) tail with dark terminal band. *Immature:* Buffy neck and breast. *Habits:* Often feeds on carrion along the road. *Voice:* A low croak. *Similar species:* The whitish neck, breast, primaries and tail with black bar are distinctive. *Habitat:* Thorn forest, savanna, prairie, arid scrub. *Texas:* Common to rare resident* in South and south-central Texas. *Range:* Southwestern U.S. to southern Argentina, southern Florida, Cuba.

130. American Kestrel

Falco sparverius (L—10 W—22)
A small falcon; gray crown; black and white facial pattern; orange buff back and underparts spotted with brown; blue-gray wings; orange tail with black subterminal bar edged in white. *Female:* Rusty back and wings barred with brown. *Habits:* Perches or hovers a few feet off the ground while foraging; often seen on telephone wires along the road. *Voice:* A rapid, high-pitched "kle-kle-kle-kle-kle," etc. *Similar species:* Merlin shows a distinctly dark tail barred with white; lacks facial pattern of Kestrel. *Habitat:* Open areas. *Texas:* Common winter resident (Sept.–Mar.) throughout; uncommon to rare summer resident* in northern half. *Range:* Breeds nearly throughout western hemisphere from subarctic Alaska and Canada to southern Argentina, West Indies; winters from northern temperate regions south through breeding range.

131. Merlin

Falco columbarius (L—11 W—25)
A small falcon; slate above, buffy below with dark brown spots and streaks; white throat; brown eyes, yellow cere and legs; black tail, white at base, with two white bars and white terminal edging. *Female:* Dark brown above. *Habits:* A bird hunter; sallies from low perches, using surprise and speed to capture prey. *Voice:* "Kwe kwe kwe kwe kwe," etc. *Similar species:* See Kestrel. *Habitat:* Open woodlands, hedgerows, second growth, savanna. *Texas:* Rare transient (Oct., Apr.) throughout; rare winter resident along central and lower coast. *Range:* Breeds across boreal and northern temperate regions of Old and New World; winters in southern temperate and tropical zones.

132. Aplomado Falcon

Falco femoralis (L—16 W—37)
A medium-sized falcon; gray above; gray crown; black facial pattern against white face; white throat and breast; black, finely barred belly; rusty thighs; black tail barred with white. *Immature:* Buffy face and breast streaked with brown. *Similar species:* Merlin lacks facial pattern and dark belly contrasting with light breast. *Habitat:* Savanna, open woodlands, grasslands. *Texas:* Casual in South Texas and westward along the Rio Grande; a hacking program was begun in 1987 at the Laguna Atascosa National Wildlife

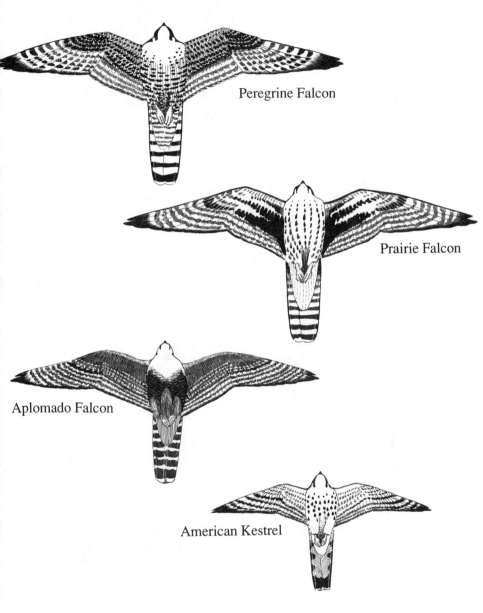

Peregrine Falcon

Prairie Falcon

Aplomado Falcon

American Kestrel

Falcons in flight

Refuge (Cameron Co.) to reintroduce this bird into its former Texas range. *Range:* Resident from southwestern U.S. (at least formerly) to southern South America.

133. Peregrine Falcon

Falco peregrinus (L—18 W—40) **Endangered**
A large falcon; dark gray above; white below with spotting and barring on belly and thighs; black crown and cheek with white neck patch; brown eye; yellow eyering, cere, and legs; in flight note large size, long, pointed wings, long tail, whitish underparts finely barred and spotted; black and white facial pattern. *Immature:* Dark brown above; buffy below spotted and streaked with brown; has facial pattern of adult. *Habits:* Forages by flying with swift, powerful wing beats, well up in the air, then stooping on prey. *Voice:* A rapid "kee kee kee kee." *Similar species:* Prairie Falcon is much paler, has two dark commas on face (not one), and shows black axillaries in flight. *Habitat:* Open areas, usually near water. *Texas:* Rare to casual transient (Sept.–Oct., Mar.–Apr.) throughout, common to uncommon along coast; rare winter resident along coast; rare summer resident in Brewster and Culberson cos. *Range:* Breeds in various boreal, temperate, and tropical localities in both the Old World and the New World. Northern birds are largely migratory. Breeding populations have been extirpated from most of temperate North America.

134. Prairie Falcon

Falco mexicanus (L—18 W—40)
Pale, sandy brown above mottled with brown and white; white below with brown spotting; sandy crown with white face; two commas extend down from crown, one through the eye, the other through the ear; tail brownish barred with white; in flight note black axillaries against otherwise pale underparts. *Habits:* A bird hunter, stooping on prey from well up in the air. *Voice:* "Kee kee kee kee," etc. *Similar species:* See Peregrine Falcon. *Habitat:* Desert, thorn forest, arid scrub, prairie—cliffs, crags, canyons, or similar situation required for nesting. *Texas:* Rare to casual winter resident (Sept.–Apr.) throughout except eastern quarter; rare summer resident* in western Panhandle and mountains of Trans-Pecos. *Range:* Breeds in western North America from southwestern

Canada to northwestern Mexico; winters from northwestern U.S. through breeding range to central Mexico.

Order Galliformes
Family Cracidae
Chachalacas

Terrestrial, chicken-like birds of tropical forests and thickets.

135. Plain Chachalaca

Ortalis vetula (L— 23 W— 26)
A pheasant-like bird with long neck, legs, and tail; olive green throughout, buffier on belly; patch of naked, red skin at chin; long, broad tail tipped with buff. *Habits:* Terrestrial, flying to trees to feed on fruits or escape predators. *Voice:* An extremely loud, raucous "ca-ca-cow" given by several members of a group in alternating cadences producing a deafening cacophony at close range; also various chuckles, clucks, and cackles. *Habitat:* Riparian forest, thorn forest, thickets, second growth, swamps. *Texas:* Common permanent resident* in Lower Rio Grande Valley. *Range:* In lowlands from South Texas and northwestern Mexico to Costa Rica.

Family Phasianidae
Pheasants, Grouse, Turkeys, and Quail

Terrestrial, heavy-bodied, mostly seed- and fruit-eating birds with short, curved wings for quick take-off.

136. Ring-necked Pheasant

Phasianus colchicus (Male, L— 33 W— 31)
A chicken-sized bird with long legs and extremely long, pointed tail; green head with naked red skin on face; white collar; body rich chestnuts, grays, golds and bronzes, spotted with white and brown; grayish-brown, long, pointed tail barred with brown; has spurs on tarsi. *Female:* Pale grayish-brown spotted with dark brown; long, pointed tail. *Voice:* A loud,

hoarse "keow-kuk." *Similar species:* Female could be mistaken for a prairie-chicken, but note long, pointed tail (short and square in prairie-chicken). *Habitat:* Pastures, agricultural fields. *Texas:* Introduced throughout the state but sustaining populations (permanent resident*) exist only in the Panhandle, and Jefferson Co. of East Texas. *Range:* Native of central Asia. Introduced throughout North America. Sustaining populations exist in cool temperate regions with extensive grain crops and moderate hunting.

137. Greater Prairie-Chicken

Tympanuchus cupido (L—18 W—28) **Endangered** (Attwater's race). This grouse is mottled brown and white above; barred brown and white below; dark tail; during displays long feathers from the nape of the neck are extended upward, and naked reddish skin at eyebrows is engorged — the male then puts his head down, stamps his feet and expands throat sacks of naked golden skin, emitting a long, low moan, "wooo-WOOO-wooo." *Female:* Lacks throat sacks and has barred tail. *Habits:* Courtship displays are given at communal arenas called "leks" or "booming grounds" where several males display at the same time in an open space. *Similar species:* Lesser Prairie-Chicken is smaller, paler, and male has red-orange throat sacks (not yellow). *Habitat:* Tall and mid-grass prairie. *Texas:* Formerly native to eastern Texas prairies; the northern race (*T. c. americanus*) has been extirpated while the endemic race (*T. c. attwateri*) has been reduced to less than 1,000 birds in the coastal prairies. *Range:* Formerly throughout the Great Plains from central Canada to South Texas, now much reduced.

138. Lesser Prairie-Chicken

Tympanuchus pallidicinctus (L—16 W—27) Mottled brown and white above; barred tan and white below; dark tail; during displays long feathers from the nape of the neck are extended upward, and naked golden skin at eyebrows is engorged — the male then puts his head down, stamps his feet and expands throat sacks of naked reddish-orange. *Female:* Lacks throat sacks and has barred tail. *Habits:* See Greater Prairie-Chicken. *Voice:* Similar to Greater Prairie-Chicken but higher pitched. *Similar species:* See Greater Prairie-Chicken. *Habitat:* Shortgrass prairie;

shinnery oak. *Texas:* Locally common resident* in eastern counties of Panhandle (Wheeler, Hemphill, Lipscomb, Gray, Donley, and Hall). *Range:* Formerly throughout western shortgrass prairie regions, now reduced to local populations in Colorado, Texas, New Mexico, Oklahoma, and Kansas.

139. Wild Turkey *Meleagris gallopavo* (Male, L—47 W—63)

Dark brown body with iridescent bronze highlights; naked red head and neck; blue skin on face with dangling red wattles; hairy beard hanging from breast; tail dark barred with buff; tarsi with spurs. *Female:* Naked facial skin is grayish; lacks beard and wattles. *Habits:* Males associate in groups of two to three, females in larger flocks. *Voice:* A rapid, high-pitched gobble. *Habitat:* Deciduous forest, oak woodlands, thorn forest. *Texas:* Formerly a common resident* in eastern two-thirds; now common in South and Central Texas but extirpated from other areas. *Range:* Formerly from southern Canada to central Mexico, now extirpated from many areas but being reintroduced.

140. Montezuma Quail *Cyrtonyx montezumae* (L—9 W—17)
Chestnut and brown with white streaking on back; spectacular black and white facial pattern (like a hockey goalie mask) and chestnut crest; chestnut breast and belly spotted with white on sides; brown wings spotted with dark brown. *Female:* Chestnut and brown above; buffy below with brown flecks; whitish throat; faint facial pattern in brown and white reminiscent of male's. *Habits:* "Freezes" when approached rather than fly (hence the name "fool's quail"). *Voice:* A softly trilled whistle. *Similar species:* Female Northern Bobwhite has tawny rather than whitish throat, and flies when approached. *Habitat:* Pine-oak and juniper-oak woodlands. *Texas:* Rare and local resident* in western Edwards Plateau and Trans-Pecos. *Range:* Southern Arizona, New Mexico, and western Texas south to central Mexico.

**141. Northern Bob-
white**

Colinus virginianus (L—10 W—15)
Brown and gray above mottled with dark brown and
white; chestnut sides spotted with white; white breast
and belly scalloped with black; chestnut crown with
short, ragged crest; white eyebrow and throat. *Female:*
Tawny eyebrow and throat. *Habits:* Coveys fly and
scatter in a burst when approached. *Voice:* Familiar,
whistled "hoo WHIT" (bob white), several other calls
including a whistled "perdeek." *Similar species:* See
Montezuma Quail. *Habitat:* Savanna, prairie, brushy
fields, pastures, agricultural areas. *Texas:* Common
permanent resident* throughout except Trans-Pecos.
Range: Eastern and central U.S. south to Guatemala;
isolated populations in Arizona and Sonora.

142. Scaled Quail

Callipepla squamata (L—11 W—15)
Grayish-brown above; scaled gray and black on neck
and nape; brown head with erect brown crest tipped
in buff (hence the name "cotton-top"); spotted and
scalloped brown and buff on flanks and belly. *Habits:*
Coveys scatter by running along the ground when approached. *Voice:* A nasal "chip CHURP." *Similar species:* Hybridizes with Northern Bobwhite in southern
Texas, producing obvious intergrades. *Habitat:* Dry
thorn forest, arid scrub, desert. *Texas:* Common permanent resident* in western half and in drier portions of South Texas to coast. *Range:* Resident from
southwestern U.S. to central Mexico.

143. Gambel's Quail

Callipepla gambelii (L—11 W—15)
Pale gray above and on breast; gray nape streaked
with black; chestnut cap with long, black, curling
topknot; black face and throat; beige lower breast and
belly with black central spot; chestnut flanks spotted
with white. *Female:* Head is brownish with buffy
throat; shorter topknot. *Habits:* Coveys escape by scat-
tering on foot. *Voice:* A hoarse, whistled "coo CUT,"
also "chi-ca-co-coo." *Habitat:* Desert thickets. *Texas:*
Uncommon to rare permanent resident* along the
Rio Grande in the Trans-Pecos. *Range:* Resident in
southwestern U.S. and northwestern Mexico.

Order Gruiformes
Family Rallidae
Rails, Gallinules, and Coots

Except for the ubiquitous, duck-like coot, these are secretive marsh birds, heard more often than seen. They have cone-shaped bills, short, rounded wings, short tails, and extremely long toes for support in walking on floating vegetation.

144. Yellow Rail

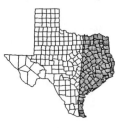

Coturnicops noveboracensis (L— 7 W—13)
A very small (cowbird-sized) rail; dark brown with tawny stripes above; dark brown crown; broad, tawny eyebrow; dark brown mask; whitish chin; tawny underparts barred with black on the flanks; short, yellowish bill and pale legs; in flight (a rarely observed event) shows white secondaries. *Habits:* Extremely secretive. *Voice:* "Tik tik tik-tik-tik, tik tik tik-tik-tik," etc., like hitting two stones together. *Habitat:* Wet prairies, marshes. *Texas:* Rare to casual transient (Sept.–Oct., Apr.) in eastern third; winter resident along coast—probably much more common than available records indicate. *Range:* Breeds in eastern and central Canada and northeastern and north-central U.S.; winters along southern Atlantic and Gulf coast of U.S.; resident in central Mexico.

145. Black Rail

Laterallus jamaicensis (L— 6 W—10)
A tiny (sparrow-sized) rail; dark gray with chestnut nape and black barring on flanks; short, black bill. *Habits:* Secretive. *Voice:* "Tic-ee-toonk." *Habitat:* Wet prairies, marshes. *Texas:* Rare to casual transient (Apr., Sept.–Oct.) in eastern third; uncommon permanent resident* along upper coast, scarcer along central and lower coast—possibly more common than records indicate. *Range:* Breeds locally in California, Kansas and along east coast from New York to Texas, also West Indies, Central and South America; winters along Gulf Coast and in tropical breeding range.

146. Clapper Rail

Rallus longirostris (L—13 W—20)
A large rail; streaked brown and tan above; buffy below with gray and white barring on flanks; head and neck buffy with dark crown; long, pinkish or yellowish bill; pale greenish legs. *Voice:* "Chik chik chik chik chik," etc., like hitting a rock with a metal rod. *Similar species:* King Rail inhabits fresh water (occasionally brackish) marshes — not salt marshes, and is rustier overall, with darker barring on flanks, and has black lores. However, plumage in both species is variable, and they are known to interbreed. *Habitat:* Salt marshes. *Texas:* Common permanent resident* along immediate coast. *Range:* Resident along coast from Connecticut to Belize, California to southern Mexico, West Indies, and much of coastal South America to southeastern Brazil and Peru.

147. King Rail

Rallus elegans (L—15 W—22)
A large rail; streaked brown and rusty above; tawny below with black and white barring on flanks; head and neck tawny with dark crown and darkish stripe through eye; long bill with dark upper and pinkish or yellowish lower mandible; pale, reddish legs. *Voice:* A series of low grunts, "ih ih ih ih ih," etc. *Similar species:* See Clapper Rail. *Habitat:* Fresh water marshes. *Texas:* Uncommon to rare transient (Oct.–Nov., Mar.–Apr.) across eastern third, rare to casual in west; uncommon to rare summer resident* in eastern third; uncommon winter resident along coast; probably more common than records indicate due to secretive habits. *Range:* Breeds in eastern half of U.S. south to central Mexico; winters along coast from Georgia to Texas south to southern Mexico; resident in Cuba.

148. Virginia Rail

Rallus limicola (L—10 W—14)
Similar to the King Rail but about half the size; streaked brown and rusty above; tawny below with black and white barring on flanks; gray head with rusty crown; white throat; long reddish bill; pale legs. *Voice:* "Kik kik kik ki-deek ki-deek ki-deek," etc. *Similar species:* The larger King Rail has tawny (not gray) face and tawny (not white) throat. *Habitat:* Fresh water and brackish marshes. *Texas:* Uncommon to rare transient (Sept., Mar.) in eastern third, rare to casual in west; uncommon winter resident along

coast; casual summer resident* in north-central Texas. *Range:* Breeds locally from southern Canada to southern South America; winters along coast and in subtropical and tropical portions of breeding range.

149. Sora

Porzana carolina (L—9 W—14)
A medium sized rail; streaked brown and rusty above; grayish below with gray and white barring on flanks; gray head with rusty crown; black at base of bill; black throat and upper breast; short, yellow bill; greenish legs. *Female:* Amount of black on throat and breast reduced. *Immature:* Browner overall, lacks black on throat and breast. *Voice:* "Ku-week," also a long descending series of whistles. *Similar species:* Same size and habitat preferences as Virginia Rail but note short, yellowish, cone-shaped bill in Sora (reddish and long in Virginia Rail). *Habitat:* Fresh water and brackish marshes. *Texas:* Uncommon transient (Sept.–Oct., Mar.–Apr.) throughout; rare and local summer resident*; common winter resident along coast. *Range:* Breeds from central Canada to southern U.S.; winters along coast and from southern U.S. to northern South America and West Indies.

150. Paint-billed Crake

Neocrex erythrops (L—9 W—14)
Olive green above; gray head with olive crown; olive bill, red at base; red eyes; gray breast fading to brownish on belly; barred white on flanks; red legs. *Habitat:* Marshes. *Texas:* Accidental—Brazos Co. *Range:* Northern and central South America.

151. Spotted Rail

Pardirallus maculatus (L—10 W—15)
Dark brown above; dark gray below; spotted with white on back, head, and breast; barred with white on flanks and belly; yellow bill with red basal half of lower mandible; reddish legs. *Voice:* "High-pitched cries and guttural booms" (Edwards 1972:49). *Habitat:* Fresh water marshes. *Texas:* Accidental—Brown Co. *Range:* Rare and local in Middle and South America and West Indies.

152. Purple Gallinule

Porphyrula martinica (L—13 W—23)
A large rail with short, cone-shaped bill and extremely long toes; iridescent green back; purple head and underparts; blue frontal shield of naked skin on forehead; red bill with yellow tip; yellow legs. *Immature:* Buffy overall, darker on back. *Habits:* The extremely long toes enable this rail to walk on lily pads and other floating vegetation without sinking. *Voice:* A chicken-like "cuk cuk cuk cuk cuk-kik cuk-kik," etc. *Similar species:* Clapper and King rails have long, pointed (not short, cone-shaped) bills; immature Common Moorhen is grayish rather than brownish, and shows white edging along folded wing. *Habitat:* Fresh water marshes. *Texas:* Uncommon to rare summer resident* (May–Aug.) in eastern third. *Range:* Breeds from eastern U.S. south to northern Argentina, West Indies; winters from southern Gulf states south through breeding range.

153. Common Moorhen

Gallinula chloropus (L—14 W—23)
A large rail with short, cone-shaped bill and extremely long toes; entirely sooty gray with white edging along wing and white undertail coverts; red frontal shield of naked skin on forehead; red bill with yellow tip; greenish legs. *Immature:* Similar to adult but with olive bill, frontal shield, and legs. *Habits:* The extremely long toes enable this rail to walk on lily pads and other floating vegetation without sinking; swims more than most other rails. *Voice:* Low croaks and whiney, high-pitched squeaks. *Similar species:* See Purple Gallinule; immature American Coot lacks white wing edging. *Habitat:* Fresh water marshes. *Texas:* Uncommon to rare summer resident* (May–Sept.) in eastern third; common winter resident along coastal plain. *Range:* Breeds locally in temperate and tropical regions of the world; winters mainly in subtropical and tropical zones.

154. American Coot

Fulica americana (L—16 W—26)
A large, black rail, more duck-like than rail-like in appearance and behavior; white bill with dark tip; red eye; greenish legs. *Immature:* Paler; pale gray bill. *Habits:* Swims in open water, tipping and diving for food instead of skulking through reeds like most rails; pumps head forward while swimming. *Voice:* Various

croaks and cat-like mews. *Similar species:* See Common Moorhen. *Habitat:* Ponds, lakes, marshes, bays. *Texas:* Locally common to rare summer resident* throughout; common winter resident. *Range:* Breeds from central Canada to Nicaragua and West Indies; winters along coast and from central U.S. to northern Colombia, West Indies.

Family Aramidae
Limpkins

The family has only one species as a member, the Limpkin; a dark, long-legged marsh bird, night heron–like in appearance.

155. Limpkin

Aramus guarauna (L— 27 W— 42)
Dark brown body with broad white streaking on back, wings and breast; finely streaked on neck; head a pale brown; red eye; bill long, slightly down-turned, orange at base, dark at tip; dark legs. *Habits:* The name derives from its odd, limping gait in which it walks in rather awkward, jerky fashion, pumping the tail upward at each step; mainly crepuscular and nocturnal. *Voice:* A loud, ringing, goose-like honking— "kow," also "keee-ooow." *Similar species:* Immature night-herons have short, heavy bills; immature ibises have much longer, down-curved bills. *Habitat:* Marshes, swamps, lagoons, mangroves. *Texas:* Hypothetical— Jefferson, Cameron cos. *Range:* Florida, southern Mexico to northern Argentina, Greater Antilles.

Family Gruidae
Cranes

Long-legged, long-necked birds of marsh and grasslands. Unlike herons, cranes fly with legs and neck extended. Unlike ducks and geese, they often glide in flight.

156. Sandhill Crane

Grus canadensis (L—42 W—74)
A tall, long-necked, long-legged, gray-bodied bird with bustle-like tail; black legs; red crown. *Immature:* Rusty tinge to gray body; lacks red crown. *Habits:* Normally in family groups of two adults and one or two young. *Voice:* A loud croaking bugle, "crrrrahh." *Similar species:* The larger Whooping Crane is white (tinged with rust in immature), not gray as in Sandhill Crane. *Habitat:* Prairie, savanna, grasslands, pasture, croplands, estuaries, lakes, ponds. *Texas:* Common transient (Oct.–Nov., Feb.–Mar.) in western two-thirds; common winter resident along coastal plain; formerly bred. *Range:* Formerly bred over much of North America; now breeds in Alaska and northern Canada, south locally in northwestern and north-central U.S., Florida; winters from southern U.S. to southern Mexico.

157. Whooping Crane

Grus americana (L—51 W—87) **Endangered**
A very tall, long-necked, long-legged, white-bodied bird; black legs; red, black, and white facial pattern. *Immature:* Rusty tinge to white body, especially on neck; lacks facial pattern of adult. *Habits:* Normally in family groups of two adults and one or two immatures. *Voice:* A loud, goose-like honk. *Similar species:* See Sandhill Crane. *Habitat:* Estuaries, prairie marshes, savanna, grasslands, pasture, croplands. *Texas:* Casual transient (Oct.–Nov., Feb.–Mar.) in eastern third; common winter resident at Aransas National Wildlife Refuge, Aransas Co. *Range:* Formerly bred over much of the Great Plains of North America; now breeds only in Wood Buffalo National Park in northern Saskatchewan; winters only at Aransas.

Order Charadriiformes
Family Burhinidae
Thick-knees

Peculiar shorebirds with long legs, thick tibio-tarsal joint, large head, and large eye.

158. Double-striped Thick-knee

Burhinus bistriatus (L— 20 W— 40)
A curlew-sized shorebird with long, greenish legs and relatively short, thick bill; mottled buff and brown above; buffy below streaked with brown on neck and breast; crown striped with buff and dark brown; large, cream-colored eye; prominent, white, supraorbital stripe; tail brown with white subterminal and black terminal band. *Habits:* Largely nocturnal. Prefers to run rather than fly when approached. *Voice:* "Its calls are loud, echoing, somewhat cackling cries, vaguely reminiscent of those of the Sandhill Crane and the Limpkin, seldom heard except at night, most commonly shortly after dusk" (Edwards 1972:64). *Habitat:* Arid open country. *Texas:* Accidental—Kleberg Co. *Range:* Southern Mexico to Costa Rica; northern South America; Hispaniola.

Family Charadriidae
Plovers

Plovers are rather compact shorebirds with relatively long legs, short necks, and short, thick bills.

159. Black-bellied Plover

Pluvialis squatarola (L—12 W—25)
A Killdeer-sized plover; checked black and white on back; white crown, nape, and shoulder; black face, throat, and breast; white belly and undertail coverts. *Winter:* Heavy black bill contrasts with whitish area at base of bill; pale eyebrow; crown and back brownish mottled with white; breast is mottled with brown; belly white; black legs. *Voice:* A gull-like "keee keee kee-a-wee keee," etc. *Similar species:* Lesser Golden-Plover has pale legs, Blackbelly has black legs, and Golden lacks the black axillaries of the Black-bellied Plover (visible only in flight). *Habitat:* Beaches, bays, mud flats, estuaries. *Texas:* Common to uncommon transient (Aug.–Sept., Apr.–May) in eastern third, rare to casual in west; common winter resident along coast; uncommon in summer along coast. *Range:* Breeds in the high arctic of Old and New World; winters along temperate and tropical coasts of the world.

160. Lesser Golden-Plover

Pluvialis dominica (L—11 W—23)
A Killdeer-sized plover; checked black, white, and gold on back and crown; white "headband" running from forehead, over eye and down side of neck; black face and underparts. *Winter:* Heavy black bill contrasts with white at base of bill; pale eyebrow; crown and back brown and white often flecked with gold; underparts white, speckled with brown on breast; pale legs. *Voice:* A whistled "kew-wee." *Similar species:* See Black-bellied Plover. *Habitat:* Shortgrass prairie, overgrazed pasture, plowed fields, mud flats. *Texas:* Common to uncommon spring transient (Mar.–Apr.) across eastern third, rare to casual in west; rare to casual fall transient across eastern third. *Range:* Breeds in high arctic of Old and New World; winters mainly in southern hemisphere.

161. Snowy Plover

Charadrius alexandrinus (L—7 W—14)
A small plover; grayish-brown crown, back, and wings; white forehead, face, collar, and underparts; broad, dark line behind eye; partial dark band across breast, broken in the middle; black bill; black legs. *Immature:* Similar to adult but paler with dark gray legs. *Voice:* A low, whistled "pew-weet." *Similar species:* The other small, pale plover (Piping) has a white rump, visible in flight (brown in Snowy Plover); adult Piping has dull orange legs, even in winter (Snowy's are black). *Habitat:* Mud flats, estuaries, bays. *Texas:* Common permanent resident* along coast; rare summer resident in Panhandle (Randall and Roberts cos.); rare to casual transient (Mar.–May, July–Oct.) throughout. *Range:* Breeds locally in temperate and tropical regions of the world; winters mainly in subtropical and tropical areas.

162. Wilson's Plover

Charadrius wilsonia (L—8 W—16)
A smallish plover with a heavy, black bill; brown back and head; white forehead; black lores; white chin and collar; black band across throat; white underparts; pinkish legs. *Female and immature:* Brown breast band. *Voice:* "Peet peet peet," etc. *Similar species:* The smaller, short-billed Semipalmated Plover has orange (not pinkish) legs. *Habitat:* Bays, mud flats. *Texas:* Common summer resident* (Apr.–Sept.) along coast. *Range:* Breeds along both coasts from Califor-

nia and New Jersey south to northern South America, West Indies; winters mainly in tropical portions of breeding range.

163. Semipalmated Plover

Charadrius semipalmatus (L—7 W—15)
A small plover; brown back and head; white forehead; white postorbital stripe; orange eyering; orange bill, black at tip; black lores; white chin and collar; black band across throat; white underparts; orange or yellow legs. *Winter:* Brown breast band; dull, dark bill (may show some orange at base). *Immature:* Similar to adult but eyering yellow, bill black at tip, brown at base, legs brown anteriorly, yellow posteriorly. *Voice:* A whistled "tew-wee." *Similar species:* See Wilson's Plover; the other small plovers are paler and have incomplete breast bands. *Habitat:* Beaches, mud flats, estuaries. *Texas:* Common to uncommon transient (Aug.–Sept., Mar.–Apr.) across eastern third, rare to casual in west; common winter resident along coast, rare in summer. *Range:* Breeds in high arctic of North America; winters mainly along temperate and tropical coasts from Georgia and California to southern South America, West Indies.

164. Piping Plover

Charadrius melodus (L—7 W—15)
A small plover; grayish-brown crown, back and wings; white forehead with distinct black band across forecrown; white chin, throat collar, and underparts; partial or complete black band across breast; orange bill tipped with black; orange legs; white rump. *Winter:* Lacks black breast and crown bands; dark bill. *Voice:* "Peep," repeated. *Similar species:* See Snowy Plover; Semipalmated is dark brown on back (not pale) and has a complete breast band, even in winter. *Habitat:* Beaches. *Texas:* Uncommon winter resident along coast (Aug.–May), rare in summer; rare to casual transient in eastern third. *Range:* Breeds locally in southeastern and south-central Canada, northeastern and north-central U.S.; winters along coast from South Carolina to southern Veracruz, also in West Indies.

165. Killdeer

Charadrius vociferus (L—10 W—20)
A medium-sized plover; brown back and head; orange rump; white forehead; white postorbital stripe; orange eyering; dark bill; black lores; white chin and collar; two black bands across throat and upper breast; white underparts; pale legs. *Habits:* Feigns broken wing when young or nest are approached. *Voice:* "Kill de-er," also various peeps. *Similar species:* The Killdeer is the only plover with two black bars across breast. *Habitat:* Open areas. *Texas:* Common summer resident* throughout; withdraws from Panhandle in winter. *Range:* Breeds from subarctic Canada and Alaska south to central Mexico, Greater Antilles, western South America; winters along coast and from southern U.S. to northern and western South America, West Indies.

166. Mountain Plover

Charadrius montanus (L—9 W—19)
Nondescript, medium-sized plover; brown back, nape, and crown; white forehead and eyebrow; brown cheek; whitish below washed with buff on sides of breast; bill black; legs tan. *Habits:* Forages in typical plover fashion—quick runs followed by brief stops. *Voice:* A soft whistle. *Similar species:* Winter Lesser Golden-Plover has mottled back with some gold flecks, not plain brown. *Habitat:* Shortgrass prairie, overgrazed pasture, plowed fields, deserts. *Texas:* Rare summer resident* in western Panhandle and Trans-Pecos; rare transient throughout except eastern quarter where absent; rare winter resident in southern half. *Range:* Breeds in dry, western Great Plains from southern Canada to western Texas; winters in California, Arizona, Texas, and northern Mexico.

Family Haematopodidae
Oystercatchers

Stout, gull-like birds; black or black and white with a long, brilliant orange bill.

167. American Oystercatcher

Haematopus palliatus (L—19 W—35)
Gull-sized bird; black hood; long, bright orange bill; red eyering; brown back; white breast and belly; pinkish legs; broad white bars on secondaries and white base of tail show in flight. *Immature:* Brown head; dull orange bill. *Habits:* Feeds on oysters and other bivalves by prying open'the shells. *Voice:* A strident "weeep." *Habitat:* Beaches, bays. *Texas:* Uncommon to rare and local permanent resident* along immediate coast. *Range:* Breeds locally along coast from northwestern Mexico and Maine south to South America, West Indies.

Family Recurvirostridae
Stilts and Avocets

A small family of medium-sized, long-legged, long-billed, long-necked shorebirds.

168. Black-necked Stilt

Himantopus mexicanus (L—14 W—27)
Spindly shorebird with long neck, needle-like bill, and long legs; black head, nape, and back; white at base of bill, throat and underparts; white patch behind eye; pink legs. *Female:* Similar to male but paler. *Immature:* Brown rather than black. *Voice:* A rapid, buzzy "keer-keer-keer," etc. *Habitat:* Mud flats, marshes, estuaries, ponds. *Texas:* Common summer resident* (Apr.–Oct.) along coast, rare in winter; rare, local breeder inland; rare to casual transient throughout except eastern quarter where absent. *Range:* Breeds locally in western U.S. and along coast in east from Maine south locally along coasts of Middle and South America to northern Argentina, West Indies; winters from North Carolina south through breeding range.

169. American Avocet

Recurvirostra americana (L—18 W—32)
Long-legged, long-necked shorebird with long, upturned bill; black and white back and wings; white belly; rusty orange head; whitish at base of bill; gray legs. *Winter:* Head and neck mostly whitish with little rusty tinge. *Habits:* Forages by swinging submerged bill from side to side as it walks along. *Voice:*

"Kleet kleet kleet," etc. *Habitat:* Estuaries, ponds, lakes, mud flats, flooded pastures, bays. *Texas:* Common to uncommon summer resident* along coast and in western third; common to uncommon transient nearly throughout except eastern quarter; common winter resident along coast. *Range:* Breeds in western and central Canada south through western U.S. to northern Mexico; winters from southern U.S. to southern Mexico.

Family Jacanidae
Jacanas

Rail-like shorebirds with long legs and extremely long toes; wings with spurs at the wrist. Females are polyandrous.

170. Northern Jacana

Jacana spinosa (L—10 W—12)
Gallinule-sized bird; rich chestnut body; dark head and neck; yellow forehead; two-tone bill, white at base, yellow at tip; long, grayish-green legs with extremely long toes; chestnut wing linings and coverts; yellow flight feathers; spurs at wrist on wings. *Immature:* Brown above; white below; broad white stripe extending behind eye and down neck; yellow bill and frontal shield. *Habits:* Walks on lily pads and other floating vegetation; often raises wings while foraging. *Voice:* "A loud, grating, cackling chatter, and a musical whistle" (Edwards 1972:53). *Habitat:* Fresh water marshes. *Texas:* Rare to casual visitor along coastal plain, mainly in winter (Oct.–Mar.); has bred.*
Range: Northern Mexico to Panama; Greater Antilles.

Family Scolopacidae
Sandpipers

Scolopacids constitute a diverse assemblage of shorebirds. Breeding plumage for most sandpipers is worn for only a short time, most of which is spent on arctic breeding grounds. As a result it is the winter plumage that is most often critical for identification of Texas shorebirds. Many second-year birds and other nonbreeders remain in Texas and elsewhere on the wintering ground or migration route through the summer.

Hayman et al. (1986) provide a useful identification guide for this difficult group.

171. Greater Yellow-legs

Tringa melanoleuca (L—14 W—25)
Mottled grayish-brown above; head, breast and flanks white heavily streaked with grayish brown; white belly and rump; long, yellow legs; bill long, often slightly upturned and darker at tip than at base. *Winter:* Paler overall; streaking on breast and head is reduced. *Voice:* A rapid sequence of three, descending notes, "tew tew tew." *Similar species:* Lesser Yellowlegs is half the size of the Greater; Lesser's "pew" call is generally given as a single note or series of notes on the same pitch, not a descending three-note sequence; bill is shorter, thinner, and straight. *Habitat:* Mud flats, estuaries, marshes, prairies, flooded agricultural fields. *Texas:* Common to uncommon transient (Mar.–May, Aug.–Oct.) throughout; rare winter resident (Aug.–May) throughout except along coastal plain where common; rare in summer along coast (June–July). *Range:* Breeds in muskeg bogs and tundra of northern Canada and Alaska; winters in coastal U.S. south to southern South America, West Indies.

172. Lesser Yellowlegs

Tringa flavipes (L—11 W—20)
Mottled grayish-brown above; head, breast and flanks white heavily streaked with grayish brown; white belly and rump; yellow legs. *Winter:* Paler overall; streaking on breast is reduced. *Voice:* Single "pew" alarm note, repeated. *Similar species:* See Greater Yellowlegs. *Habitat:* Mud flats, pond borders, flooded prairies, swales, estuaries. *Texas:* Common to uncommon transient (Mar.–May, July–Oct.) throughout; common winter resident (July–Apr.) along coastal plain, rare inland. *Range:* Breeds in northern Canada and Alaska; winters from Atlantic (South Carolina) and Pacific (southern California) coasts of U.S. south to southern South America, West Indies.

**173. Spotted Red-
shank**

Tringa erythropus (L—13 W—23)
Black body; long bill with drooping tip and red lower mandible; red legs. *Winter:* Grayish above and on head and breast; whitish below; bill and legs as in breeding plumage. *Voice:* "Tsuweet." *Habitat:* Mud flats, estuaries. *Texas:* Hypothetical—Aransas Co. *Range:* Breeds in Old World arctic; winters in southern temperate and tropical regions of Old World.

**174. Solitary Sand-
piper**

Tringa solitaria (L—9 W—17)
Dark gray back and wings with white spotting; heavily streaked with grayish-brown on head and breast; white eyering; long, greenish legs; tail dark in center, barred white on outer portions. *Winter:* Streaking on head and breast reduced or faint. *Habits:* Often bobs while foraging. *Voice:* A high-pitched "tseet-eet." *Similar species:* Spotted Sandpiper is found in similar habitats; however it bobs almost continuously, shows white on wings in flight (none on Solitary), has a pale eyebrow (no eyering), and no white spotting on folded wings; tail barring is much more prominent in the Solitary. Stilt Sandpiper and yellowlegs show white rump in flight (dark in Solitary). *Habitat:* Ponds, rivers, lakes. *Texas:* Common (eastern half) to uncommon or rare (western half) transient (Mar.–May, July–Oct.); rare in summer and winter along coast. *Range:* Breeds across arctic and boreal North America; winters along southern Atlantic (Georgia, Florida) and Gulf coasts of U.S. south to southern South America, West Indies.

175. Willet

Catoptrophorus semipalmatus (L—15 W—27)
Large, heavy-bodied, long-billed shorebird; mottled grayish-brown above and below; whitish belly; broad white stripe on wing is conspicuous in flight. *Winter:* Gray above, whitish below. *Voice:* Shrill "will will-it," repeated. *Similar species:* Large size, white wing stripes and flight call separate this from other shorebirds. *Habitat:* Estuaries, beaches, coastal ponds, marshes, mud flats. *Texas:* Common resident* along coast; uncommon to rare spring transient (Mar.–May) inland, scarcer in fall (July–Sept.). *Range:* Breeds in southwestern and south-central Canada and northwestern and north-central U.S, along Atlantic and Gulf coasts (Nova Scotia to Texas), West Indies;

winters from coastal North America (California and Virginia) south to northern half of South America, West Indies.

176. Spotted Sand-
piper

Actitis macularia (L— 8 W—13)
Grayish-brown above, white with dark spots below; white eyebrow. *Winter:* Lacks spots; white below extending toward back at shoulder; grayish smear on side of breast. *Habits:* Teeters almost continually while foraging; flight peculiar, with stiff-winged bursts and brief glides. *Voice:* "Peet weet." *Similar species:* See Solitary Sandpiper. *Habitat:* Streams, ponds, rivers, lakes, beaches. *Texas:* Locally common transient (Mar.–May, July–Oct.) throughout; uncommon to rare winter resident in southern half; rare to casual summer resident in northern half; has bred.* *Range:* Breeds throughout temperate and boreal North America; winters from southern U.S. south to northern Argentina, West Indies.

177. Upland Sand-
piper

Bartramia longicauda (L—12 W— 22)
The shape of this bird is unique — large, heavy body, long legs, long neck, small head, and short bill. Plumage is light brown with dark brown streaks on back and wings; buff head, neck and breast mottled with brown; large brown eye. *Voice:* "Kip-ip," repeated. *Similar species:* The Buff-breasted Sandpiper is found in similar habitats; however, it has clear, unstreaked, buffy underparts contrasting with white wing linings in flight. *Habitat:* Prairie, pastures, plowed fields. *Texas:* Common transient (Mar.–May, July–Oct.) in eastern half, uncommon to rare in western half; rare summer resident in northern third; has nested.* *Range:* Breeds across northeastern and north-central U.S. and in Great Plains of Canada; winters South America.

178. Eskimo Curlew

Numenius borealis (L—14 W— 28) **Endangered**
A yellowlegs-sized curlew with relatively short, slightly decurved bill; mottled brown above; buffy flecked with brown below; brown and buff striped crown; rusty wing linings visible in flight. *Voice:* A soft twitter. *Similar species:* Whimbrel is larger, lacks rusty wing linings. *Habitat:* Prairies, pastures, plowed

fields, estuaries. *Texas:* Formerly abundant, now casual (?) along coast in spring. Possibly extinct. *Range:* Formerly bred in arctic of north-central Canada; wintered in southeastern South America.

179. Whimbrel

Numenius phaeopus (L—18 W—33)
Mottled gray and brown above; grayish below with dark flecks; crown striped with dark brown and gray. *Voice:* "Kee kee kee kee." *Similar species:* Long-billed Curlew is larger, buffy, has a very long, decurved bill, and is not striped prominently on crown. *Habitat:* Tallgrass prairies, estuaries, oyster reefs. *Texas:* Common spring (May) and rare fall transient along coast; rare to casual inland; rare along coast in winter. *Range:* Breeds in high arctic of Old and New World; winters in subtropical and tropical regions.

180. Bristle-thighed Curlew

Numenius tahitiensis (L—17 W—32)
Similar to Whimbrel but with buffy rump (not mottled) and buffy, barred tail. *Voice:* "Kew-wit." *Habitat:* Mud flats, estuaries, beaches. *Texas:* Hypothetical. *Range:* Breeds in western Alaska; winters in islands of South Pacific.

181. Long-billed Curlew

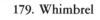

Numenius americanus (L—23 W—38)
A large, heavy-bodied bird with very long, decurved bill; mottled brown and buff above; uniformly buffy below; rusty wing linings visible in flight. *Voice:* A strident "per-leee," repeated. *Similar species:* See Whimbrel. *Habitat:* Prairies, pastures, lawns, golf courses. *Texas:* Common to uncommon transient in all but eastern quarter; common to uncommon summer resident on coastal plain; rare in northern Panhandle and Central Texas, has bred*; common winter resident along coastal plain, uncommon in southern Panhandle and Central Texas. *Range:* Breeds in prairie regions of western U.S. and southwestern Canada; winters in central California, southern Arizona, Texas, and southern Louisiana south to southern Mexico.

182. Hudsonian Godwit

Limosa haemastica (L—16 W—27)
Mottled dark and light brown and white above; rufous below; white eyebrow; long, upturned bill red at base, dark at tip; white rump; dark wings with white wing stripe visible in flight. *Winter:* Gray above, whitish below with white eyebrow. *Voice:* "Quee quee." *Similar species:* The Marbled Godwit is mottled brown and buff at all seasons (not gray or cinnamon). *Habitat:* Prairie ponds, swales, marshes, beaches, mud flats. *Texas:* Common spring (Apr.–May) and rare fall (Aug.–Sept.) transient along coast, scarcer inland. *Range:* Breeds in northern North America; winters in southern South America.

183. Bar-tailed Godwit

Limosa lapponica (L—16 W—27)
Mottled brown and buff above, rusty below with long, two-toned, upturned bill, reddish at base, dark at tip; black and white barring on tail. *Winter:* Gray above, whitish below. *Similar species:* Marbled Godwit is buffy and mottled in all plumages; the Bar-tailed has a mottled or barred tail and rump unlike the Hudsonian in which the tail basal half is white and the terminal half is dark with a white edging. *Habitat:* Marshes, swales, estuaries. *Texas:* Hypothetical— Gonzales Co. *Range:* Breeds in Old World arctic and western Alaska; winters in temperate and tropical regions of Old World.

184. Marbled Godwit

Limosa fedoa (L—18 W—31)
Mottled buff and dark brown above; buffy below barred with brown; long, upturned bill pink at base, dark at tip; rusty wing linings. *Winter:* Ventral barring faint or lacking. *Voice:* "Koo-wik," repeated. *Similar species:* See Hudsonian Godwit. *Habitat:* Bay shores, mud flats, estuaries, flooded prairies. *Texas:* Common in winter, uncommon to rare in summer along coast; rare to casual inland during migration. *Range:* Breeds in northern Great Plains of Canada and extreme northern U.S.; winters in coastal U.S. from California and South Carolina south to northern South America.

185. Ruddy Turn-stone

Arenaria interpres (L—10 W—19)
A plump bird with slightly upturned bill; rufous above, white below with black breast; black and white facial pattern; two white stripes on wings; white band across tail; orange legs. *Winter:* Grayish above; white below with varying amounts of black on breast and face. *Voice:* A single, whistled "tew," also a low chatter. *Habitat:* Beaches, mud flats. *Texas:* Common winter, uncommon summer resident along coast; uncommon to rare transient elsewhere in eastern half. *Range:* Breeds in high arctic of Old and New World; winters in southern temperate and tropical regions.

186. Surfbird

Aphriza virgata (L—10 W—17)
Mottled black, brown and white above; white below with black checks; rump white; tail white with black terminal wedge; white wing stripe on dark wings; bill dark with yellowish basal half of lower mandible. *Winter:* As in breeding but slate gray above and below with white belly; white eyebrow and throat. *Voice:* "Tew tew tew." *Habitat:* Rocky shores. *Texas:* Casual along coast in spring (Apr.). *Range:* Breeds in mountain tundra of central Alaska; winters along Pacific Coast of North America and both coasts of Middle and South America.

187. Great Knot

Calidris tenuirostris (L—11 W—21)
Chunky shorebird with long bill; mottled gray and white above, reddish on upper back; breast mostly black; whitish belly with black spotting on flanks. *Winter:* Grayish above with fine streaking on head and back; whitish below. *Voice:* "Chuker-chuker-chuker." *Similar species:* The winter Red Knot lacks streaking on head and back and has a distinct whitish eye line, which is indistinct in the Great; Great Knot has darker spotting on breast. *Habitat:* Rocky beaches, bay shorelines, mud flats. *Texas:* Hypothetical—one record from upper coast. *Range:* Breeds in northeastern Siberia; winters in the tropics from the Persian Gulf to the Philippines.

188. Red Knot

Calidris canutus (L—11 W—21)
A plump bird, mottled brown and russet above and on crown; rusty below. *Winter:* Pale gray above; grayish breast; whitish belly; white eyebrow; white, finely barred rump. *Voice:* A hoarse "kew kew."
Similar species: Dowitchers are white up the back; Sanderling is smaller and lacks white rump; other peeps of similar plumage are sparrow-sized. *Habitat:* Beaches, bay shorelines, mud flats. *Texas:* Common transient (Mar.–May, Aug.–Oct.), uncommon winter resident, and rare summer resident along coast.
Range: Breeds in Old and New World high arctic; winters in temperate and tropical regions.

189. Sanderling

Calidris alba (L—8 W—16)
A chunky, feisty peep of the beaches; dappled brown, white and black on back and crown; rusty flecked with white on face and breast; short black legs and bill; white wing stripe. *Winter:* As in breeding but mottled gray and white above; white below; white eyebrow; grayish shoulder patch extends to side of breast. *Habits:* Spends considerable time in chases and fights with other Sanderlings. *Voice:* "Kwit."
Similar species: Other winter peeps are more or less streaked with grayish on throat and breast (white on winter Sanderling); Sanderling has palest back. *Habitat:* Beaches. *Texas:* Common resident along coast; uncommon to rare transient (Apr.–May, July–Oct.) elsewhere in eastern half. *Range:* Breeds in high arctic of Old and New World; winters on temperate and tropical beaches.

190. Semipalmated Sandpiper

Calidris pusilla (L—6 W—12)
Dark brown, russet and white above; finely streaked brown and white on head and breast; pale eyebrow with some rusty on crown and cheek; white belly. *Winter:* Grayish above with grayish wash on head and breast; white belly. *Voice:* "Chit" or "chek." *Similar species:* Winter-plumaged Western Sandpiper is essentially identical to winter Semipalmated. They can be separated by voice ("chek" in Semipalmated, "zheet" in Western). The bill of the Western *averages* longer than that of Semipalmated, and in longer-billed birds there is a noticeable droop at the tip. However, there is considerable overlap in this and

Red Knot

Pectoral Sandpiper

Dunlin

Sanderling

White-rumped Sandpiper

Baird's Sandpiper

Semipalmated Sandpiper

Western Sandpiper

Least Sandpiper

Calidris sandpipers in flight

all other characters used to separate the winter-plumaged birds in the field, except voice. *Habitat:* Mud flats, ponds, lakes. *Texas:* Common fall and spring transient (Mar.–May, Aug.–Sept.) along coast; uncommon to rare inland. *Range:* Breeds in high arctic of North America; winters along both coasts of Middle and South America to Paraguay (east) and northern Chile (west), West Indies.

191. Western Sandpiper

Calidris mauri (L— 6 W—12)
Similar to Semipalmated but whiter on back, and with distinct rusty cheek and supraorbital patches. *Winter:* As described for Semipalmated Sandpiper. *Voice:* "Zheet." *Similar species:* See Semipalmated Sandpiper. *Habitat:* Beaches, mud flats, ponds, lakes, estuaries, swales. *Texas:* Common winter resident along coast, uncommon in summer; uncommon to rare transient (Mar.–May, July–Nov.) inland. *Range:* Breeds in high arctic of northern Alaska and northeastern Siberia; winters along both U.S. coasts from California and North Carolina south to northern South America, West Indies.

192. Least Sandpiper

Calidris minutilla (L— 6 W—12)
Dark brown and buff on back and wings; head and breast streaked with brown and white; relatively short, thin bill; white belly; yellowish legs (sometimes brown with caked mud). *Winter:* Brownish-gray above; buffy wash on breast. *Voice:* "Preep." *Similar species:* Yellow legs are distinctive, as is call note. *Habitat:* Ponds, lakes, swales, mud flats. *Texas:* Common to uncommon in winter (Nov.–Mar.) throughout except northern Panhandle, Trans-Pecos, and East Texas where scarce; uncommon in summer along coast. *Range:* Breeds across northern North America; winters from coastal (Oregon, North Carolina) and southern U.S. south to northern half of South America, West Indies.

193. White-rumped Sandpiper

Calidris fuscicollis (L—8 W—15)
Dark and tan on back and wings; finely streaked brown and white on head, breast, and flanks; white rump; dark legs; wings extend beyond tail. *Winter:* As in breeding but gray above, white below with gray wash on breast, and white eyebrow. *Voice:* "Teet." *Similar species:* Curlew Sandpiper is also white-rumped but has long, decurved bill. *Habitat:* Swales, mud flats, lakes, ponds. *Texas:* Common spring transient (May) along coast, uncommon to rare inland; uncommon fall transient (Aug.–Sept.), rare to casual inland. *Range:* Breeds in high arctic of North America; winters in South America east of the Andes.

194. Baird's Sandpiper

Calidris bairdii (L—8 W—15)
A medium-sized sandpiper, dark brown and buff on back and wings; buffy head and breast flecked with brown; wings extend beyond tail. *Voice:* "Chureep." *Similar species:* Brownish (rather than grayish) winter plumage makes this bird look like a large Least Sandpiper. Long wings, black bill and legs, and dark rump separate it from the Least and other peeps. *Habitat:* Ponds, lakes, swales. *Texas:* Common to uncommon spring transient (Apr.–May) over most of state, uncommon to rare in fall (Sept.). *Range:* Breeds in high arctic of North America and northeastern Siberia; winters in western and southern South America.

195. Pectoral Sandpiper

Calidris melanotos (L—9 W—17)
Dark brown, tan, and white on back and wings; head and breast whitish, densely flecked with brown; belly white, the dividing line between mottled brown breast and white belly distinct; dark bill; yellow legs. *Voice:* "Prip." *Similar species:* No other sandpiper shows sharp contrast of breast and belly coloration. *Habitat:* Wet prairies, ponds, lakes, swales, agricultural fields. *Texas:* Common fall (Sept.–Oct.) and spring (Mar.–May) transient in eastern third (except Piney Woods), uncommon to rare in west. *Range:* Breeds in the high arctic of North America; winters in southern half of South America.

**196. Sharp-Tailed
Sandpiper**

Calidris acuminata (L—9 W—17)
Dappled brown, rusty, and white on wings and back;
dark crown contrasts with buffy eyebrow; buffy throat
and breast flecked with brown; white belly. *Winter:*
Buffier above; few brown flecks on breast. *Similar species:* Looks like a faded Pectoral Sandpiper with contrasting buff breast and white belly (Pectoral's breast
is mottled brown). *Habitat:* Ponds, lakes, flooded agricultural areas. *Texas:* Hypothetical—Galveston Co.
Range: Breeds in northern Siberia; winters in New
Guinea, New Caledonia, Australia and vicinity.

197. Purple Sandpiper

Calidris maritima (L—9 W—15)
Dark brown back and wings; head finely streaked
with brown and white; belly white; breast and flanks
whitish spotted with brown; bill yellow-orange at
base, dark at tip; yellow-orange legs; white eyering.
Winter: Back marked with gray and buff; head and
breast slate gray with gray streaking on flanks. *Voice:*
"We-it." *Similar species:* The Surfbird is also gray in
winter with yellow legs, but it shows a broad white
band on the tail in flight (tail is dark in Purple Sandpiper). *Habitat:* Rocky shores. *Texas:* Casual winter
visitor mainly to upper coast. *Range:* Breeds in arctic
of northeastern North America, Greenland, Iceland,
northern Scandinavia, and Siberia; winters along Atlantic Coast of North America from New Brunswick
to Maryland; also shores of North and Baltic seas in
Old World.

198. Dunlin

Calidris alpina (L—9 W—16)
Rusty and dark brown on back and wings; white
streaked with black on neck and breast; crown streaked
with russet and black; large black smudge on belly;
long bill droops at tip. *Winter:* As in breeding but
with dark gray back; head and breast pale gray with
some streaking; white eyebrow; white belly. *Voice:* A
hoarse "zheet." *Similar species:* Dark gray back and
long, drooping bill distinguish the winter Dunlin
from other gray-breasted peeps. *Habitat:* Ponds,
lakes, beaches, mud flats. *Texas:* Common winter resident (Nov.–May) along coast. *Range:* Breeds in arctic
of Old and New World; winters in temperate and
northern tropical regions.

199. Curlew Sand-piper

Calidris ferruginea (L—8 W—16)
Rusty above and below with long, decurved bill. *Winter:* Dark gray back; head and breast pale gray; white eyebrow; white belly. *Voice:* "Si-rip." *Similar species:* Winter Dunlin is similar, but winter Curlew Sandpiper has white rump. *Habitat:* Mud flats, beaches. *Texas:* Casual transient (Apr.–May, Sept.), mainly along coast. *Range:* Breeds in Old World arctic; winters in Old World temperate and tropical regions.

200. Stilt Sandpiper

Calidris himantopus (L—9 W—17)
A trim, long-necked, long-legged sandpiper, dark brown and buff on back and wings; crown streaked with dark brown and white; white eyebrow; chestnut pre- and postorbital stripe; white streaked with brown on neck; white barred with brown on breast and belly; long, yellow-green legs; white rump; long, straight bill (twice length of head). *Winter:* Gray and white mottling on back; gray head with prominent eyebrow; gray throat and breast; whitish belly with gray flecks. *Habits:* Often feeds with rapid up-and-down motion in breast-deep water. *Voice:* A low "whurp." *Similar species:* Winter Lesser Yellowlegs has barred (not gray) tail; winter dowitchers have longer bill (three times length of head), flanks with dark bars or spots, and show white on lower back in flight. *Habitat:* Mud flats, flooded pastures, lakes, ponds. *Texas:* Common to uncommon transient (July–Sept., Apr.–May) in eastern third; rare to casual in west; rare summer and winter resident along coast. *Range:* Breeds in arctic of north-central Canada; winters in central South America.

201. Buff-breasted Sandpiper

Tryngites subruficollis (L—8 W—17)
Dark brown feathering edged in buff or whitish on back; buffy head and underparts, spotted with brown on breast; streaked crown; large, dark eye; pale legs; wing linings appear white in flight. *Habits:* Often seen in small flocks that twist and turn erratically in flight over freshly plowed fields. *Voice:* A low trill. *Similar species:* See Upland Sandpiper. *Habitat:* Shortgrass prairie, stubble fields, overgrazed pastures. *Texas:* Common to uncommon transient (July–Aug., Apr.) in eastern third. *Range:* Breeds in arctic of

Alaska and northwestern Canada; winters in Paraguay, Uruguay and northern Argentina.

202. Ruff *Philomachus pugnax* (Male, L—12 W—24; Female L—10 W—21)
Dark brown, tan, and white on back; spectacular collar of ruffled feathers around neck and breast—black, chestnut, or white; black below; bill and legs yellowish; rump white except for dark central line. *Female:* (called a reeve): Dark gray above and below; white belly; white rump with dark central line; yellow legs and base of bill. *Winter:* Dark gray and white on back; grayish head and breast; whitish belly; bill yellowish at base; legs yellowish. *Voice:* "Tew-ee." *Similar species:* Lesser Yellowlegs has white rump with no dark, central line. *Habitat:* Beaches, estuaries, mud flats. *Texas:* Casual winter visitor (Oct.–Apr.), mainly along coast. *Range:* Breeds in Old World arctic; winters in Old World temperate and tropical regions.

203. Short-billed Dowitcher

Limnodromus griseus (L—11 W—19)
A rather squat, long-billed sandpiper (bill is three times length of head); mottled black, white, and buff on back wings, and crown; cinnamon buff on neck and underparts spotted with dark brown; white face with dark eyeline; white tail barred with black; white on rump extending in a wedge up back. *Winter:* Grayish crown, nape, and back; whitish face and underparts; flanks and undertail coverts spotted with black. *Habits:* Often feeds with rapid up-and-down motion, breast-deep in water, usually in small flocks. *Voice:* A rapid "wik-ee" or "wik-ee-kee," repeated. *Similar species:* Long-billed Dowitcher in breeding plumage is barred, not spotted, on flanks; winter plumages of the dowitchers are very similar but calls are quite different: Short-billed has a two- or three-note whistle while the Long-billed has a thin "eek." *Habitat:* Mud flats, flooded pastures, ponds, lakes, estuaries. *Texas:* Uncommon winter resident (Aug.–May), rare in summer along coast; uncommon to rare transient (Apr.–May, Aug.–Oct.) inland. *Range:* Breeds across central Canada and southern Alaska; winters in coastal U.S. (California, South Carolina) south to northern South America, West Indies.

204. Long-billed Dowitcher

Limnodromus scolopaceus (L—11 W—19)
See Short-billed Dowitcher. *Voice:* A thin "eek," often repeated. *Similar species:* See Short-billed Dowitcher. *Habitat:* Mud flats, flooded pastures. *Texas:* Common winter resident (Sept.–May), uncommon in summer, along coast; common to uncommon transient inland (Apr.–May, Aug.–Oct.) *Range:* Breeds in coastal Alaska, northwestern Canada, and northeastern Siberia; winters from southern U.S. to Guatemala.

205. Common Snipe

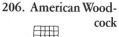

Gallinago gallinago (L—11 W—17)
Dark brown back with white stripes; crown striped with dark brown and gray; neck and breast streaked grayish brown and white; whitish belly; tan rump; tail banded with rust and black; very long bill (three times length of head). *Habits:* Normally solitary, retiring, and wary; gives an explosive "zhrrt" when flushed and flies in erratic swoops and dips. *Voice:* Song, given on wing—"cheek cheek cheek cheek," etc., plus a winnowing sound (made by air passing through the tail feathers). *Habitat:* Marshes, bogs, flooded pastures, wet ditches. *Texas:* Common winter resident (Oct.–Mar.) in eastern half of state; uncommon to rare in west. *Range:* Breeds in northern temperate and boreal regions of Old and New World; winters in southern temperate and tropical regions.

206. American Woodcock

Scolopax minor (L—11 W—17)
A fat, short-legged, long-billed bird with no apparent neck and hardly any tail; dark and grayish brown above; gray-brown neck and breast becoming rusty on belly and flanks; dark brown crown with thin, transverse gray stripes; large, brown eye; overall impression of flushed bird is cinnamon buff because of underparts and wing linings. *Habits:* Nocturnal; feeds, sings, and displays at night. *Voice:* A buzzy, nasal "peent," also a flight song composed of a long trill followed by various "chik," "cheek," and "cherk" sounds made by air passing through the bird's feathers as it descends; wings make a whistling sound when bird is flushed. *Habitat:* Moist woodlands, swamp borders. *Texas:* Uncommon to rare winter resident (Nov.–Feb.) in eastern third, rare to casual summer resident, has bred.* *Range:* Breeds across eastern half of U.S. and southeastern Canada; winters in southern

half of breeding range into South Texas and southern Florida.

207. Wilson's Phalarope

Phalaropus tricolor (L—9 W—17)
Female: A trim, thin-billed, long-necked bird; chestnut and gray on the back; gray crown and nape; black extending from eye down side of neck; white chin; chestnut throat; white breast and belly. *Male:* Similar but paler. *Winter:* Grayish-brown above, white below; gray head with white eyebrow; white chin; rusty throat. *Habits:* Unlike other shorebirds, phalaropes often swim, whirling in tight circles, while foraging. *Voice:* A nasal "wak," repeated. *Similar species:* Other phalaropes have white foreheads and black and white facial pattern in winter. *Habitat:* Ponds, lakes, mud flats, flooded pastures. *Texas:* Common transient (July–Aug., Apr.–May) nearly throughout; rare in summer (has nested* in Panhandle); casual in winter. *Range:* Breeds in western U.S., southwestern Canada, and Great Lakes region; winters in western and southern South America.

208. Red-necked Phalarope

Phalaropus lobatus (L—8 W—14)
Female: Black with rusty striping on back and flanks; white below; neck and nape orange; head black; chin white. *Male:* Similar in pattern but paler. *Winter:* Black back with white striping; white below; white forehead; gray-black crown; white eyebrow; black postorbital stripe. *Habits:* See Wilson's Phalarope. *Voice:* A hoarse "chik" or "ker-chik." *Similar species:* Winter Red Phalarope has a pearl gray, unstreaked back (Red-necked is almost black, striped with white). *Habitat:* Marshes, ponds, lakes; but mainly pelagic. *Texas:* Rare to casual transient (Apr.–May, Aug.–Oct.) throughout. *Range:* Breeds in northern tundra bogs of Old and New World; winters at sea in southern Pacific and Indian oceans.

209. Red Phalarope

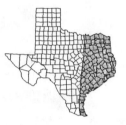

Phalaropus fulicaria (L—9 W—17)
Female: Black back striped with buff; neck and underparts rusty orange; black cap; white cheek; relatively short, heavy bill is yellow at base, black at tip. *Male:* Similar in pattern but paler. *Winter:* Uniform pearl gray on back; white below; white forehead and front half of crown; gray rear half of crown and nape line; dark postorbital stripe; bill blackish. *Habits:* See Wilson's Phalarope. *Similar species:* See Red-necked Phalarope. *Habitat:* Beaches, mud flats, but mainly pelagic in winter. *Texas:* Casual fall transient in eastern half. *Range:* Breeds in Old and New World arctic; winters in southern Pacific and Atlantic oceans.

Family Laridae
Jaegers, Gulls, and Terns

This family is subdivided into four distinct groupings: jaegars and skuas, gulls, terns, and skimmers. Identification to species of the immatures for some groups within the Laridae can be difficult or impossible in the field. Harrison (1985) and Grant (1986) provide detailed descriptions and keys for advanced students of these birds.

210. Pomarine Jaeger

Stercorarius pomarinus (L— 22 W— 48)
Protruding central tail feathers are twisted; dark brown above; white collar tinged with yellow; whitish below with dark breast band and undertail coverts. *Dark phase:* Completely dark brown with white at base of primaries; cheeks tinged with yellow; dark cap. *Immature:* Barred brown or brown and white below. *Similar species:* Parasitic Jaeger has pointed (not twisted) tail feathers; Long-tailed Jaeger has very long central tail feathers (half of body length). *Habitat:* Pelagic, beaches. *Texas:* Rare winter visitor on Gulf beaches, probably uncommon offshore. *Range:* Breeds in Old and New World arctic; winters in temperate and tropical oceans.

211. Parasitic Jaeger

Stercorarius parasiticus (L—19 W—42)
Dark brown above; white collar and white below with
faint brown breast band; pointed, protruding central
tail feathers; wings dark but whitish at base of primaries. *Dark phase:* Completely dark brown. *Immature:* Dark brown above; barred reddish brown or
brown and white below. *Similar species:* See Pomarine
Jaeger. *Habitat:* Pelagic, beaches. *Texas:* Rare in
winter along barrier beaches, probably uncommon
offshore. *Range:* Breeds in Old and New World arctic;
winters in temperate and tropical oceans.

212. Long-tailed Jaeger

Stercorarius longicaudus (L—32 W—40)
Gray-brown above; white collar and white below with
gray-brown undertail coverts; very long central tail
feathers. *Dark Phase:* Completely dark gray-brown
(extremely rare). *Immature:* Dark throat, white breast
and belly. *Similar species:* See Pomarine Jaeger.
Habitat: Pelagic, beaches. *Texas:* Casual fall visitor
(Aug.–Nov.), probably rare offshore. This is the rarest
of the three jaegers in Texas. *Range:* Breeds in Old
and New World arctic; winters mainly in tropical
oceans.

213. South Polar Skua

Catharacta maccormicki (L—21 W—52)
A thick-bodied, Herring Gull–sized bird. *Dark phase:*
Dark brown throughout with white patch at base of
primaries; light ruff at nape. *Light phase:* Gray
throughout; patterned like dark phase; nape ruff is
whitish; thick scapulars give the bird a definite
"hunched" appearance in flight. *Habits:* Chases other
seabirds to rob them of food. *Immature:* Patterned
like adult but generally paler in color with some
streaking on breast. *Similar species:* Great Skua has
overall rusty tint. *Habitat:* Pelagic, beaches. *Texas:*
Hypothetical—15 mi. offshore from Aransas Co. in
the Gulf of Mexico. *Range:* Breeds on South Shetland
Islands and coastal Antarctica; wanders during nonbreeding season over most of the world's oceans south
of the Arctic.

214. Laughing Gull

Larus atricilla (L—17 W—40)
Black head; gray back and wings with black wing tips; white collar, underparts, and tail; scarlet bill and black legs; partial white eyering. *Winter:* As in breeding but head whitish with dark gray ear patch; black bill. *Immature:* Brownish above and on breast; white belly and tail with black terminal bar. *Voice:* A raucous, derisive "kaah kah-kah-kah-kah kaah kaah," also a single "keeyah." *Similar species:* Franklin's Gull shows white tips on black primaries and a darkish hood in winter. *Habitat:* Beaches, bays, lakes, agricultural areas. *Texas:* Common resident* along coast, less common in winter. *Range:* Breeds along both coasts in North America from New Brunswick on the east and northern Mexico on the west, south to northern South America, West Indies.

215. Franklin's Gull

Larus pipixcan (L—15 W—36)
Black head; gray back and wings; white bar bordering black wing tips spotted terminally with white; white collar, underparts, and tail; underparts variously tinged with rose; scarlet bill and legs; partial white eyering. *Winter:* As in breeding but head with a partial, dark hood; black bill. *Immature:* Similar to winter adult but with black terminal tail band. *Voice:* "Ayah." *Similar species:* See Laughing Gull. *Habitat:* Tallgrass prairie, pastures, flooded fields, bays. *Texas:* Common transient (Oct.–Nov., Apr.–May) in eastern half, uncommon to rare in west; rare along coast in winter. These birds occur in large flocks during migration. *Range:* Breeds north-central U.S. and south-central Canada; winters along Pacific coast of Middle and South America.

216. Little Gull

Larus minutus (L—11 W—22)
A small gull; black head; gray back; wings dark below and gray above with white border; white collar, underparts, and tail; black bill; red legs. *Winter:* Light forehead, incomplete gray hood, black ear patch. *Immature:* Black tail band and black stripe running diagonally across gray upper wing; pinkish legs. *Voice:* "Ki-ki-ki-ki," etc. *Similar species:* Other black-headed gulls have black or black and white wing tips; those of the adult Little Gull are white; the immature Little Gull has dark primaries but lacks

Breeding Adult   Winter Adult   First Year

Herring

Ring-billed

Laughing

Franklin's

Bonaparte's

Adult and immature (first year) gulls in flight

dark subterminal band on secondaries of Franklin's, Common Black-headed, and Bonaparte's gulls. *Habitat:* Marshes, bays, rivers, estuaries. *Texas:* Accidental — Dallas and Travis cos. *Range:* Breeds in central and western Asia, northern Europe, and locally in Great Lakes of North America; winters in coastal regions of Baltic, Mediterranean, Black, and Caspian seas, and is rare in North America in Great Lakes and Atlantic coast from Maine south to Virginia.

217. Common Black-headed Gull

Larus ridibundus (L—16 W—40)
Front two-thirds of head with dark brown hood; otherwise white with gray back and wings; red bill and legs; white outer primaries with black tips. *Winter:* White head with black ear patch. *Immature:* Like winter adult but with black tail band and brown stripe running diagonally across gray wing; pinkish-beige bill with dark tip; pinkish-beige legs; incomplete brown hood in first breeding plumage. *Voice:* "Keerrip." *Similar species:* Primaries of Bonaparte's Gull appear white or grayish from below; Common Black-headed primaries appear dark; Common Black-headed has red bill (black in Bonaparte's). *Habitat:* Marshes, lakes, grasslands, estuaries. *Texas:* Casual — San Jacinto, Nueces, Tarrant, McClennan cos. *Range:* Breeds in northern regions of Old World, casual in Newfoundland; winters in temperate and northern tropical regions of Old World and along the Atlantic Coast of North America from Labrador to New York.

218. Bonaparte's Gull

Larus philadelphia (L—14 W—32)
A small gull; black head; gray back; wings gray with white outer primaries tipped in black; white collar, underparts, and tail; black bill; red legs. *Winter:* White head with black ear patch. *Immature:* Like winter adult but with black tail band and brown stripe running diagonally across gray wing; pinkish-beige legs; black bill. *Voice:* A high-pitched, screechy "aaaanhh." *Similar species:* See Common Black-headed Gull. *Habitat:* Marine, bays, estuaries. *Texas:* Uncommon winter resident (Nov.–Apr.) along coast, scarcer inland. *Range:* Breeds across north-central and northwestern North America in Canada and Alaska; winters southward along both coasts, from Washington on the west and Nova Scotia on the east to central

Mexico; also the Great Lakes, Bahamas, and Greater Antilles.

219. Heermann's Gull

Larus heermanni (L—19 W—51)
Dark gray above, pearl below with white head; red bill with black tip; rump pale gray; tail black with narrow white terminal band; wings dark with white tips; legs dark. *Winter:* Head streaked with gray. *Immature:* Dark brown throughout; bill pale at base, black at tip. *Voice:* A "whistled whine, and a *co-wak,* sometimes repeated" (Edwards 1972:65). *Habitat:* Marine, beaches. *Texas:* Accidental—Reagan, Nueces cos. *Range:* Breeds from central California to southern Mexico, mainly (exclusively?) on coastal islands; Pacific Coast from southern British Columbia to Guatemala during nonbreeding period.

220. Mew Gull

Larus canus (L—16 W—43)
White body and tail; dark gray back; gray wings, primaries tipped in black and white; short, yellow bill; greenish legs; dark eye. *Winter:* Like summer, but mottled with brown on head and breast. *Immature:* First year—Grayish-brown back; white head mottled with brown; brown below; dark wings and tail; pale legs; two-tone bill, pale at base, dark at tip; second year—Gray back; white body, mottled with brown on head and breast; pale legs; two-tone bill. *Voice:* "A low mewing . . . *quee'u* or *mee'u.* Also *hiyah-hiyah-hiyah,* etc., higher than other gulls" (Peterson 1961: 132). *Similar species:* Solid yellow bill and dark eye separate adults of this species from Ring-billed Gulls; most first-year Mew Gulls have a dark tail, whereas first-year Ring-billed Gulls have a distinct, dark, subterminal band on light tail. *Habitat:* Marshes, lakes, bays. *Texas:* Accidental—Hudspeth, Tarrant cos. *Range:* Breeds in western North America (Alaska to Washington) and northern Eurasia; winters along Pacific Coast of North America (southeastern Alaska to southern California), Mediterranean Sea, Middle East and southern Asia.

221. Ring-billed Gull

Larus delawarensis (L—16 W—48)
White body; gray back; gray wings with black outer primaries tipped with white; bill orange-yellow with black, subterminal ring; legs pale yellow. *Immature:* Like adult but mottled with brown or gray; bill pale with black tip; whitish tail with black terminal band. *Voice:* A strident "Ayah." *Similar species:* Immature Herring Gulls are much larger; tail is mostly dark in Herring Gull, without a subterminal band as in immature Ring-billed Gull, and lacks white terminal band. *Habitat:* Lakes, bays, beaches, estuaries. *Texas:* Common to uncommon winter resident (Aug.–May) in eastern half, scarcer west; uncommon summer resident along coast. *Range:* Breeds in Great Plains region of central Canada, scattered areas in northern U.S.; winters across most of U.S. except northern plains and mountains, south to Panama.

222. California Gull

Larus californicus (L— 21 W— 40)
White body; gray back; gray wings with black outer primaries tipped with white; bill yellow with red spot on lower mandible; feet pale yellow. *Winter:* Head and breast smudged with brown. *Immature:* Mottled dark brown in first winter; bill pale with black tip; legs pinkish; tail dark; grayish above, whitish below in second winter; legs pale greenish. *Similar species:* Immature Herring Gull has all black (not two-tone) bill in first winter and pinkish (not greenish) legs in second winter. *Habitat:* Lakes, bays, beaches, estuaries, marine. *Texas:* Casual winter visitor (Oct.–May) mainly along coast and at large lakes in western Texas. *Range:* Breeds in west-central Canada and northwestern U.S.; winters along Pacific Coast from Vancouver to central Mexico.

223. Herring Gull

Larus argentatus (L— 24 W— 57)
White body; gray back; gray wings with black outer primaries tipped with white; bill yellow with red spot on lower mandible; feet pinkish; yellow eye. *Winter:* Head and breast smudged with brown. *Immature:* Mottled dark brown in first winter; bill black; feet pinkish; tail dark; in second and third winter, grayish above, whitish below variously mottled with brown; tail with broad, dark, terminal band; bill pinkish with black tip; legs pinkish. *Voice:* The familiar, rusty

gate squawking "qeeyah kwa kwa kwa kwa" of all Hollywood shows that include an ocean scene. *Similar species:* See California Gull. *Habitat:* Beaches, bays, marine, lakes, rivers. *Texas:* Common (along coast) to uncommon (eastern half) winter resident (Oct.– Mar.), scarcer in west; rare summer resident along coast – single breeding record from Laguna Madre.* *Range:* Breeds in boreal and northern temperate regions of both Old and New World; winters along coasts of far north southward into temperate and northern tropical regions.

224. Thayer's Gull

Larus thayeri (L– 23 W– 55)
White body; gray back; gray wings with outer primaries dark gray tipped with white; bill yellow with red spot on lower mandible; brown eye (sometimes yellow shot with brown); legs pinkish. *Winter:* Head and breast smudged with brown. *Immature:* Mottled dark brown in first winter; bill black; feet pinkish; tail dark; grayish above, whitish below mottled with brown in second and third winters; bill pinkish with black tip; legs pinkish. *Similar species:* Thayer's Gull can be distinguished (with difficulty) from Herring Gull by paler gray back, underwing and primary tips, dark eye, and darker legs. *Habitat:* Beaches, bays, estuaries. *Texas:* Casual winter visitor (Nov.–Apr.), mainly along coast. *Range:* Breeds on polar islands of northern Canada; winters along Pacific Coast from southwestern Canada to Baja California.

225. Iceland Gull

Larus glaucoides (L– 23 W– 42)
White body; gray back and upper wing coverts; white primaries and terminal edge of secondaries; yellow eye; bill pinkish or yellowish with red spot on lower mandible; feet pinkish; long-winged – wing tips extend beyond tail in sitting bird. *Winter:* Head and breast smudged with brown; wing tips with some gray. *First winter:* White with light brown markings; bill black; legs pinkish; tail white marked with brown. *Second and third winter:* Paler than adult; some brown smudging; bill pinkish with black tip. *Similar species:* Glaucous Gull is larger, has more massive bill and proportionately shorter wings (wings extend well beyond tail in standing Iceland Gull). Glaucous Gull lacks contrasting darker gray wing tips

of winter Iceland Gull, *Habitat:* Seacoasts. *Texas:* Hypothetical—Starr Co. *Range:* Breeds on islands of far north in North Atlantic; winters along northern coasts of North Atlantic and Baltic Sea.

226. Lesser Black-backed Gull

Larus fuscus (L—21 W—45)
White body; dark gray back and wings; outer primaries black sparsely tipped with white, appearing an almost uniform gray below; bill yellow with red spot on lower mandible; eyes and legs yellow. *Winter:* Head and breast streaked with brown. *First winter:* White heavily marked with brown; bill black; feet pale pinkish. *Second winter:* Body white marked with brown; back and wings dark gray marked with brown; bill pinkish with black tip; legs pale yellow or pink. *Similar species:* First-winter birds very similar to first-winter Herring Gull but have paler rump; older birds are darker on the back and have yellow legs (pinkish in Great Black-backed Gull). *Habitat:* Beaches, marine. *Texas:* Casual winter visitor (Oct.–Mar.), mainly along coast. *Range:* Breeds in Iceland and coastal northern Europe; winters along coasts of Europe and eastern North America.

227. Slaty-backed Gull

Larus schistisagus (L—25 W—58)
White body; dark gray back; black outer primary tips separated from dark gray wing by a whitish bar; pink legs; yellow bill with red spot on lower mandible; yellow eye. *Winter:* Head and breast flecked with gray. *Immature:* Pale mottled brown in first winter; bill black, feet pinkish; in second and third winter, gray above, whitish below variously mottled with brown; pinkish legs; yellowish bill with dark tip. *Similar species:* Darker back than adult Herring Gull; broad white band along trailing edge of wing, narrower in Lesser Black-backed and Western gulls. May be conspecific with Herring Gull. *Habitat:* Coastal marine and pelagic. *Texas:* Hypothetical—Cameron Co. *Range:* Breeds in coastal Siberia and islands of the northwestern Pacific. Winters in the breeding range south to coastal China and Japan.

228. Western Gull

Larus occidentalis (L— 25 W— 58)
White body; dark gray back and wings; outer primaries black above sparsely tipped with white, gray below; bill very large, yellow with red spot on lower mandible; legs and eyes yellow. *Winter:* Head and breast streaked with brown. *First winter:* White heavily marked with brown; rump paler; bill black; feet pale pinkish. *Second and third winter:* Body white streaked with brown; dark gray mottled with brown on back and wings; tail mostly dark; bill yellowish with black tip; legs pale pink. *Similar species:* Wings of Great Black-backed Gull appear uniform black from above, but Western shows dark gray with black tips; second- and third-winter birds and adults are darker-backed than Herring Gulls of comparable age. *Habitat:* Coastal regions. *Texas:* Accidental—El Paso Co. *Range:* Breeds along Pacific Coast from southwestern Canada to Baja California; winters in breeding range south to central Pacific coast of Mexico.

229. Glaucous Gull

Larus hyperboreus (L— 27 W— 60)
A very large gull; white body; pale gray back; yellow eye; wings pale gray with outer primaries broadly tipped with white above, mostly white from below; bill yellow with red spot on lower mandible; feet pinkish; wing tips barely extend beyond tail in sitting bird. *Winter:* Head and breast smudged with brown. *First winter:* Mostly white or with light brown markings; bill pinkish with black tip; legs pinkish; tail white marked with brown. *Second and third winter:* Back grayish; bill yellowish with dark tip. *Similar species:* See Iceland Gull. *Habitat:* Coastal regions. *Texas:* Casual in winter (Sept.–Apr.) along coast; resemblance to immatures of other pale gulls confuses status. *Range:* Breeds in circumpolar regions of Old and New World; winters in coastal regions of northern Eurasia and North America.

230. Great Black-backed Gull

Larus marinus (L— 30 W— 66)
A very large gull; white body; black back; yellow eye; wings appear black above with white trailing edge, outer primaries tipped with white; bill very large, yellow with red spot on lower mandible; legs pinkish. *First winter:* White checked with brown above, paler below; rump paler; bill black; legs pale pink. *Second*

and third winter: Body white streaked with brown; black mottled with brown on back and wings; bill pinkish or yellowish with black tip; legs pale pinkish. *Voice:* Hoarse, low squawks and chuckles. *Similar species:* See Western and Lesser Black-backed gulls. *Habitat:* Seacoasts and large lakes. *Texas:* Casual in winter (Oct.–Apr.) on coast. *Range:* Breeds in coastal northeastern North America and northeastern Eurasia; winters in breeding range and south to southeastern U.S. and southern Europe.

231. Black-legged Kittiwake

Rissa tridactyla (L—17 W—36)
A small gull; white body; gray back; white, slightly forked tail; dark eye; wings gray above, white below tipped with black; bill yellow; legs dark. *Winter:* Nape and back of crown gray with dark ear patch. *First winter:* White marked with black half "collar" on nape; gray back; dark diagonal stripe on upper wing; black ear patch; tail white with black terminal band; bill and legs black. *Voice:* "Kitt-ee-waak." *Similar species:* Immature Bonaparte's Gull lacks black "collar." *Habitat:* Pelagic, coasts. *Texas:* Rare in winter (Nov.–Mar.), mainly along coast. *Range:* Breeds in circumpolar regions of Old and New World; winters in northern and temperate seas of northern hemisphere.

232. Sabine's Gull

Xema sabini (L—14 W—33)
Dark hood; white collar, underparts, and forked tail; gray back; distinctive pattern of white wing with black primaries and gray shoulder; black bill tipped with yellow; black legs. *Winter:* Similar to breeding but head is white with gray on crown and nape. *Immature:* Mottled brown and white above; white below; forked tail white with black terminal band; bill black; legs gray. *Habitat:* Pelagic and coasts. *Texas:* Casual in fall (Sept.–Oct.), mainly along coast. *Range:* Breeds in circumpolar regions of Old and New World; winters in tropical seas.

233. Gull-billed Tern

Sterna nilotica (L—15 W—36)
A medium-sized tern with a heavy, black bill; black cap and nape; white face, neck, and underparts; gray back and wings; tail with shallow fork; black legs. *Winter:* Crown white finely streaked with black. *Habits:* Does not dive like most terns. It swoops and sails over marshland for insects. *Voice:* A harsh, nasal "kee-yeek" or "ka-wup." *Similar species:* Black bill and shallow tail fork are distinctive. *Habitat:* Marshes, wet fields, prairies, bays. *Texas:* Common summer resident* (Mar.–Oct.) along coast; uncommon in winter. *Range:* Breeds locally in temperate and tropical regions of the world; winters in subtropics and tropics.

234. Caspian Tern

Sterna caspia (L—21 W—52)
A large tern with large, heavy, blood orange bill; black cap and nape; white face, neck, and underparts; gray back and wings; tail moderately forked; black legs. *Winter:* Black cap streaked with white. *Voice:* A low squawk, "aaaak," repeated. *Similar species:* Primaries of Royal Tern appear whitish from below, Caspian primaries are dark; Royal has white forehead (not black flecked with white) most of the year; Royal's call is a screechy "keee-eer," not a squawk like the Caspian's. *Habitat:* Beaches, bays, marine, estuaries, lakes. *Texas:* Common permanent resident* along coast. *Range:* Breeds locally inland and along the coast in temperate, tropical, and boreal areas of the world; winters in southern temperate and tropical regions.

235. Royal Tern

Sterna maxima (L—20 W—45)
A large tern with yellow or yellow-orange bill; black cap with short, ragged crest; black nape; white face, neck, and underparts; gray back and wings; tail forked; black legs. *Winter:* White forehead and crown; black nape. *Voice:* A screechy "keee-eer." *Similar species:* See Caspian Tern. *Habitat:* Beaches, bays, *Texas:* Common summer resident* (Mar.–Nov.) along coast; uncommon in winter. *Range:* Breeds locally in temperate and tropical regions of western hemisphere and West Africa; winters in warmer portions of breeding range.

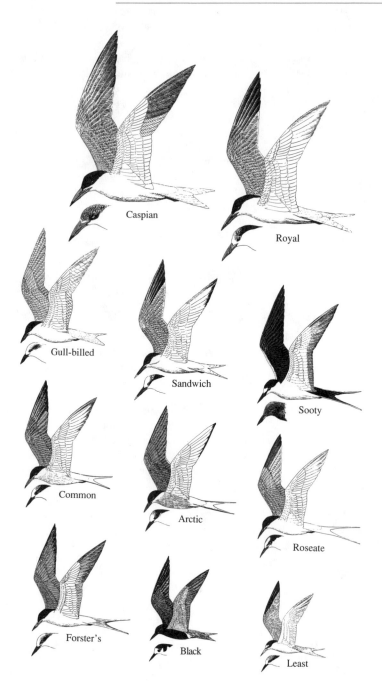

Adult terns in flight. *Top:* breeding plumage, *bottom:* winter plumage; except Sooty Tern: *top:* adult, *bottom:* immature

236. Elegant Tern

Sterna elegans (L—17 W—42)
A large tern with long, pointed orange-yellow bill; black cap often with a ragged crest; black nape; white face, neck, and underparts (often tinged with rose); gray back and wings; tail deeply forked; black legs. *Winter:* White forehead and crown; black nape. *Voice:* A screechy "kerr-eek." *Similar species:* Bill relatively long and thin compared with Royal Tern; call ends in an upward "eek," Royal ends in a downward "err"; in winter plumage, black of crest extends to eye in Elegant Tern, but usually not in Royal Tern. *Habitat:* Seacoasts. *Texas:* Accidental—Nueces, Reeves cos. *Range:* Breeds along Pacific Coast from southern California to central Mexico; winters along Pacific Coast from Guatemala to Chile.

237. Sandwich Tern

Sterna sandvicensis (L—15 W—34)
A trim, medium-sized tern with long, pointed black bill, tipped with yellow; black cap and short, ragged crest; black nape; white face, neck, and underparts; gray back and wings; tail deeply forked; black legs. *Winter:* White forehead; crown white, finely streaked with black; black nape. *Voice:* "Keerr-rik." *Similar species:* The combination of slim, yellow-tipped, black bill and black legs is distinctive. *Habitat:* Marine, bays, often associated with Royal Tern. *Texas:* Common summer resident* (Mar.–Nov.) along coast; uncommon in winter. *Range:* Breeds locally along Atlantic, Gulf, and Caribbean coasts of North and South America from Virginia to Argentina, West Indies; winters through subtropical and tropical portions of breeding range and on the Pacific Coast of Middle and South America from southern Mexico to Peru.

238. Roseate Tern

Sterna dougallii (L—16 W—28)
A medium-sized tern; black bill reddish at base; black cap and nape; white face and neck; underparts white tinged with pink; gray back and wings; black outer primaries; tail very long, white, and deeply forked, extends well beyond folded wings in sitting bird; red legs. *Winter:* White forehead and crown; back of crown and nape black; bill black. *First breeding:* Like adult but with white forehead. *Habits:* Flies with distinctive rapid, shallow wing beats. *Voice:* "Che-

wee," mellow (for a tern). *Similar species:* Roseate has completely white tail; Common Tern has gray outer edgings and white inner edgings; Forster's Tern has white outer edgings and gray inner edgings; Common Tern tail does not extend beyond the folded wings of sitting bird as it does in the Roseate; also the Roseate Tern "chewee" call is distinctive ("kee-arr" in Forster's, "keeeyaak" or "keyew" in Common). *Habitat:* Beaches, marine, bays. *Texas:* Casual along coast. *Range:* Breeds locally along coasts of temperate and tropical regions of the world (in U.S. from Maine to North Carolina); winters mainly in tropical portions of breeding range.

239. Common Tern

Sterna hirundo (L—14 W—31)
A medium-sized tern; red bill, black at tip; black cap and nape; white face, neck, and underparts; gray back and wings; entire outer primary, tips, and basal portions of other primaries are black (gray from below); forked tail with gray outer edgings, white inner edgings; red legs. *Winter:* White forehead and crown; back of crown and nape black; bill black; sitting bird shows a dark bar at the shoulder (actually upper wing coverts). *First breeding:* Similar to adult winter plumage. *Voice:* A harsh "keeeyaak," also "keyew keyew keyew." *Similar species:* Winter Arctic Tern has white (not dark) basal portions of primaries from below; also see Roseate Tern. *Habitat:* Beaches, bays, marshes, lakes, rivers. *Texas:* Common transient (Sept.–Oct., May–June) along coast, uncommon to rare inland in eastern third; rare summer* and winter resident along coast; bred formerly. *Range:* Breeds locally in boreal and temperate regions of Old and New World (mostly Canada, northeastern U.S., and West Indies); winters in southern temperate and tropical regions.

240. Arctic Tern

Sterna paradisaea (L—16 W—31)
A medium-sized tern; red bill; black cap and nape; white face; grayish neck, breast, and belly; white undertail coverts; gray back; wings gray above with dark outer edge of outer primary. white below with primaries narrowly tipped in black; tail deeply forked; red legs. *Winter:* white forehead and crown; back of crown and nape black; bill black. *Voice:* A high, nasal

"ki-kee-yah"; also "kaaah." *Similar species:* See Common Tern. *Habitat:* Mostly marine, beaches. *Texas:* Casual along coast. *Range:* Breeds in the Arctic; winters in the Antarctic.

241. Forster's Tern

Sterna forsteri (L—15 W—31)
A medium-sized tern; orange or yellow bill with black tip; black cap and nape; white face and underparts; gray back and wings; forked tail, white on outer edgings, gray on inner; orange legs. *Winter:* White head with blackish ear patch; bill black. *Voice:* "Chew-ik." *Similar species:* Winter Common and Arctic terns have back of crown and nape black (usually white in Forster's). *Habitat:* Marshes, bays, beaches, marine. *Texas:* Common permanent resident* along coast; common to uncommon transient in eastern third. *Range:* Breeds locally across northern U.S., south-central and southwestern Canada, and Atlantic and Gulf coasts; winters coastally from southern U.S. to Guatemala; also Greater Antilles.

242. Least Tern

Sterna antillarum (L—9 W—20)
A small tern; yellow bill with black tip; black cap and nape with white forehead; white face and underparts; gray back and wings; tail deeply forked; yellow legs. *Winter:* White head with blackish postorbital stripe and nape; bill brown; legs dull yellow. *Voice:* A high-pitched "ki-teek ki-teek ki-teek," etc. *Similar species:* Winter Forster's Tern is much larger and has whitish (not black) nape. *Habitat:* Bays, beaches, rivers, lakes, ponds. *Texas:* Common summer resident* (Mar.–Sept.) along coast; rare inland breeding population along Red River; uncommon to rare transient in eastern third. *Range:* Breeds along both coasts from central California (west) and Maine (east) south to southern Mexico; rare inland population bred along rivers of Mississippi drainage; West Indies; winters along coast of northern South America.

243. Bridled Tern

Sterna anaethetus (L—15 W—30)
Dark gray above, white below; black cap with white forehead and eyebrow; white collar; black bill and feet; deeply forked, brown tail edged in white. *Similar species:* Sooty Tern lacks collar, and white stripe extends to, but not behind, eye (extends behind eye in Bridled Tern). *Habitat:* Mostly marine. *Texas:* Casual—Nueces, Cameron, Brazoria, Galveston cos.—after hurricanes; may be regular in open Gulf. *Range:* Breeds locally on islands in tropical seas (including West Indies).

244. Sooty Tern

Sterna fuscata (L—17 W—32)
Black above, white below; black cap with white forehead; black bill and feet; tail deeply forked, black with white edging. *Immature:* Dark brown throughout with white spotting. *Habits:* Does not dive for fish as other terns do. It plucks fish from surface. *Voice:* A creaky "waky wak." *Similar species:* See Bridled Tern. *Habitat:* Marine, bays, beaches. *Texas:* Uncommon summer resident* (Apr.–Sept.) along central and lower coast. *Range:* Breeds locally on tropical and subtropical coasts and islands throughout the world.

245. Black Tern

Chlidonias niger (L—10 W—24)
A small tern; dark gray throughout except white undertail coverts; slightly forked tail. *Winter:* Dark gray above, white below with dark smudge at shoulder; white forehead; white crown streaked with gray; gray nape; white collar. *Voice:* A high-pitched "kik kik kik," etc. *Habits:* Note swallow-like flight in pursuit of insects. *Habitat:* Marshes, bays, estuaries, lakes, ponds. *Texas:* Common summer resident (May–Sept.) along coast; does not breed; common to uncommon transient (May–June, Aug., Sept.) in eastern half, scarcer in west. *Range:* Breeds in temperate and boreal regions of northern hemisphere; winters in tropics.

246. Brown Noddy

Anous stolidus (L—16 W—32)
Brown except for grayish forehead and crown. *Immature:* Almost entirely brown, somewhat paler on forehead. *Habits:* Picks fish from surface rather than diving for them. *Voice:* A squawk, "karrr-rrak." *Similar species:* Black Noddy has a darker body contrasted with a whiter cap, limited mostly to the forehead, and a relatively thin bill. *Habitat:* Marine, beaches. *Texas:* Casual (June–Sept.) along coast. *Range:* Resident of southern temperate and tropical seas; nearest breeding areas to Texas are Yucatán and Dry Tortugas.

247. Black Noddy

Anous minutus (L—14 W—30)
Entirely black except for whitish forehead. *Immature:* Like adult, but crown is less distinct. *Habits:* Picks fish from surface rather than diving for them. *Similar species:* See Brown Noddy. *Habitat:* Marine, beaches. *Texas:* Accidental—Padre Island, Nueces Co. *Range:* Resident of tropical seas.

248. Black Skimmer

Rynchops niger (L—18 W—45)
Black above; white below; extremely long, straight razor-shaped bill, red with black tip; lower mandible is longer than the upper. *Immature:* Like adult but mottled brown and white above. *Habits:* Flies above the water with the lower mandible dipped below the surface to capture fish. *Voice:* A mellow "kip," "kee-yip," or "kee-kee-yup." *Habitat:* Beaches, bays, estuaries. *Texas:* Common summer resident* (Apr.–Oct.) along coast, uncommon in winter. *Range:* Breeds from southern California (west) and New York (east) south to southern South America along coasts and on major river systems; winters in southern temperate and tropical portions of breeding range, West Indies.

Order Columbiformes
Family Columbidae
Doves and Pigeons

These are small to medium-sized, chunky birds with relatively small heads. Larger species are generally referred to as "pigeons" while smaller ones are "doves." They feed on fruits and seeds, and produce "crop milk" (specialized cells sloughed from the esophagus) to feed their young.

249. Rock Dove

Columba livia (L—13 W—23)
The domestic pigeon is highly variable in color, including various mixtures of brown, white, gray, and dark blue; the "average" bird shows gray above and below with head and neck iridescent purplish-green; white rump; dark terminal band on tail. *Voice:* A series of low "coo"s. *Habitat:* Cities, towns, agricultural areas. *Texas:* Common permanent resident* throughout. *Range:* Resident of Eurasia and North Africa; introduced into western hemisphere where resident nearly throughout near cities.

250. White-crowned Pigeon

Columba leucocephala (L—14 W—23)
A large, slate-colored bird; iridescent nape; white crown and eye; bill purple at the base, pale green at tip; legs purple. *Female:* Like male but with grayer crown and less iridescence. *Voice:* "Kroo-ko-kooo" with an accent on the last syllable (Howell 1932:277). *Habitat:* Mangroves and adjacent coastal woodlands. *Texas:* Hypothetical—Cameron Co. *Range:* Southern tip of Florida, West Indies, Caribbean coast of Middle America.

251. Red-billed Pigeon

Columba flavirostris (L—15 W—25)
Slaty blue body with iridescent purple cast on head and breast; red legs; red bill, yellow at tip. *Voice:* "Coo-oo-ooo" followed by "coot-coo-coo-oooo," repeated. *Habitat:* Riparian forest, open woodlands, secondary forest, pastures with scattered trees. *Texas:* Rare summer resident* (Mar.–Aug.) in Lower Rio Grande Valley. *Range:* Breeds from South Texas and northwestern Mexico south in lowlands to Costa Rica.

252. Band-tailed Pigeon

Columba fasciata (L—15 W—25)
Gray above and below with purplish cast on head and breast; bronze terminal band on tail bordered by a dark brown subterminal band; white half-collar on nape; iridescent bronze upper back; yellow legs and bill with black tip. *Voice:* A low "hoo-ooo." *Habitat:* Montane oak, pine-oak and coniferous forest. *Texas:* Common summer resident* in Trans-Pecos mountains. *Range:* Breeds locally in mountains from southwestern Canada south through western U.S. and Mexico to northern Argentina; winters in breeding range from southwestern U.S. southward.

253. Ringed Turtle-Dove

Streptopelia risoria (L—12 W—20)
Body entirely a pale beige; wings with somewhat darker primaries; square tail, the outer rectrices tipped with white; usually with a black half-collar at the nape; black bill; orange eye; red legs. *Voice:* A guttural "coo-curroo." *Habitat:* Semiarid and arid scrub, parks, savanna. *Texas:* May be established as a feral population in Harris Co. *Range:* Numerous feral populations, often in or near cities, worldwide. Origin unknown but closely related to *S. roseogrisea* of Africa and *S. decaocto* of Eurasia.

254. White-winged Dove

Zenaida asiatica (L—12 W—20)
Grayish brown above, grayish below; gray wings with broad white band on secondaries (visible as a broad white stripe along front edge of folded wing); light blue skin around red-orange eye; black whisker; red legs; broad white corners on square tail. *Voice:* A hoarse "caroo-co-coo" ("who cooks for you") or "carroo coo-ooo coo-wik coo-ooo coo-wik." *Habitat:* Thorn forest, residential areas, agricultural areas. *Texas:* Common summer resident* (Apr.–Sept.) in southern Texas north to San Antonio and Trans-Pecos along the Rio Grande; disjunct population in Galveston; uncommon winter resident in towns in breeding range. *Range:* Breeds from southwestern U.S. through Middle America and western South America to Chile; also in Bahamas and Greater Antilles; winters from northern Mexico south through breeding range.

255. Mourning Dove

Zenaida macroura (L—12 W—18)
Tan above, orange-buff below; brownish wings spotted with dark brown; tail long, pointed, and edged in white; gray cap; black whisker; purplish-bronze iridescence on side of neck; blue eyering; brown eye and bill; pink feet. *Voice:* A low, hoarse "hoo-wooo hooo ho hooo." *Similar species:* The long, pointed tail separates this from all other doves except the tiny Inca Dove, which has rusty wings, and body feathers that appear scale-like. *Habitat:* Prairie, thorn forest, woodlands. *Texas:* Common permanent resident* throughout. *Range:* Breeds from southern Canada south through U.S. to highlands of central Mexico, Costa Rica, Panama, Bahamas, Greater Antilles; winters in southern temperate and tropical portions of breeding range.

256. Passenger Pigeon

Ectopistes migratorius (L—16 W—24) **Extinct.**
Tan above with gray wash; buffy below with rusty wash; red eyes, eyering, and legs; long, pointed tail. *Habits:* Formerly associated in huge flocks. *Similar species:* Mourning Dove has blue eyering and black whisker (no whisker in Passenger Pigeon). *Habitat:* Deciduous forests. *Texas:* Formerly an irregular migrant to northeastern portion. *Range:* Bred across eastern half of U.S. south to Georgia, Kansas, and Oklahoma; wintered in southeastern U.S.

257. Inca Dove

Columbina inca (L—9 W—11)
A very small dove; light brown above with dark brown markings—giving the bird a scaly appearance; buffy below with brown barring; long, pointed tail with white outer tail feathers; rusty wing patches show in flight; red eye; brown bill; pink legs. *Voice:* A plaintive "hoo hoo" ("no hope"). *Similar species:* Ground-Doves have short, square tail, and lack scaly appearance on back. *Habitat:* Thorn forest, savanna, residential areas. *Texas:* Common permanent resident* in South and Central Texas. *Range:* Resident from southwestern U.S. to Costa Rica.

258. Common Ground-Dove

Columbina passerina (L—7 W—11)
A very small dove; grayish-brown above with dark brown spotting on wing; gray tinged with pink below with scaly brown markings on breast; gray crown and nape; red eye; pink bill; pinkish-beige legs; rusty wing patches show in flight; black outer tail feathers with white edgings. *Female:* Like male but grayish below (not pinkish), and gray crown is less distinct. *Habits:* Thrusts head forward while walking. *Voice:* "Hoo-wih," repeated. *Similar species:* See Inca Dove. *Habitat:* Thorn forest, savanna. *Texas:* Common permanent resident* in southern half. *Range:* Southern U.S. south to northern half of South America, West Indies.

259. Ruddy Ground-Dove

Columbina talpacoti (L—7 W—11)
Rusty brown above; ruddy below with gray cap; rufous wing patches; brown spotting on wings; black outer tail feathers. *Female:* More brownish than rusty. *Voice:* "Hoo-doo." *Similar species:* Female Common Ground-Dove has scaly breast; female Ruddy has plain breast. *Habits:* Jerks head while walking like Common Ground-Dove. *Habitat:* Tropical savannas, pasture, hedgerows. *Texas:* Casual in Lower Rio Grande Valley. *Range:* Northern Mexico to southern South America.

260. Blue Ground-Dove

Claravis pretiosa (L—8 W—12)
Bluish-gray above and below; brown spots on wings; black outer tail feathers. *Female:* Brownish above; buffy below; reddish-brown wing spots. *Voice:* A soft "hoot." *Similar species:* Female Blue Ground-Dove is a buffy yellow rather than brown or scaly gray. *Habitat:* Riparian forest, second growth woodlands, brushy pastures. *Texas:* Hypothetical—Cameron Co. *Range:* Lowlands of central Mexico to southern South America.

261. White-tipped Dove

Leptotila verreauxi (L—12 W—19)
A large, plump, short-legged dove; brown above; beige below; buffy forehead; rusty wing linings; dark, square-tipped tail with white terminal edgings on outer feathers; gray bill; red legs; white eye. *Habits:* Almost entirely terrestrial; seldom seen off the ground except when calling or nesting; flies low to the ground

with long, swooping glides. *Voice:* A very low, soft "hooo oooo." *Similar species:* Has square tail (not pointed as in Mourning Dove); no white on wings (as in Whitewing). *Habitat:* Riparian forest, tropical woodlands, scrub. *Texas:* Common permanent resident* in Lower Rio Grande Valley. *Range:* S Texas to southern South America.

Order Psittaciformes
Family Psittacidae
Parrots and Parakeets

Parrots are brightly colored (often shades of green), noisy birds with large, hooked bills. They usually travel in pairs within flocks.

The status of parrots in Texas is not clear. There are many early sight records of "parrots" from the riparian woodlands of South Texas, particularly along the Rio Grande. However, if these brids were present they had disappeared by the early 1900s. In recent years there have been increasing numbers of sightings — of Yellow-headed Parrots, Red-crowned Parrots, and Green Parakeets — all of which are native to the riparian forests of northern Tamaulipas. However, along with these birds are reports of Burrowing Parrots, Budgerigars, and many other species not native to the region that are presumably escapees. Therefore, essentially all parrot sightings have been written off as escaped cage birds despite the fact that records of those species native to northern Mexico may represent recolonization.

Within the past two years it has become evident from the large flocks in towns, citrus groves, and native riparian forest that the first-mentioned three species are now resident in the Rio Grande Valley. A study is needed to determine the status of these birds — are they breeding, or migratory?

262. Monk Parakeet

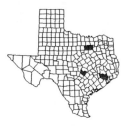

Myiopsitta monachus (L—12 W—21)
Green above; blue-green outer primaries and rectrices; grayish-white forehead and face; grayish-white breast with faint barring; yellowish band across belly; green undertail coverts; long, pointed tail. *Immature:* Like adult but with greenish forehead. *Habits:* Builds large colonial nests of sticks and grasses placed on poles or trees; feeds in flocks—often on agricultural crops. *Voice:* A harsh, screeching "eeeh," repeated. *Habitat:* Open woodland, savanna, riparian forest, agricultural and residential areas. *Texas:* Feral populations in metropolitan areas of Dallas, Fort Worth, Austin, and Houston. *Range:* Central Bolivia, Paraguay, and southern Brazil south to central Argentina; now established in many parts of the eastern and southern U.S.

263. Black-hooded Parakeet

Nandayus nenday (L—12 W—21)
Green above; face and crown brown; breast bluish-green; belly yellowish-green; thighs red; dark flight and tail feathers bluish on outer webs, gray from below; white eyering; long, pointed tail. *Immature:* Similar to adults but mostly green on breast (not blue). *Voice:* A loud "kreeah," repeated. *Habitat:* Savannas, palm groves. *Texas:* Rio Grande Valley, Corpus Christi, Rockport. *Range:* Southern Bolivia, Paraguay, and southern Brazil south to central Argentina.

264. Carolina Parakeet

Conuropsis carolinensis (L—13 W—22) **Extinct.**
Bright green body; yellow head; long, pointed tail. *Habits:* Feed in large flocks, often on agricultural crops. *Voice:* A screeching "Ki ki ki," etc. *Habitat:* Deciduous woodlands. *Texas:* Formerly resident in East Texas. *Range:* Eastern half of U.S.

265. Green Parakeet

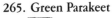

Aratinga holochlora (L—11 W—20)
Bright green body; long, pointed tail. *Habits:* Almost always in noisy flocks at tree-top level. *Voice:* A raucous "screeek," repeated. *Habitat:* Riparian forest, residential areas, citrus. *Texas:* Rare but evidently increasing in numbers in the Lower Rio Grande Valley. *Range:* Lowlands from northern Mexico to Nicaragua.

266. White-fronted Parrot

Amazona albifrons (L—10 W—18)
Green above; white crown; reddish lores and eyering; blue cheek and nape; white throat; blue breast; green belly; basal half of outside tail feathers red; red at bend of wing. *Female:* Lacks red on wing. *Voice:* A harsh "ka-ka-ka-ka," etc. *Habitat:* Thorn forest, arid tropical scrub; dry pinelands. *Texas:* Rio Grande Valley. *Range:* Western and southern Mexico to northwestern Costa Rica.

267. Red-crowned Parrot

Amazona viridigenalis (L—12 W—20)
Green body; red crown and wing patch. *Habits:* Parrots are almost always seen in pairs, even in flocks in flight. *Voice:* Loud screams, "keek bereeek keek keek." *Habitat:* Riparian forest, open woodlands. *Texas:* Rare but perhaps increasing in the Lower Rio Grande Valley; Corpus Christi. *Range:* Gulf lowlands of northeastern Mexico.

268. Lilac-crowned Parrot

Amazona finschi (L—13 W—22)
Green body; lilac crown and nape; red forehead and patch on primaries. *Voice:* "A harsh, rolling screech" (Forshaw 1973:529). *Habitat:* Open deciduous woodlands, pine, pine-oak, agricultural land. *Texas:* Lower Rio Grande Valley. *Range:* Western Mexico from Sinaloa to Oaxaca.

269. Red-lored Parrot

Amazona autumnalis (L—13 W—22)
Green body; grayish wash on crown; yellow cheek; red forehead and patch on primaries. *Voice:* Harsh screeches, "ky-ake," repeated. *Similar species:* Lilac-crowned Parrot has green (not yellow) cheek. *Habitat:* Riparian and wet, lowland forest, but foraging out into second growth and cultivated areas. *Texas:* Lower Rio Grande Valley. *Range:* Caribbean slope of Middle America from northern Mexico to Panama; coastal Colombia, western Venezuela, and Ecuador; Amazon Basin of central Brazil.

270. Yellow-headed Parrot

Amazona oratrix (L—14 W—24)
Green body; yellow head; red patch at bend of wing and base of tail. *Voice:* A loud "wa-ow." *Habitat:* Riparian forest, open woodlands. *Texas:* Casual to rare (increasing?) in Lower Rio Grande Valley. *Range:* Gulf and Pacific lowlands of Mexico; Belize.

Order Cuculiformes
Family Cuculidae
Cuckoos, Roadrunners, and Anis

Cuckoos are a family of trim, long-tailed birds found in both the Old and New World; several species lay their eggs in other birds' nests. Like parrots, woodpeckers, and some other avian groups, cuckoos perch with two toes forward and two toes backward (most birds have three toes forward and one toe backward).

271. Black-billed Cuckoo

Coccyzus erythropthalmus (L—12 W—16)
A thin, streamlined bird with long, graduated tail; red eyering; black bill; brown above; white below; dark brown tail with white tips. *Habits:* Slow, deliberate, reptilian foraging movements. *Voice:* A mellow "coo-coo-coo," repeated. *Similar species:* Yellow-billed Cuckoo has yellow eyering and lower mandible; more prominent white tail spots; rusty wing patch visible in flight. *Habitat:* Deciduous and mixed forest. *Texas:* Uncommon spring transient (May) along coast, rare in fall; scarcer inland in eastern third; has bred.* *Range:* Breeds northeastern quarter of U.S. and southeastern Canada; winters in northern half of South America.

272. Yellow-billed Cuckoo

Coccyzus americanus (L—12 W—17)
A thin, streamlined bird with long, graduated tail; dark bill with yellow lower mandible and eyering; brown above; white below; dark brown tail with white tips; rusty wing patches visible in flight. *Habits:* Slow, deliberate, reptilian foraging movements. *Voice:* A metallic "ka-ka-ka-ka-ka-ka cow cow cow," also a low

hoarse "cow" similar to that of roadrunner. *Similar species:* See Black-billed Cuckoo. *Habitat:* Deciduous and thorn forest, scrub, second growth, savanna. *Texas:* Common to uncommon summer resident* (Apr.–Sept.) throughout. *Range:* Breeds from south-eastern Canada and nearly throughout U.S. into northern Mexico and West Indies; winters in north and central South America.

273. Mangrove Cuckoo

Coccyzus minor (L—12 W—17)
Grayish-brown above; buffy below; black mask; dark, graduated tail with white tips. *Voice:* Similar to that of Yellow-billed Cuckoo but faster and lower pitched. *Similar species:* Other cuckoos lack black mask and have white (not buffy) breast. *Habitat:* Mangrove swamps, coastal woodlands, and scrub. *Texas:* Casual along coast. *Range:* Breeds from southern Florida, coastal Mexico and Central America to Panama; West Indies; winters in all except northernmost portions of breeding range and along Venezuelan coast.

274. Greater Road-runner

Geococcyx californianus (L— 22 W— 22)
Olive above with white feather edgings; buffy streaked with brown below; dark brown, ragged crest; ex-tremely long, graduated tail with white tips, held cocked; bare skin behind eye is white anteriorly, pink posteriorly. *Female:* Skin behind eye is blue anteriorly. *Habits:* Almost entirely terrestrial, seldom flies. *Voice:* A descending series of soft, low, "coo"s; also a rattle — made by vibrating upper and lower mandibles to-gether. *Habitat:* Thorn forest, desert. *Texas:* Common to uncommon permanent resident* throughout. *Range:* Southwestern U.S. to central Mexico.

275. Smooth-billed Ani

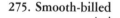

Crotophaga ani (L—14 W—16)
Black throughout; large, smooth, parrot-like bill; very long tail. *Habits:* Anis crawl around in shrubs in a rat-like fashion. They associate in groups throughout the year, and nest communally. *Voice:* An ascending "kar-eek." *Similar species:* Smooth-billed Ani bill has a raised central ridge; also the bill is smooth rather than grooved as in the Groove-billed Ani; calls are different. *Habitat:* Scrub, hedgerows, pastures. *Texas:* Hypothetical—Jefferson, Chambers cos. *Range:* South-

ern Florida south through West Indies, parts of southern Central America to southern South America.

276. Groove-billed Ani

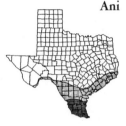

Crotophaga sulcirostris (L—14 W—16)
Black throughout; large, grooved, parrot-like bill; very long tail. *Habits:* Anis crawl around in shrubs in a rat-like fashion. They associate in groups throughout the year, and nest communally; often seen with cattle. *Voice:* "Chik bereek." *Similar species:* See Smooth-billed Ani. *Habitat:* Thorn forest, scrub, pastures, hedgerows. *Texas:* Common summer resident* (Apr.–Sept.) in central and southern coastal plain, uncommon to rare in winter. *Range:* South Texas and northwestern Mexico to northern Argentina and Chile.

Order Strigiformes
Family Tytonidae
Barn-Owls

This small, cosmopolitan family is comprised of 12 species, of which only one, the Common Barn-Owl, occurs regularly in North America.

277. Common Barn-Owl

Tyto alba (L—16 W—45)
Tawny and gray above; white sparsely spotted with brown below; white, monkey-like face, and large, dark eyes; long legs. *Habits:* Almost strictly nocturnal. *Voice:* Eerie screeches and hisses. *Habitat:* Savanna, prairie, farmland, thorn forest. *Texas:* Common to uncommon permanent resident* except in Trans-Pecos where rare. *Range:* Resident in temperate and tropical regions nearly throughout the world.

Family Strigidae
Typical Owls

Owls comprise a large family of fluffy-plumaged, mainly nocturnal raptors. Plumage coloration is mostly muted browns and grays; two toes forward and two backward when perched.

278. Flammulated Owl

Otus flammeolus (L—7 W—16)
A small owl with dark brown eyes, tawny facial disk, and relatively short ear tufts; mottled dark brown, gray, tawny, and white above; gray and white below streaked with dark brown. *Habits:* Almost strictly nocturnal. *Voice:* A whistled "poot" or "poo-poot." *Similar species:* Screech-owls have yellow eyes; screech-owl calls are trills or quavering whistles. *Habitat:* Montane pine, pine-oak, and juniper woodlands. *Texas:* Rare summer resident* (Mar.–Sept.) in mountains of the Trans-Pecos. *Range:* Breeds in western North America from southwestern Canada through mountains of western U.S. to southern Mexico; winters from central Mexico to Guatemala.

279. Eastern Screech-Owl

Otus asio (L—9 W—22)
A small, long-eared, yellow-eyed owl with a pale bill. *Red phase:* Rufous above; streaked with rust, brown and white below; rusty facial disk with white eyebrows. *Gray phase:* Similar to red phase but gray rather than rusty. *Voice:* A quavering, descending whistle; also a low, quavering whistle on a single pitch. *Similar species:* Western Screech-Owl usually has a dark (not pale) bill; calls are different. *Habitat:* Woodlands, thorn forest, residential areas. *Texas:* Common to uncommon permanent resident* in eastern half; uncommon to rare in Panhandle. *Range:* Resident from southeastern Canada and eastern half of U.S. to northeastern Mexico.

280. Western Screech-Owl

Otus kennicottii (L—9 W—22)
A small, long-eared, yellow-eyed owl with a dark bill; mottled gray, dark brown, and white above; streaked with gray, brown, and white below; gray facial disk with whitish eyebrows. *Voice:* A sequence of increasingly rapid whistles; also a set of two trills, the second larger than the first. *Similar species:* See Eastern Screech-Owl. *Habitat:* Riparian and oak woodland, desert scrub, residential areas. *Texas:* Uncommon permanent resident* in Trans-Pecos. *Range:* Western North America from southeastern Alaska to central Mexico.

281. Great Horned Owl

Bubo virginianus (L– 22 W– 52)
A large owl; mottled brown, gray, buff, and white above; grayish-white below barred with brown; yellow eyes; rusty facial disc; white throat (not always visible); long ear tufts. *Voice:* A series of low hoots, "ho-hoo hooo hoo"; female's call is higher-pitched than male's. *Similar species:* The smaller Long-eared Owl is streaked rather than barred below and ear tufts are placed more centrally; other large owls lack long ear tufts. *Habitat:* Woodlands. *Texas:* Common permanent resident* throughout. *Range:* New World except polar regions.

282. Snowy Owl

Nyctea scandica (L– 24 W– 60)
White with various amounts of gray and black barring; yellow eyes. *Immature:* Much more buff and brown spotting and barring than adults. *Voice:* A harsh "ka-ow," but usually silent. *Habitat:* Tundra, fields, pastures. *Texas:* Casual winter visitor (Dec.– Mar.) to northern and central Texas. *Range:* Resident in northern polar regions of Old and New World.

283. Northern Pygmy-Owl

Glaucidium gnoma (L– 7 W– 13)
A small, long-tailed owl; rufous above with black "eyespots" on the nape; rufous breast spotted with white; white belly, heavily streaked with brown; crown spotted with white; yellow eyes; tail brown barred with white. *Gray phase:* Brownish-gray rather than rufous. *Habits:* Crepuscular. *Voice:* Monotonously repeated whistles at two- to three-second intervals. *Similar species:* Ferruginous Pygmy-Owl has white streaks (not spots) on breast and a barred brown and rusty tail; lacks crown spotting; Northern Pygmy-Owl call is slower than that of Ferruginous Pygmy-Owl. *Habitat:* Highland forests of pine, pine-oak, and juniper. *Texas:* Casual transient (Apr.–May, Aug.– Sept.) in Guadalupe Mountains National Park, Culberson Co. *Range:* Resident in western North America from southwestern Canada through western U.S. and Mexico to Honduras.

284. Ferruginous Pygmy-Owl

Glaucidium brasilianum (L— 7 W—14)
A small, long-tailed owl; rufous above with black "eyespots" on the nape; white below, heavily streaked with rufous; rufous breast and crown; yellow eyes; tail brown barred with rust. *Habits:* Crepuscular. *Voice:* A whistled "whit whit whit whit whit whit," etc. *Similar species:* See Northern Pygmy-Owl. *Habitat:* Riparian forest, savanna, second growth, brushy pastures. *Texas:* Rare permanent resident* in the Lower Rio Grande Valley. *Range:* Southern Arizona and Texas to central Argentina.

285. Elf Owl

Micrathene whitneyi (L— 6 W—15)
A small, short-tailed, yellow-eyed owl; mottled brownish-gray and white above; rusty brown and gray on head and breast barred with dark brown; brownish streaks on belly; white stripe on wing. *Habits:* Nocturnal. *Voice:* A series of rapid, high-pitched whistles, "whit-whit-whit," etc. *Similar species:* Short tail and lack of ear tufts separates this species from other small, Texas owls. *Habitat:* Desert scrub, thorn forest, pinyon-juniper. *Texas:* Uncommon summer resident* (Mar.–Sept.) in Big Bend region of Trans-Pecos; rare and local in Lower Rio Grande Valley. *Range:* Breeds from southwestern U.S. to central Mexico; winters in southern portion of breeding range to southern Mexico.

286. Burrowing Owl

Athene cunicularia (L— 9 W— 24)
A long-legged, terrestrial owl; brown spotted with white above; white collar, eyebrows, and forehead; white below with brown barring. *Habits:* Often associated with prairie dog towns, this owl spends most of its time on the ground or perched on fence posts. *Voice:* A whistled "coo-hoo"; various other squeaks and whistles. *Similar species:* The long legs and terrestrial habits are distinctive. *Habitat:* Prairies, pastures, agricultural areas. *Texas:* Common to uncommon summer resident* in western half, formerly further east; uncommon to rare winter resident over most of state except eastern quarter. *Range:* Breeds in southwestern Canada and western U.S. south to central Mexico, Florida, West Indies, and locally in South America.

287. Mottled Owl

Ciccaba virgata (L—14 W—38)
A medium-sized, dark-eyed owl; brown mottled with white above; buff heavily streaked with brown below. *Voice:* A descending series of sharply whistled notes, "whew whew whew whew." *Habitat:* Riparian forest, lowland tropical forest. *Texas:* Accidental—Hidalgo Co. *Range:* Northern Mexico to northern Argentina.

288. Spotted Owl

Strix occidentalis (L—18 W—42)
A large, dark-eyed owl; brown spotted with white above and below. *Voice:* A series of three to four hoarse, high-pitched "haaw"s. *Similar species:* Barred Owl has white belly streaked with brown (not brown spotted with white), and is not spotted with white on crown. *Habitat:* Montane coniferous and riparian forest. *Texas:* Rare permanent resident in mountains of the Trans-Pecos; may breed. *Range:* Local resident of western montane regions from southwestern Canada to central Mexico.

289. Barred Owl

Strix varia (L—18 W—42)
A large, dark-eyed owl; brown mottled with white above; white barred with brown on throat and breast, streaked with brown on belly. *Voice:* "Haw haw haw ha-hoo-aw" ("who cooks for you all"). *Similar species:* See Spotted Owl. *Habitat:* Deciduous and mixed forest. *Texas:* Common permanent resident* of eastern third south to San Patricio Co. *Range:* Resident in southern Canada, eastern half of U.S., locally in northwestern U.S., and in central plateau of Mexico.

290. Long-eared Owl

Asio otus (L—14 W—39)
Medium-sized, trim, yellow-eyed owl with long ear tufts; mottled brown and white above; whitish streaked with brown below; rusty facial disks. *Habits:* Nocturnal. *Voice:* "Haaaaaa"—like a baby's call; also three to four quick, high-pitched "hoh"s. *Similar species:* See Great Horned Owl. *Habitat:* Coniferous and mixed woodland. *Texas:* Rare winter resident (Nov.–Apr.) throughout, has bred.* *Range:* Breeds in temperate and boreal regions of the northern hemisphere; winters in temperate areas and mountains of northern tropical regions.

291. Short-eared Owl

Asio flammeus (L—15 W—42)
A medium-sized owl; brown streaked with buff above; buff streaked with brown below; round facial disk with short ear tufts and yellow eyes; buffy patch shows on upper wing in flight; black patch at wrist visible on wing lining. *Habits:* Crepuscular. Forages by coursing low over open areas—reminiscent of Northern Harrier. *Voice:* A sharp "chik-chik" and various squeaks. *Similar species:* Tawny color and lack of ear tufts separate this from other owl species. *Habitat:* Savanna, prairie, marshes, estuaries. *Texas:* Uncommon winter resident (Oct.–Apr.) in eastern third. *Range:* Breeds in tundra, boreal and northern temperate areas of northern hemisphere, also in Hawaiian Islands; winters in southern portions of breeding range south to northern tropical regions.

292. Northern Saw-whet Owl

Aegolius acadicus (L—8 W—20)
A small owl; dark brown above with white spotting; white below with broad chestnut stripes; facial disk with gray at base of beak, gray eyebrows, the rest finely streaked brown and white; yellow eyes. *Immature:* Dark brown back spotted with white; solid chestnut below; chestnut facial disk with white forehead and eyebrows. *Habitat:* A tame owl, easily approached. *Voice:* A whistled monotone "hoo hoo hoo hoo," etc.; also a raspy note, given in series of three ("saw whetting noises"). *Similar species:* Chestnut underparts are distinctive among Texas owls. *Habitat:* Coniferous forest. *Texas:* Casual in winter in northern half; has bred* in Culberson Co. *Range:* From central Canada south to northern U.S. and in western mountains south to southern Mexico; winters in breeding range south and east to southern U.S.

Order Caprimulgiformes
Family Caprimulgidae
Goatsuckers

Most of the species in this family have soft, fluffy plumage of browns, grays, and buff. Long, pointed wings and extremely large, bristle-lined mouth are also distinctive characters of the group. Usually crepuscular or nocturnal, they forage for insects in bat-like fashion with characteristic swoops and dives.

293. Lesser Night-hawk

Chordeiles acutipennis (L— 9 W— 22)
Mottled dark brown, gray, and white above; whitish below with black bars; white throat; white band across primaries and tail; tail slightly forked. *Female:* Buffy rather than white on throat and wing, lacks white tail bar. *Habits:* Normally forages with a fluttering flight low over the ground. *Voice:* A quavering trill. *Similar species:* Common Nighthawk call is different (a sharp, nasal "bezzzt"); Common Nighthawk forages high above ground, and white on primaries is closer to wrist than in Lesser Nighthawk. *Habitat:* Thorn forest, desert scrub. *Texas:* Common summer resident* (Apr.–Sept.) in south and west; casual in winter along lower coast. *Range:* Breeds from southwestern U.S. south to southern Brazil; winters from southern Mexico south through breeding range.

294. Common Night-hawk

Chordeiles minor (L— 9 W— 23)
Mottled dark brown, gray and white above; whitish below with black bars; white throat; white band across primaries and tail; tail slightly forked. *Female:* Buffy rather than white on throat. *Habits:* Crepuscular. Normally forages high above the ground; has a dive display in which the bird plummets toward the ground, swerving up at the last moment and making a whirring sound with the wings. *Voice:* "Bezzzt." *Similar species:* See Lesser Nighthawk. *Habitat:* Savannas, grasslands, thorn forest, and a variety of other open and semi-open situations. *Texas:* Common to uncommon summer resident* (Apr.–Sept.) throughout. *Range:* Breeds locally from central and southern Canada south through U.S. to Panama; winters in South America.

295. Common Pauraque

Nyctidromus albicollis (L—12 W— 25)
Tawny brown, gray, black, and buff above; chestnut cheek patch; white throat; buffy barred with gray below; white wing patches; outer tail feathers black bordered by white; inner feathers barred brown and gray; tail long and rounded; wing rounded. *Female:*

Tail is barred brown and gray with white tips. *Habits:* Nocturnal. *Voice:* "Whit-whit whit-whit-whit-whit whit-whit wheeeezeerrrr." *Similar species:* Nighthawks, which also have white wing patches, have notched (not rounded) tails and pointed (not rounded) wings. *Habitat:* Thorn forest, arid scrub, riparian woodland. *Texas:* Common permanent resident* in South Texas. *Range:* South Texas to northern Argentina.

296. Common Poor-will

Phalaenoptilus nuttallii (L—8 W—17)
A small nightjar; grayish-brown above with dark brown markings; white throat; breast whitish closely barred with gray; wings and tail rounded; outer tail feathers broadly tipped in white. *Habits:* Nocturnal. Hibernates in cold weather. *Voice:* A whistled "poor-will" or "poor-will-ip." *Similar species:* Nighthawks and Pauraques have white bar on wing; Whip-poor-will is dark brown, not grayish, and has much more white on tail. *Habitat:* Deserts, dry thorn forest. *Texas:* Common summer resident* (Mar.–Oct.) in western two-thirds except Panhandle; rare eastward to central coast in dry cycles. *Range:* Breeds from extreme southwestern Canada south through western U.S. to central Mexico; winters in southern parts of breeding range.

297. Chuck-will's-widow

Caprimulgus carolinensis (L—12 W—25)
A large nightjar; tawny, buff, and dark brown above; chestnut and buff barred with dark brown below; white throat; long, rounded tail with white inner webbing on outer three feathers; rounded wings. *Female:* Has buffy tips rather than white inner webbing on outer tail feathers. *Habits:* Nocturnal. *Voice:* "Chuck-wills-widow," also moaning growls. *Similar species:* Lacks white wing patches of nighthawks; the smaller, darker Whip-poor-will has extensive white on tail in male, buff in female. *Habitat:* Deciduous and mixed woodlands, thorn forest. *Texas:* Common summer resident* (Apr.–Sept.) in eastern third south to Lavaca Co., further west on Edwards Plateau to Kinney Co.; common transient (Apr.–May, Sept.–Oct.) in southern Texas. *Range:* Breeds across eastern half of U.S., mainly in southeast; permanent resident in parts of West Indies; winters from eastern Mexico south

through Central America to Colombia, southern Florida, West Indies.

298. Whip-poor-will

Caprimulgus vociferous (L—10 W—19)
Dark brown mottled with buff above; grayish barred with dark brown below; dark throat and breast with white patch; rounded tail with white outer three feathers; rounded wings. *Female:* Has buffy tips rather than white on outer tail feathers. *Habits:* Nocturnal. *Voice:* A rapid, whistled "whip-poor-will" monotonously repeated. *Similar species:* See Chuckwills-widow. *Habitat:* Woodlands. *Texas:* Common summer resident* (Mar.–Oct.) in mountains of Trans-Pecos; common transient in eastern half (Apr.–May, Sept.–Oct.); formerly bred in north-central Texas. *Range:* Breeds across southeastern and south-central Canada and eastern U.S., also in southwestern U.S. through the highlands of Mexico and Central America to Honduras; winters from northern Mexico to Panama, Cuba, also rarely along Gulf and Atlantic coasts of southeastern U.S.

Order Apodiformes
Family Apodidae
Swifts

Swifts are small to medium-sized, stubby-tailed birds with long, pointed wings. In flight, an extremely rapid, shallow wing beat is characteristic.

299. Black Swift

Cypseloides niger (L—7 W—15)
Uniformly black with slightly forked tail. *Habits:* Crepuscular. *Habitat:* Mainly montane, especially near cliffs and crags. *Texas:* Hypothetical—Randall, Brewster, Harris, Chambers cos. *Range:* Breeds in western Canada and northwestern U.S.; also in scattered localities of Mexico, Central America, and West Indies; winters from southern Mexico to Costa Rica, and in West Indies.

300. White-collared Swift

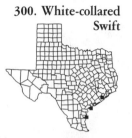

Streptoprocne zonaris (L—9 W—18)
Uniformly black with white collar; notched, swallow-like tail. *Habitat:* Widely distributed over forest and open country in the tropics; often seen near cliffs or cataracts. *Texas:* Casual—Aransas, Kleberg, Brazoria cos. *Range:* Mexico to Argentina; Greater Antilles.

301. Chimney Swift

Chaetura pelagica (L—5 W—12)
Dark throughout; stubby, square tail; long narrow wing. *Voice:* Rapid series of "chip"s. *Similar species:* Insect-like chatter of Vaux's Swift is distinctly different from the more musical twittering of the Chimney Swift. *Habitat:* Widely distributed over most habitat types wherever appropriate nesting and roosting sites are available (chimneys, cliffs, caves, crevices, hollow trees). *Texas:* Common summer resident* (Mar.–Oct.) over eastern two-thirds; rare in west. *Range:* Breeds throughout eastern North America; winters mainly in Peru.

302. Vaux's Swift

Chaetura vauxi (L—5 W—12)
Dark throughout; somewhat paler below and on rump; stubby tail and long, narrow wings. *Voice:* A high-pitched, dry rattle. *Similar species:* See Chimney Swift. *Habitat:* Widely distributed over most habitat types during migration. *Texas:* Hypothetical transient and winter resident in north and west. Scattered sight records. *Range:* Breeds in coastal California, north-western U.S., Alaska, and southwestern Canada; Mexico, Central, and northern South America; winters in tropical portions of breeding range.

303. White-throated Swift

Aeronautes saxatalis (L—6 W—13)
Patterned black and white above and below; notched tail; long, narrow wings. *Voice:* Rapid series of "chee"s. *Similar species:* Violet-green Swallow lacks black sides, rapid wing beat, and narrow wings of the swift. *Habitat:* Montane regions. *Texas:* Common summer resident* in mountains of the Trans-Pecos; rare in winter. *Range:* Breeds in mountains of western U.S. and southwestern Canada south through Mexico and Central America to Honduras; winters in southern portions of breeding range.

Family Trochilidae
Hummingbirds

Tiny birds with short, pointed wings, short tail, and long, thin, pointed bill. Plumages often show metallic tints. Their ability to fly backward is unique. Many hummingbirds have spectacular flight displays that are as characteristic of a species as its plumage. Distribution of western hummingbirds apparently has been affected by the proliferation of nectar feeders. Several of the species recorded below are found regularly during migration and in winter at South Texas feeders, hundreds of miles from their normal wintering range.

304. Green Violet-ear

Colibri thalassinus (L—4 W—5)
Iridescent green throughout with violet ear and belly patch. *Female:* duller; violet reduced or lacking. *Voice:* A series of high-pitched chips. *Habitat:* Highland forests and edges. *Texas:* Casual; scattered records from Central Texas and along coast. *Range:* Southern Mexico to northern South America.

305. Green-breasted Mango

Anthracothorax prevostii (L—5 W—8)
Dark green body; black throat bordered with emerald green; purple tail. *Female:* Green back and head; dark throat and breast broadly bordered with white. *Habitat:* Open woodlands, scrub, and mangroves, often along coast. *Texas:* Hypothetical—Nueces Co. *Range:* Southern Mexico south through Middle America to northern and western South America.

306. Antillean Crested Hummingbird

Orthorhynchus cristatus (L—4 W—5)
Iridescent green above, dark below; crested; white-tipped tail. *Female:* Paler below. *Habitat:* Open woodlands and edge, gardens. *Texas:* Hypothetical—Galveston Co. Single specimen of questionable origin. *Range:* Lesser Antilles.

307. Black-crested Coquette

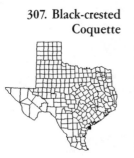

Lophornis helenae (L— 3 W— 4)
Bronzy green above with white bar across lower back; long greenish-black crest; green throat; black breast with buffy tufts; belly white spotted with bronze. *Female:* Bronzy green above; throat, belly, and crissum buffy; breast bronze; tail bronze with ventral black bar. *Habitat:* Wet lowland forest and edge. *Texas:* Hypothetical— two sight records from central coast. *Range:* Caribbean slope of Middle America from Veracruz to Costa Rica.

308. Broad-billed Hummingbird

Cynanthus latirostris (L— 4 W— 5)
Iridescent green above; blue throat, green breast and belly; white undertail coverts; bill red with black tip; tail notched with blue tint. *Female:* Green above; grayish below with narrow grayish postorbital stripe; square tail; bill brown with reddish base. *Similar species:* Female White-eared Hummingbird has dark rather than grayish-white cheek of female and immature Broad-billed; female White-eared also has green on throat, breast, and flanks—grayish in female Broad-billed. *Habitat:* Arid scrub. *Texas:* Rare summer resident* (Apr.–Sept.) in Chisos Mountains of Big Bend. *Range:* Breeds from southeastern Arizona, New Mexico, and Big Bend of Texas south through arid highlands to southern Mexico; winters mainly in southern portion of breeding range.

309. White-eared Hummingbird

Hylocharis leucotis (L— 4 W— 5)
Iridescent purple crown and chin; white postorbital stripe; green back and breast; whitish belly; orange bill with black tip; dark, square-tipped tail. *Female:* Greenish crown and chin. *Voice:* Metallic chatter. *Similar species:* See Broad-billed Hummingbird. *Habitat:* Highland pine and pine-oak forests and edges. *Texas:* Casual summer straggler (Apr.–Aug.) to Chisos Mountains of Big Bend. *Range:* Highlands of Mexico to Nicaragua.

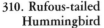

310. Rufous-tailed Hummingbird

Amazilia tzacatl (L—4 W—5)
Green head, breast, and back; belly grayish with bronze flanks; rufous crissum and tail; bill red basally. *Similar species:* Buff-bellied Hummingbird has tawny rather than grayish belly. *Habitat:* Humid, lowland forest and edges, gardens. *Texas:* Accidental—Cameron Co. *Range:* Eastern lowlands of Mexico and Caribbean lowlands of Central America to Nicaragua; Pacific and Caribbean slopes of Costa Rica.

311. Buff-bellied Hummingbird

Amazilia yucatanensis (L—4 W—6)
Green body except buffy orange belly; rufous tail; red bill with black tip. *Voice:* A quick, angry "tsee tsi tsi tsoo." *Similar species:* See Rufous-tailed Hummingbird. *Habitat:* Thorn and riparian forest, oak woodlands, second growth, suburban areas. *Texas:* Uncommon summer resident* in Lower Rio Grande Valley north along coastal plain to San Patricio Co.; rare fall visitor to upper coast; rare winter resident (feeders) along central and lower coast. *Range:* From southern Texas to northern Honduras.

312. Violet-crowned Hummingbird

Amazilia violiceps (L—5 W—7)
Green above; white below; violet crown; red bill with black tip. *Female:* Like male but with dull greenish-blue crown. *Voice:* A loud chatter. *Habitat:* Riparian woodlands in arid regions. *Texas:* Accidental—El Paso Co. *Range:* Southeastern Arizona and southwestern New Mexico south through arid regions of western Mexico to Chiapas.

313. Blue-throated Hummingbird

Lampornis clemenciae (L—5 W—8)
A large hummingbird; green above, grayish below with blue throat; black and white face pattern; dark blue tail tipped with white. *Female:* Lacks blue throat. *Voice:* "Tsip," and "tseet." *Similar species:* Female Magnificent Hummingbird has square, dark green tail with grayish tips (not rounded, dark blue tail with extensive white tips of female Blue-throated). *Habitat:* Arid scrub, desert riparian scrub, pine and pine-oak woodlands. *Texas:* Uncommon summer resident (Apr.–Sept.) in Big Bend region; rare elsewhere in Trans-Pecos. *Range:* Southern Arizona and West Texas south in central highlands to southern Mexico.

314. Magnificent Hummingbird

Eugenes fulgens (L—6 W—7)
A large hummingbird; green above and dark below with brilliant green throat and purple crown; white postorbital spot; white at base of tail; notched, green tail. *Female:* Green above, grayish below; white postorbital stripe; square, greenish tail tipped with gray. *Voice:* "Chip." *Similar species:* See Blue-throated Hummingbird. *Habitat:* Montane coniferous forest, pine-oak, and oak woodlands. *Texas:* Rare summer resident (Apr.–Sept.) in mountains of Trans-Pecos. *Range:* Breeds locally in southeastern Arizona, western Colorado, and West Texas south through highlands of Mexico and Central America to Nicaragua; winters from northern Mexico south through breeding range.

315. Lucifer Hummingbird

Calothorax lucifer (L—4 W—5)
Green above; purple throat; buff below with greenish flanks; black, scimitar-shaped bill; forked tail. *Female and immature male:* Green above, buff below with white postorbital stripe; rounded, white-tipped tail. *Similar species:* Only Texas hummer with decurved bill. *Habitat:* Desert scrub. *Texas:* Rare summer resident* (Apr.–Oct.) in mountains of Trans-Pecos. *Range:* Breeds in southern Arizona and West Texas south through highlands to southern Mexico; winters in central and southern Mexico.

316. Ruby-throated Hummingbird

Archilochus colubris (L—4 W—4)
Green above; whitish below; red throat. *Female and immature:* Green above, whitish below; rounded green tail with white tips; immature male often shows red feathers on throat. *Voice:* Song—"chip chipit chip chipit chipit," etc. *Similar species:* Female Blackchin is indistinguishable from female Rubythroat in the field. *Habitat:* Woodlands, second growth, brushy pastures and fields. *Texas:* Common summer resident* in eastern third south to Refugio Co.; common transient in eastern half; rare to casual in west; rare winter resident along coast. *Range:* Breeds in southern Canada and eastern half of U.S.; winters from southern Mexico to Costa Rica; also southern Florida and Cuba.

317. Black-chinned Hummingbird

Archilochus alexandri (L−4 W−4)
Green above; whitish below; black throat. *Female and immature:* Green above, whitish below; rounded green tail with white tips. *Voice:* Song—a series of high-pitched "tsip" notes. *Similar species:* See Ruby-throated Hummingbird. *Habitat:* Thorn forest, arid scrub, desert riparian scrub. *Texas:* Common summer resident* (Apr.–Aug.) in South Texas, Edwards Plateau, and Trans-Pecos; rare in Panhandle. *Range:* Breeds in arid portions of southwestern Canada and western U.S. south to northern Mexico; winters in central and southern Mexico.

318. Anna's Hummingbird

Calypte anna (L−4 W−5)
Green above, white below with brilliant rose crown and throat. *Female and immature male:* Green above; grayish below; whitish postorbital stripe; brownish tinge on crown; varying amounts of dark or rose spotting on throat. *Voice:* Song—a series of squeaky chips and buzzes. *Similar species:* Female and immature male Anna's usually have rose spotting on throat and breast, and greenish-bronze wash on lower breast and flanks which Blackchin, Costa's, and Rubythroat lack. *Habitat:* Oak chaparral, thorn forest, second growth, brushy pastures. *Texas:* Rare to casual winter visitor to southern half. *Range:* Breeds in coastal regions from southwestern Canada to northern Baja California; winters in breeding range and eastward in northern Mexico and southwestern U.S. borderlands.

319. Costa's Hummingbird

Calypte costae (L−4 W−5)
Green above, whitish below with purple head and throat. *Female:* Green above, whitish below. *Immature male:* Like female but with purple spotting on throat and head. *Voice:* A nasal "tsink." *Similar species:* See Anna's Hummingbird. *Habitat:* Desert scrub, oak chaparral. *Texas:* Casual visitor to West and South Texas. *Range:* Breeds from central California, southern Nevada and Utah to southwestern New Mexico, southern Arizona, and northwestern Mexico; winters in southern California, Arizona, and northwestern Mexico.

320. Calliope Hummingbird

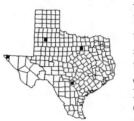

Stellula calliope (L—3 W—4)
A tiny bird, green above and white below with streaked white and purple throat. *Female:* Green above, buff below, with orange buff on flanks; dark throat spotting; tail green with white terminal spots. *Immature male:* Like female but with some purple spotting on throat. *Voice:* Song—"tsee-ree." *Similar species:* Lack of rufous in tail separates females from Rufous, Broad-tailed, and Allen's hummingbirds. *Habitat:* Open montane coniferous forests and meadows, oak chaparral, desert scrub. *Texas:* Casual fall (Aug.) visitor in western half. *Range:* Breeds in mountains of southwestern Canada and western U.S. south to southern California and northern Baja California; winters in northwestern and central Mexico.

321. Broad-tailed Hummingbird

Selasphorus platycercus (L—4 W—5)
Bronzy green above; whitish below; red throat; rounded green tail; wings make an insect-like whine in flight. *Female:* Green above; buffy below with dark or purplish-red throat spots; tail a complex pattern of rufous (base), green, black, and white (tips). *Similar species:* The sound made by male Broadtail wings is diagnostic; male differs from male Rubythroat by having purplish rather than orange-red throat and unnotched tail; female differs from female Rufous and Allen's by buffy (not rusty) flanks, relatively limited rufous on tail, and (when present) purplish-red rather than orange-red throat spots. *Habitat:* Montane coniferous forest, pinyon-juniper and pine-oak woodlands, desert scrub. *Texas:* Uncommon summer resident* in mountains of Trans-Pecos; rare transient (Mar.–Apr., Aug.–Oct.) in western half; rare winter resident at feeders along central and lower coast. *Range:* Breeds in mountains of western U.S. south through the highlands of Mexico to Guatemala; winters in breeding range from northern Mexico south.

322. Rufous Hummingbird

Selasphorus rufus (L—4 W—4)
Rufous above; whitish below with rufous flanks and tail; orange-red throat; green crown and wings; wings whistle as in Broadtail. *Female:* Green above; white below with contrasting rufous flanks; throat often flecked with orange-red; tail rufous at base with white tips. *Similar species:* Male Allen's has green (not

rufous) back; female is inseparable from female Allen's in the field, but can be distinguished in the hand (Stiles 1972); see Broad-tailed Hummingbird. *Habitat:* Montane coniferous and mixed forest and meadows, desert scrub. *Texas:* Uncommon fall visitor in Trans-Pecos, Central Texas, and coastal plain; rare transient across Texas; rare winter visitor along coast. *Range:* Breeds in western Canada and northwestern U.S.; winters from southern California and South Texas to southern Mexico.

323. Allen's Hummingbird

Selasphorus sasin (L—4 W—4)
Green crown and back; red throat; rufous flanks and tail; wings whine in flight as in Rufous and Broad-tailed. *Female:* Green above; white below with contrasting rufous flanks; throat often flecked with orange-red; tail rufous at base with white tips. *Similar species:* See Rufous Hummingbird. *Habitat:* Oak chaparral, brushy fields and thickets. *Texas:* Casual winter visitor (Oct.–Mar.) along coast and in Trans-Pecos. *Range:* Breeds along coastal regions of southern Oregon and California; winters from southern California and northwestern Mexico to central Mexico.

Order Trogoniformes
Family Trogonidae
Trogons

Kestrel-sized tropical birds, often brilliantly colored with metallic greens, reds, and blues.

324. Elegant Trogon

Trogon elegans (L—13 W—16)
Bright green above and below to breast; white breast band; belly red; tail is bronze above, white below with dark tip; yellow bill. *Female:* Like male but brown rather than green; white ear spot. *Immature:* Like female but barred below; spotted wing coverts. *Voice:* A croaking "coah," repeated. *Habitat:* Riparian forest. *Texas:* Casual—Starr, Hidalgo, Cameron, and Brewster cos. *Range:* Southern Arizona and New Mexico south through Mexico and Pacific slopes of Central America to Costa Rica.

Order Coraciiformes
Family Alcedinidae
Kingfishers

Stocky, vocal birds; predominantly green or slate blue with long, chisel-shaped bills, and shaggy crests; generally found near water where they dive from a perch or from the air for fish.

325. Ringed Kingfisher

Ceryle torquata (L—17 W—28)
A crow-sized bird; blue-gray above with ragged crest, chestnut below; white throat, collar, and undertail coverts. *Female:* Breast blue-gray (chestnut in male) with white band. *Voice:* A loud series of "chak"s, like a slow Belted Kingfisher; also a more rapid series of "chak"s. *Similar species:* Smaller Belted Kingfisher has white belly. *Habitat:* Rivers, lakes, bays. *Texas:* Uncommon permanent resident* along Lower Rio Grande (Webb Co. east); casual elsewhere in South Texas. *Range:* Mexico north to Sinaloa on the west coast and to South Texas on the east; Central and South America; Lesser Antilles.

326. Belted Kingfisher

Ceryle alcyon (L—13 W—22)
Blue-gray above with ragged crest; white collar, throat, and belly; blue-gray breast band. *Female:* Like male but with chestnut band across belly in addition to blue-gray breast band. *Voice:* A loud rattle. *Similar species:* See Ringed Kingfisher. *Habitat:* Rivers, lakes, ponds, bays. *Texas:* Common summer resident* throughout except southern Panhandle and Central and South Texas; winters throughout. *Range:* Breeds throughout most of temperate and boreal North America excluding arid southwest; winters from southern portion of breeding range south through Mexico and Central America to northern South America; West Indies; Bermuda.

327. Green Kingfisher

Chloroceryle americana (L—9 W—12)
Green above; white collar and belly; chestnut breast band. *Female:* Greenish breast band. *Voice:* Series of sharp "tic"s. *Habitat:* Streams, rivers, ponds. *Texas:* Uncommon permanent resident* in southern Edwards Plateau and along Lower Rio Grande; rare along coastal plain river bottoms from central coast south. *Range:* Northwestern Mexico and Central Texas to Argentina.

Order Piciformes
Family Picidae
Woodpeckers

A distinctive family of birds with plumages of mainly black and white. Long claws, stubby, strong feet, and stiff tail feathers enable woodpeckers to forage by clambering over tree trunks. The long, heavy, pointed bill is used for chiseling, probing, flicking, or hammering for arthropods. Most species fly in a distinct, undulating manner.

328. Lewis' Woodpecker

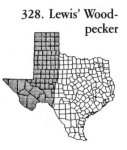

Melanerpes lewis (L—11 W—21)
Black with greenish sheen above, reddish below; grayish throat and collar streaked with black on chin; reddish face. Robin size, crow-like flight, and fly-catching habits are distinctive. *Immature:* Similar to adult but head, neck, and underparts are brownish. *Voice:* "Churr," "cheeurr," harsh rattle. *Habitat:* Open, coniferous woodlands, burned-over forest, and cottonwood belts along streams and rivers. *Texas:* Rare winter visitor to western third. *Range:* Western North America from British Columbia and Alberta south to northern Baja California, Sonora, and Chihuahua.

329. Red-headed Woodpecker

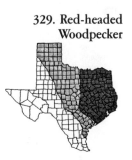

Melanerpes erythrocephalus (L—10 W—18)
Black above, white below with scarlet head. *Immature:* Head brownish. *Voice:* A loud "keeeer." *Habitat:* Eastern deciduous forest, oak woodlands, savanna. *Texas:* Uncommon permanent resident* in Panhandle and East Texas south to Calhoun Co.; irregular in winter in South and West Texas. *Range:* Eastern

North America from central plains and southern Canada to Texas and Florida.

330. Acorn Wood-pecker

Melanerpes formicivorus (L—9 W—17)
Black back, wings, breast, and tail; white rump, belly; throat tinged with yellow; black and white face pattern; crown red. *Female:* Like male but front portion of crown black. *Voice:* A loud, jeering "ja-cob," repeated; also similar sounds—"kerack," "charrr," "cheerrup." *Habitat:* Open oak and pine-oak woodlands. *Texas:* Common permanent resident* in mountains of the Trans-Pecos; formerly in juniper-oak woodlands of Kerr and Real cos. *Range:* Northwestern Oregon, California, Baja California; Arizona and New Mexico south through central and western Mexico, Central America, to the northern Andes of Colombia.

331. Golden-fronted Woodpecker

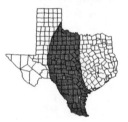

Melanerpes aurifrons (L—10 W—17)
Nape yellow; crown red; barred black and white on back; white rump; black tail; dirty white below with golden tinge on belly. *Female:* Crown whitish. *Voice:* A rapid series of "kek"s; a strident "cheeurr." *Similar species:* Red-bellied Woodpecker has red nape and barred tail. *Habitat:* Mesquite thorn forest; riparian woodlands. *Texas:* Common to uncommon permanent resident* from north-central Texas south through Edwards Plateau and South Texas. *Range:* Southwestern Oklahoma through Texas and eastern Mexico to Nicaragua.

332. Red-bellied Woodpecker

Melanerpes carolinus (L—10 W—16)
Nape and crown red; barred black and white on back and tail; white rump; dirty white below with reddish tinge on belly. *Female:* Crown whitish. *Voice:* "Querr querr querr querr." *Similar species:* See Golden-fronted Woodpecker. *Habitat:* Riparian forests and mixed woodlands. *Texas:* Common resident* in East Texas south to Calhoun Co. *Range:* Eastern U.S.

333. Yellow-bellied Sapsucker

Sphyrapicus varius (L—8 W—15)
Black and white above; creamy yellow below with dark flecks on sides; breast black; throat, forehead, and crown red; black and white facial pattern. The western subspecies (*S. v. nuchalis*) has red (rather than black) on back of crown. *Female: S. v. varius*—white throat; *S. v. nuchalis*—white chin. *Immature:* Black wings with white patch, white rump, and checked black and white tail of adults; but barred brownish and cream on head, back, breast and belly. *Voice:* A thin, nasal "cheerr." *Habitat:* Woodland, savanna, thorn forest, riparian forest. *Texas:* Common winter resident (Oct.–Mar.) throughout. *S. v. nuchalis* is a rare permanent resident in mountains of the Trans-Pecos. *Range:* Breeds in temperate and boreal wooded regions of Canada and the U.S.; winters from southern U.S. south to Panama and the West Indies.

334. Williamson's Sapsucker

Sphyrapicus thyroideus (L—9 W—16)
Black above; black breast and yellow belly; throat red; white rump and wing patch; white postorbital and suborbital stripes. *Female:* Barred brown and white; black patch on breast; head brownish. *Voice:* A nasal "queeer." *Similar species:* Black patch on breast, brown head, and lack of white wing patch separates female from immature Yellow-bellied Sapsucker. *Habitat:* Coniferous forest. *Texas:* Rare winter resident (Oct.–Mar.) in Trans-Pecos, western Panhandle, and Edwards Plateau. *Range:* Breeds in western North America from southern British Columbia and Alberta south to southern California, Nevada, Arizona, and western Colorado; winters in southern portion of breeding range south to Baja California and western Mexico south to Jalisco and Michoacán.

335. Ladder-backed Woodpecker

Picoides scalaris (L—7 W—13)
Barred black and white above; dirty white below, flecked with black on sides; black triangle framing white cheek is distinctive; red crown and forehead. *Female:* Black crown and forehead. *Voice:* A sharp "peek"; a rapid, descending series of "pik"s. *Similar species:* Only barred-backed woodpecker with black facial triangle framing white cheek. *Habitat:* Thorn forest, oak woodland, riparian forest, fence rows. *Texas:* Common resident* throughout except East

Texas. *Range:* Southwestern U.S. south through Mexico to Nicaragua.

336. Downy Wood-pecker

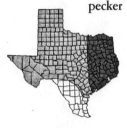

Picoides pubescens (L—7 W—12)
Black and white above; white below; red cap on back portion of crown; short bill—less than half length of head; black tail with white outer feathers spotted with black. *Female:* Black cap. *Voice:* A sharp "peek"; a rapid, descending series of "pik"s. *Similar species:* Larger Hairy Woodpecker has bill as long as head, lacks black spotting on black outer tail feathers, and has lower call note. Ladder-backed Woodpecker has ladder back. *Habitat:* Forests, second growth, and park lands. *Texas:* Common permanent resident* in Eastern Texas south to Calhoun Co., rare winter resident in west. *Range:* Temperate and boreal North America south to southern California, Arizona, New Mexico, and Texas.

337. Hairy Wood-pecker

Picoides villosus (L—9 W—15)
Black and white above; white below; red cap on back portion of crown; chisel-shaped bill as long as head; black tail with white outer feathers. *Female:* Black cap. *Voice:* A sharp "pick"; a descending series of "pick"s. *Similar species:* See Downy Woodpecker. *Habitat:* Forested regions. *Texas:* Common permanent resident* in East Texas south to Houston area, and in Guadalupe Mountains of Trans-Pecos; rare winter resident in Panhandle and Central Texas. *Range:* Temperate and boreal North America south through the mountains of western Mexico and Central America to Panama; Bahamas.

338. Red-cockaded Woodpecker

Picoides borealis (L—8 W—15) **Endangered**
Barred black and white above; white below flecked with black along sides; white cheek bordered below by black stripe; red spot behind eye. *Female:* No red spot behind eye. *Voice:* A "srip" call is given by family group members regularly as they forage. *Similar species:* Only ladder-backed woodpecker with unbroken white cheek patch. *Habitat:* Coniferous forest —especially mature longleaf and loblolly pine stands. *Texas:* Rare resident* of extreme eastern Texas. *Range:* Southeastern U.S.

339. Northern Flicker

Colaptes auratus (L—12 W—20)
Barred brown and black above; tan with black spots below; black breast; white rump. Eastern forms (e.g., *C. a. auratus, C. a. luteus, C. a. borealis*) have yellow underwings and tail linings, gray cap and nape with red occiput, tan face and throat with black mustache. Western forms (e.g., *C. a. colaris, C. a. nanus*) have red underwings and tail linings, brown cap and nape, gray cheek and throat with red mustache. *Female:* Lacks mustache. *Voice:* A long series of "kek"s first rising, then falling; a "kleer" followed by several "wika"s. *Habitat:* Forested regions. *Texas:* Uncommon permanent resident* (*C. a. auratus*) in East Texas south to Houston area; also in Panhandle (*C. a. collaris*) and Big Bend (*C. a. nanus*); common winter resident throughout. *Range:* Nearly throughout temperate and boreal North America, south in highlands of Mexico to Oaxaca. Leaves northern portion of breeding range in winter.

340. Pileated Woodpecker

Dryocopus pileatus (L—17 W—27)
Black, crow-sized bird; black and white facial pattern; red mustache and crest; white wing lining. *Female:* Has black mustache. *Voice:* A series of five or six "kuk"s, stopping abruptly, not trailing off like Northern Flicker; also a characteristic drumming made on a hollow log—a loud rattle of two to three seconds, first increasing, then decreasing in speed. *Similar species:* Ivory-billed Woodpecker has white secondaries visible when perched and in flight. *Habitat:* Forested regions. *Texas:* Common permanent resident* in eastern half south to Calhoun Co. *Range:* Much of temperate and boreal North America excluding Great Plains and Rocky Mountain regions.

341. Ivory-billed Woodpecker

Campephilus principalis (L—20 W—33) **Endangered**
Large black bird with whitish bill; white secondaries; white stripe on face and neck; red crest. *Female:* Black crest. *Voice:* A high, nasal "yant." *Similar species:* See Pileated Woodpecker. *Habitat:* Mature cypress swamps. *Texas:* Probably extinct. Formerly in eastern third. *Range:* Southeastern U.S., Cuba.

Order Passeriformes
Family Tyrannidae
Flycatchers and Kingbirds

A large group of mostly tropical songbirds, robin-sized or smaller. They are characterized by erect posture, muted plumage coloration (olives, browns, and grays), a broad bill, hooked at the tip, and bristles around the mouth. Flycatchers are insectivorous, often catching their prey on the wing.

342. Northern Beardless-Tyrannulet

Camptostoma imberbe (L— 5 W— 7)
Olive above; whitish below with olive wash on breast; buffy wing bars. *Voice:* Descending "peeer peeer peeer." *Similar species: Empidonax* flycatchers have erect posture and thicker bill; kinglets have eyering; verdin has straight, pointed bill, tyrannulet has downcurved upper mandible. *Habitat:* Thorn forest, riparian woodlands. *Texas:* Rare permanent resident* in Lower Rio Grande Valley. *Range:* South Texas, New Mexico, and Arizona south to northern Costa Rica; winters from northern Mexico south through breeding range.

343. Greenish Elaenia

Myiopagis viridicata (L— 6 W— 9)
Olive above; olive crown with inconspicuous yellow crest; white eyering; gray throat and breast; yellow below; brown wings with yellowish outer webs on flight feathers. *Voice:* "Cheez" or "cheez weez" (Slud 1964). *Habitat:* Lowland tropical forest. *Texas:* Accidental — Galveston Co. *Range:* Northern Mexico to central South America.

344. Tufted Flycatcher

Mitrephanes phaeocercus (L— 5 W— 7)
Dark brown above; rusty below; brown crest; buffy lores, eyering, and wing bars. *Voice:* "Che che che che che tse tse tse," (Peterson and Chalif 1973: 148). *Habitat:* Mid-elevation tropical forest (cloud forest, pine-oak forest) and openings. *Texas:* Hypothetical — Brewster Co. *Range:* Northern Mexico south through Middle and western South America in the Andes to Peru and Bolivia.

345. Olive-sided Fly-catcher

Contopus borealis (L−8 W−13)
Olive above; white below with olive on sides of breast and belly; white tufts on lower back (often difficult to see). *Voice:* "Whit whew whew" (quick three beers). *Similar species:* Eastern Wood-Pewee is smaller, has wing bars, and lacks dark olive along sides of breast and belly; Greater Pewee is olive below, lacking white on breast and belly. *Habitat:* Coniferous forest, thorn and riparian woodlands. *Texas:* Uncommon summer resident (Apr.–Oct.) in Guadalupe Mountains; uncommon transient (Apr.–May, Aug.–Oct.) in eastern third. *Range:* Breeds in boreal forest across the northern tier of North America and through western mountains south to Texas and northern Baja California.

346. Greater Pewee

Contopus pertinax (L−8 W−13)
Brownish-olive above; similar but lighter below; slight crest; no wing bars; yellowish lower mandible. *Voice:* A plaintive "wheway wheweeaa" (jose maria). *Similar species:* Similar in size to Olive-sided Flycatcher but entire underparts are darkish (not just sides), and lower mandible is noticeably lighter in color than upper. *Habitat:* Pine-oak woodlands. *Texas:* Few records (Apr.–Nov.) from the mountains of the Trans-Pecos. *Range:* Breeds from central Arizona and New Mexico south in highlands of Middle America to northern Nicaragua; winters from northern Mexico through Central American breeding range.

347. Western Wood-Pewee

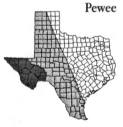

Contopus sordidulus (L−6 W−10)
Dark olive above; grayish throat; olive wash on breast; belly whitish; white wing bars. *Voice:* Nasal "peeaar" song, raspy "peezer" call. *Similar species:* Cannot safely be separated in the field from Eastern Wood-Pewee except by its raspy "peezer" call note, which is generally harsher than the "peeyer" of the Eastern Wood-Pewee. Pewees lack eyering of *Empidonax* species. *Habitat:* Riparian forest, pine-oak woodlands. *Texas:* Common summer resident* (Apr.–Oct.) in Trans-Pecos, rare transient (Apr.–May, Aug.–Oct.) elsewhere. *Range:* Breeds throughout western U.S. and Canada south to the highlands of Honduras; winters in northern South America.

348. Eastern Wood-Pewee

Contopus virens (L—6 W—10)
Dark olive above; greenish wash on breast; belly whitish; white wing bars. *Voice:* Plaintive "peeeaweee, peeeaweee, peeyer" song; "peeyer" call. *Similar species:* See Western Wood-Pewee. *Habitat:* Riparian forest, oak woodland, mesquite thorn forest. *Texas:* Common summer resident* (Apr.–Oct.) in eastern Texas south to San Antonio; common transient (Apr.–May, Aug.–Oct.) throughout eastern half; uncommon to rare west. *Range:* Breeds in eastern U.S. and southeastern Canada; winters from Costa Rica south to northern South America.

349. Yellow-bellied Flycatcher

Empidonax flaviventris (L—5 W—8)
Greenish above; yellowish below; creamy wing bars and eyering. *Voice:* Song a whistled "perweee," call a distinctive "squeeup." Both sexes sing and call during migration and on wintering ground. *Similar species:* All *Empidonax* are similar. The three yellowish species are Yellow-bellied, Acadian, and Cordilleran. Calls are distinctive for each. Acadian usually has white throat, is not as yellow below as the other two, and has bluish legs. Yellow-bellied and Cordilleran legs are usually dark brown or black. See Phillips et al. (1964) for details. *Habitat:* Riparian forest, thorn forest. *Texas:* Common transient (Apr.–May, Aug.–Oct.) in eastern third; rare to casual west; casual in winter along coast. *Range:* Breeds in northern U.S. and southern Canada west to British Columbia; winters from central Mexico to Panama.

350. Acadian Flycatcher

Empidonax virescens (L—6 W—9)
Green above; whitish below; yellow on flanks; white wing bars; whitish eyering. *Voice:* Song a repeated "pit see," call a thin "peet." *Similar species:* See Yellow-bellied Flycatcher. *Habitat:* Swamp forest; riparian forest; oak woodlands. *Texas:* Common summer resident* (Apr.–Oct.) in swamp forests of East Texas and riparian forests of the Balcones Escarpment near Austin and San Antonio; common transient (Apr.–May, Aug.–Oct.) over eastern third. *Range:* Breeds over eastern half of U.S.; winters from Nicaragua to northern South America.

351. Alder Flycatcher

Empidonax alnorum (L—6 W—9)
Brownish olive above; whitish below; greenish on flanks; white wing bars and eyering. *Voice:* Song— "fee-bee-o," call "pep." *Similar species:* All of the whitish *Empidonax* are similar but distinguishable by song or in the hand using the key by Phillips et al. (1964). *Habitat:* Swamp thickets, riparian forest, thorn forest, oak woodlands. *Texas:* Common transient (Apr.–May, Aug.–Oct.) across eastern third. *Range:* Breeds across northern tier of continent in boreal bogs of Canada and Alaska and south through Appalachians to northern Georgia; winters in northern South America.

352. Willow Flycatcher

Empidonax traillii (L—6 W—9)
Brownish-olive above; whitish below; greenish on flanks; white wing bars and eyering. *Voice:* A buzzy "fitz-bew" song. *Similar species:* See Alder Flycatcher. *Habitat:* Swamp thickets, riparian forest, thorn forest, oak woodlands. *Texas:* Rare summer resident* (Apr.–Aug.) in mountainous regions of the Trans-Pecos; common transient (Apr.–May, Aug.–Oct.) over eastern third. *Range:* Breeds through much of northern and central U.S.; winters in northern South America.

353. Least Flycatcher

Empidonax minimus (L—5 W—8)
Brownish above; white below; wing bars and eyering white; bobs tail. *Voice:* Song, "che bec," is given by both sexes during migration and on wintering grounds; call is a brief "wit." *Similar species:* See Alder Flycatcher. *Habitat:* Open woodlands, thorn forest. *Texas:* Common transient (Apr.–May, Aug.–Oct.) in eastern half; uncommon to rare in west; rare to casual in winter along coast and in South Texas. *Range:* Breeds in northern U.S. and southern and central Canada west to British Columbia, south in Appalachians to northern Georgia; winters from central Mexico to Panama.

354. Hammond's Flycatcher

Empidonax hammondii (L— 6 W— 9)
Olive gray above; whitish throat; grayish below with yellow wash on belly; wing bars and eyering white. *Voice:* "Tseeput" song is similar to that of Dusky Flycatcher. *Similar species:* See Alder Flycatcher. *Habitat:* Highland coniferous forest, riparian forest. *Texas:* Uncommon transient (Mar.–May, Aug.–Oct.) in Trans-Pecos; casual in northwestern Texas. *Range:* Breeds in western mountains from Alaska to central California and northern New Mexico; winters from southeastern Arizona and northern Mexico through the highlands of Central America to Nicaragua.

355. Dusky Flycatcher

Empidonax oberholseri (L— 6 W— 9)
Gray tinged with olive above; grayish below; white throat; tinge of yellow on belly; eyering and wing bars white. *Voice:* Song is a series of "tseeup"s, "seet"s, and "chupit"s in no particular sequence — similar but supposedly more varied than Hammond's Flycatcher song. *Similar species:* See Alder Flycatcher. *Habitat:* Montane mixed woodlands and thickets. *Texas:* Uncommon transient (Apr.–May, Aug.–Oct.) in Trans-Pecos; may breed in mountains of Trans-Pecos. *Range:* Breeds in mountains of western North America from southern Alaska to southern California, Arizona, New Mexico; winters in highlands from southern Arizona and northeastern Mexico south to Guatemala.

356. Gray Flycatcher

Empidonax wrightii (L— 6 W— 9)
Gray above; grayish-white below; eyering and wing bars white. *Voice:* Song "chi bit," call "wit." *Similar species:* See Alder Flycatcher; Gray Flycatcher reportedly dips tail smoothly down instead of jerking it up and down like other *Empidonax*. *Habitat:* Arid scrub, thorn forest. *Texas:* Uncommon transient (Apr.–May) in Trans-Pecos. *Range:* Breeds in Great Basin from southern Washington, Idaho, and Wyoming south to southern California, Arizona, and New Mexico; winters from southern Arizona through arid regions of Mexico.

357. Cordilleran Fly-catcher

Empidonax occidentalis (L—6 W—9)
Green above; yellowish below; wing bars and eyering creamy. *Voice:* Song "ter chip." *Similar species:* See Yellow-bellied Flycatcher. *Habitat:* Riparian woodlands and canyons. *Texas:* Uncommon summer resident* (Apr.–Sept.) in Trans-Pecos. *Range:* Breeds throughout much of western U.S., north along coast to Alaska, south into the highlands of Mexico; winters from northern Mexico south to Guatemala. Southern records may represent the closely related *E. flavescens.*

358. Buff-breasted Flycatcher

Empidonax fulvifrons (L—5 W—8)
Brown above; orange-buff breast; yellow belly; wing bars and eyering creamy. *Voice:* Song "chikee wheew"; call "pwip." *Similar species:* No other *Empidonax* has orange-buff in plumage. *Habitat:* Pine, pine-oak, and riparian woodlands of arid regions. *Texas:* Hypothetical—Chisos Mountains of Big Bend. *Range:* Southeastern Arizona south through highlands of western Mexico, Guatemala, and El Salvador to central Honduras.

359. Black Phoebe

Sayornis nigricans (L—7 W—11)
All black except for white belly and crissum. *Voice:* Rising "fibee" followed by descending "fibee," repeated. *Habitat:* Sparse vegetation of shoals, banks, and bars along rivers and streams. *Texas:* Uncommon permanent resident* in Trans-Pecos and southwestern Edwards Plateau; rare elsewhere in western half. *Range:* Western U.S. (California, southern Nevada, Arizona, New Mexico, West Texas) south through Middle and South America to Argentina.

360. Eastern Phoebe

Sayornis phoebe (L—7 W—11)
Dark brown above; whitish or yellowish below; dark cap often has crest-like appearance; bobs tail. *Voice:* Song—"Febezzt feebezzt," repeated; call—a clear "tship." *Similar species:* Eastern Wood-Pewee has distinct wing bars; *Empidonax* have wing bars and eyering. *Habitat:* Riparian forest, thorn forest; good nest site localities seem to determine breeding habitat—cliffs, eaves, bridges. *Texas:* Uncommon summer resident* (Feb.–Aug.) in north-central Texas and Edwards Plateau; rare in eastern Texas and Trans-Pecos;

common winter resident (Oct.–Mar.) along coastal plain; uncommon to rare inland. *Range:* Breeds from eastern British Columbia across southern Canada south through eastern U.S. (except southern coastal plain); winters from southeastern U.S. south through eastern Mexico to Oaxaca and Veracruz.

361. Say's Phoebe

Sayornis saya (L—8 W—13)
Entirely grayish-brown except for cinnamon buff belly and crissum. *Voice:* "Pitseeeurr," often given in flight; mournful "peeeurr." *Habitat:* Dry thorn forest, desert scrub. *Texas:* Uncommon to rare permanent resident* in western third; uncommon to rare winter resident (Nov.–Mar.) in southern and central Texas. *Range:* Breeds in western North America from Alaska to western Mexico; winters from southwestern U.S. to southern Mexico.

362. Vermilion Flycatcher

Pyrocephalus rubinus (L—6 W—10)
Black above; scarlet below with scarlet cap. *Female:* Brownish above; white eyebrow; white throat; white breast, faintly streaked with brown; orangish or yellowish belly. *Immature Male:* Like female with increasing amounts of black above and red below in successive molts, achieving full male plumage in third winter. *Voice:* "Pit-a-see," repeated, often given in flight. *Habitat:* Mesquite thorn forest, dry thorn forest, desert scrub, often near water. *Texas:* Uncommon permanent resident* in Trans-Pecos, Edwards Plateau, and drier (southern and western) portions of southern Texas; uncommon to rare along coastal plain in winter; casual spring transient in northern and eastern Texas. *Range:* From southwestern U.S. south in drier parts of Middle and South America to northern Argentina and Chile.

363. Dusky-capped Flycatcher

Myiarchus tuberculifer (L—8 W—11)
Olive brown above with dark crest; throat and chest gray; belly yellow. *Voice:* A plaintive "wheeeurrr," often given from the highest available perch. *Similar species:* This species is the slimmest of the Texas *Myiarchus* flycatchers; best distinguished by voice; a weak, plaintive "wheeurrr" in Dusky-capped; a shrill "wheep" in Great Crested; a sharp series of "quip"

notes in Brown-crested; a harsh "zheep" or "zhrrt" often preceded by a "quip" for the Ash-throated. See National Geographic Society (1983:283) for useful characters in the hand. *Habitat:* Pine-oak forest, riparian woodland. *Texas:* Rare summer visitor (Apr.–Oct.) in Chisos Mountains of Big Bend; casual elsewhere in Trans-Pecos and Lower Rio Grande Valley. *Range:* Breeds in southeastern Arizona, southern New Mexico to northern Argentina; winters from southern Mexico south through breeding range.

364. Ash-throated Flycatcher

Myiarchus cinerascens (L—9 W—13)
Brown above; grayish-white throat and breast; pale yellow belly. *Voice:* A harsh "zheep" or "zhrt" often preceded by a sharp "quip." *Similar species:* The palest of the Texas *Myiarchus;* see Dusky-capped Flycatcher. *Habitat:* Dry thorn forest, mesquite thorn forest, oak savanna, desert scrub, oak-juniper woodlands. *Texas:* Common summer resident* (Mar.–Sept.) in western half east to central coast; rare to casual in winter along the Rio Grande and southern coastal plain. *Range:* Breeds in western U.S. from Washington, Idaho, and Colorado south to southern Mexico; winters from southern California, Arizona and northern Mexico to Honduras on Pacific slope.

365. Great Crested Flycatcher

Myiarchus crinitus (L—9 W—13)
Brown above; throat and breast gray; belly yellow. *Voice:* "Wheep." *Similar species:* This species shows the most contrast of the Texas *Myiarchus* (brighter yellow, deeper gray, darker brown); see Dusky-capped Flycatcher. *Habitat:* Broadleaf forest, mesquite thorn forest. *Texas:* Common summer resident* (Apr.–Sept.) in eastern third south to the San Antonio River; common transient (Apr.–May, Aug.–Oct.) in eastern half. *Range:* Breeds in eastern U.S., central and southeastern Canada; winters from southern Florida, Cuba, and southern Mexico to Colombia and Venezuela.

366. Brown-crested Flycatcher

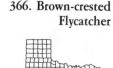

Myiarchus tyrannulus (L—9 W—13)
Brown above; gray throat and breast; belly yellow.
Voice: A series of sharp "quip" notes; also a three-note "quip-quit-too." *Similar species:* See Dusky-capped Flycatcher. *Habitat:* Mesquite thorn forest, oak woodland, riparian forest. *Texas:* Common summer resident* (Apr.–Sept.) in South Texas; casual in winter in South Texas. *Range:* Breeds from southwestern U.S. south along both slopes in Mexico through Middle and South America to Argentina; winters from southern Mexico south through breeding range.

367. Great Kiskadee

Pitangus sulphuratus (L—11 W—17)
Rusty brown above; bright yellow below; black and white head with yellow crown patch; bright rufous in wings and tail show in flight. *Voice:* Strident "kis-ka-dee," often accompanied by raucous chattering. *Habitat:* Riparian forest, mesquite thorn forest, towns, often near water. *Texas:* Common resident* south of San Fernando Creek, Kleberg Co.; rare north to Nueces Co. and west to Val Verde Co. *Range:* South Texas and northwestern Mexico to central Argentina.

368. Sulphur-Bellied Flycatcher

Myiodynastes luteiventris (L—8 W—12)
Brown streaked with dark brown above; yellow with dark streaks below; white eyebrow and dark face patch; rufous tail. *Voice:* "Peee cheee"; also a "kip kip kip" rattle. *Habitat:* Riparian forest, scrub, open woodlands. *Texas:* Casual in summer (Apr.–Sept.) along the Rio Grande. *Range:* Breeds from southern Arizona and northeastern Mexico south through Central America to Costa Rica; winters in northern South America.

369. Tropical King-bird

Tyrannus melancholichus (L—9 W—16)
Pearl gray head; dark ear patch; yellowish back, breast, and belly; wings and tail dark brown. *Voice:* Song—a rapid "kip kip kip," etc. *Similar species:* Couch's Kingbird is indistinguishable in the field except by voice—a harsh "breezeer" accompanies the rapid "kip kip kip" rattle in Couch's; Cassin's Kingbird has buff edgings to wing coverts and outer tail feathers; Western Kingbird has white outer tail feath-

ers. *Habitat:* Tropical savanna. *Texas:* Accidental — Cameron Co. *Range:* Breeds from southern Arizona and northeastern Mexico to central Argentina; winters south from central Mexico in breeding range.

370. Couch's King-bird

Tyrannus couchii (L—9 W—16)
See Tropical Kingbird. *Voice:* Song—"kip kip kip breezeer." *Similar species:* See Tropical Kingbird. *Habitat:* Tropical thorn forest. *Texas:* Uncommon summer resident* (Apr.–Oct.) in South Texas north to Bee and Live Oak cos.; rare in winter in South Texas along coast. *Range:* South Texas, eastern Mexico and Yucatán Peninsula to northern Guatemala.

371. Cassin's Kingbird

Tyrannus vociferans (L—9 W—16)
Pearl gray head and breast; whitish throat; back and belly yellowish; wings and tail dark brown with buff feather edgings; male's red crown patch usually not visible. *Voice:* A clear "tshi peew." *Similar species:* See Tropical Kingbird. *Habitat:* Savanna, pine-oak, highland scrub. *Texas:* Uncommon summer resident* (Apr.–Oct.) in Trans-Pecos; rare transient (Apr.–May, Aug.–Oct.) in western third. *Range:* Breeds in mountains of central and southwestern U.S. south through the Mexican highlands to Oaxaca; winters from northern Mexico to Guatemala.

372. Thick-billed Kingbird

Tyrannus crassirostris (L—10 W—16)
Dark brown above; grayish breast; yellowish belly and undertail coverts; heavy bill; yellow crest is usually not visible. *Voice:* A loud "wheear." *Habitat:* Tropical savanna, riparian forest. *Texas:* Casual — Big Bend region. *Range:* Breeds from southeastern Arizona, southern New Mexico, north-central and western Mexico to southern Mexico; winters through southern portion of breeding range to northwestern Guatemala.

373. Western King-bird

Tyrannus verticalis (L—9 W—15)
Pearl gray head and breast; back and belly yellowish; wings dark brown; tail brown with white outer feathers; male's red crown patch usually concealed. *Voice:* Song—Various harsh twitters; call—a sharp "whit." *Similar species:* See Tropical Kingbird. *Habitat:* Savanna, grasslands. *Texas:* Common summer resident* (Apr.–Oct.) in western two-thirds, rare in east. *Range:* Breeds in western North America from southern British Columbia east to Manitoba, south to northern Mexico; winters from southern Mexico to Costa Rica.

374. Eastern Kingbird

Tyrannus tyrannus (L—9 W—15)
Black above; white below; terminal white band on tail; red crest is usually not visible. *Voice:* A harsh, high-pitched rattle—"kit kit kitty kitty," etc., or "tshee" repeated. *Habitat:* Savanna, wood margins, open farmland. *Texas:* Common summer resident* (Mar.–Oct.) in eastern half south to Bee Co.; common transient (Mar.–May, Aug.–Oct.) throughout eastern half, rare to casual in west. *Range:* Breeds from central Canada south through eastern and central U.S. to eastern Texas and Florida; winters in central and northern South America.

375. Gray Kingbird

Tyrannus dominicensis (L—9 W—15)
Grayish above; white below; notched tail; heavy bill; dark ear patch; red crown patch usually not visible. *Voice:* Harsh "pechurrry." *Similar species:* Eastern Kingbird is darker, smaller, and has slimmer bill. *Habitat:* Tropical savanna, mangroves. *Texas:* Accidental—Aransas, Galveston cos. *Range:* Caribbean basin, rarely north along Atlantic coast to South Carolina; winters into northern South America.

376. Scissor-tailed Flycatcher

Tyrannus forficatus (L—14 W—14)
Tail black and white, extremely long, forked. Pearl gray head, back, and breast, washed with rose on belly, crissum, wing lining; bright rose axillaries; wings black. *Immature:* Short-tailed; lacks rose color of adult. *Voice:* Series of "kip," "kyeck," and "keee" notes. *Similar species:* Immature Fork-tailed Flycatcher has darker head, contrasting with neck and

throat. *Habitat:* Savanna, prairie, agricultural lands with scattered trees. *Texas:* Common summer resident* (Mar.–Nov.) over most of state, uncommon in Trans-Pecos. *Range:* Breeds in central and southern Great Plains from Nebraska south to northern Mexico; winters from southern Mexico to Panama.

377. Fork-tailed Fly-catcher

Tyrannus savana (L—16 W—14)
Extremely long, black tail with white edging; black wings and head, yellow crown patch usually not visible; back gray; whitish below. *Immature:* Paler with short tail. *Voice:* "A pebbly *krrrrr;* a metallic *zlit;* a clicking sound produced by bill" (Peterson and Chalif 1973:141). *Similar species:* See Scissor-tailed Flycatcher. *Habitat:* Tropical savanna. *Texas:* Casual visitor in South Texas. *Range:* Southern Mexico to central South America.

378. Rose-throated Becard

Pachyramphus aglaiae (L— 7 W—14)
Grayish black above; white below; throat red. *Female and immature:* Brown above; tawny below; crown dark brown. *Voice:* Plaintive "tseeoo." *Habitat:* River forest along the Rio Grande. *Texas:* Rare permanent resident,* Lower Rio Grande Valley. *Range:* Southern-most Texas and southern Arizona to Costa Rica.

379. Masked Tityra

Tityra semifasciata (L— 8 W—14)
Pale gray body; black face and forehead; red eyering and lores; bill red at base, black at tip; black wing and tail feathers. *Female:* Similar, but crown and face brown; back with brown wash. *Voice:* A nasal croak, repeated. *Habitat:* Tropical lowland forest. *Texas:* Accidental—Hidalgo Co. *Range:* Lowlands of northern Mexico south through Central America to central South America.

Family Alaudidae
Larks

Small, terrestrial songbirds with extremely long hind claws. The breeding song of these open country inhabitants is often given in flight.

380. Horned Lark

Eremophila alpestris (L—7 W—13)
Brown above; white below with black bib; face and throat whitish or yellowish with black forehead and eyeline; black horns raised when singing; dark tail with white edging; long hind claw. *Female:* Similar pattern but paler. *Immature:* Nondescript brownish above; whitish below with light streaking; dark tail with white edging and long hind claw like adult. *Voice:* Song a series of high pitched notes, often given in flight; call a thin "tseet." *Similar species:* Immature lark is similar to pipits but is grayish white rather than buffy on face and underparts. *Habitat:* Short-grass prairie, plowed fields, roadsides, sand flats. *Texas:* Locally common permanent resident* throughout. *Range:* Breeds in North America south to southern Mexico; winters in southern portion of breeding range.

Family Hirundinidae
Swallows and Martins

Mostly small, sleek birds with pointed wings. Swallows forage on flying insects, which they take on the wing.

381. Purple Martin

Progne subis (L—8 W—16)
Iridescent midnight blue throughout. *Female and immature:* Dark blue above; dirty white, occasionally mottled with blue below; grayish collar. *Voice:* Various "quik"s and "querk"s repeated in a short harsh series. *Similar species:* Extremely rare Gray-breasted Martin resembles female but is smaller, lacks grayish collar, has darker forehead and whiter belly. *Habitat:* Open areas—limited by nesting sites. Nests colonially, originally in trees, now often in specially constructed martin houses. *Texas:* Common summer resident* (Feb.–Sept.) over most of state except Panhandle where rare or absent; common transient throughout. *Range:* Breeds in open areas over most of temperate North America south to the highlands of southern Mexico; winters in Amazon Basin of South America south to northern Argentina and southeastern Brazil.

382. Gray-breasted Martin

Progne chalybea (L—8 W—16)
See female Purple Martin description. *Voice:* Like
Purple Martin but softer. *Similar species:* See Purple
Martin. *Habitat:* Open areas, often in towns. *Texas:*
Accidental—Starr, Hidalgo cos. *Range:* Central Mex-
ico to Bolivia and Brazil.

383. Tree Swallow

Tachycineta bicolor (L—6 W—13)
Iridescent blue and green above; pure white below
with slightly forked tail. *Immature:* Grayish-brown
above; whitish below. *Voice:* Series of "weet tuwit
tuweet" with twitters. *Similar species:* Violet-Green
Swallow is greener above, has white on rump and
around eye (postloral and supraloral areas on Tree
Swallow are dark). *Habitat:* Lakes, ponds, marshes—
any open area during migration. *Texas:* Common migrant (Mar.–May, Aug.–Nov.) in eastern half, less
common in west; rare in winter along coast; casual in
summer* (Bexar Co.). *Range:* Breeds over most of
boreal and temperate North America south to southern U.S.; winters from southern U.S. south to Costa
Rica and Greater Antilles in West Indies.

384. Violet-Green Swallow

Tachycineta thalassina (L—6 W—13)
See Tree Swallow. *Voice:* "Tsip tseet tsip" with rapid
twitter. *Similar species:* See Tree Swallow. *Habitat:*
Mountain forests and canyons, open areas in migration. *Texas:* Uncommon summer resident* (Mar.–
Oct.) in mountains of Trans-Pecos. *Range:* Breeds in
mountains of western North America from Alaska to
southern Mexico; winters from southern California
and northwestern Mexico south to Costa Rica.

385. Northern Rough-winged Swallow

Stelgidopteryx serripennis (L—6 W—12)
Grayish-brown above; grayish throat and breast becoming whitish on belly. *Voice:* A harsh "treet," repeated. *Similar species:* Bank Swallow has distinct
dark breast band set off by white throat and belly.
Habitat: Lakes, rivers, ponds, streams; most open
areas during migration. *Texas:* Common transient
(Mar.–May, Aug.–Oct.) over most of state; scattered
breeding records,* mostly for eastern half; rare in

winter along coast. *Range:* Breeds locally over most of temperate North America; winters from southern Texas and northern Mexico south to Panama.

386. Bank Swallow

Riparia riparia (L—6 W—12)
Brown above; white below with brown collar. *Voice:* "Bzzt," repeated in a harsh rattle. *Similar species:* See Northern Rough-winged Swallow. *Habitat:* Lakes, rivers, ponds; most open areas during migration. *Texas:* Common transient (Apr.–May, Sept.–Oct.) over most of state; rare and local as a breeding bird.* *Range:* Cosmopolitan, breeding over much of northern hemisphere, wintering in the tropics of Asia, Africa, and the New World.

387. Cliff Swallow

Hirundo pyrrhonota (L—6 W—12)
Dark above; whitish below with dark orange or blackish throat; orange cheek; pale forehead; orange rump; square tail. *Immature:* Similar to adult but duller. *Voice:* Song—a series of harsh twitters. *Similar species:* Cave Swallow has buffy throat (rather than dark), and dark forehead (not pale). Mud nest is gourd-like (Cave Swallow's is open-topped). *Habitat:* Most open areas during migration; savanna, agricultural areas, near water. This species seems to be limited by nesting locations during the breeding season (farm buildings, culverts, bridges, cliffs—near potential mud source). *Texas:* Common migrant (Mar.–May, Aug.–Oct.) throughout; locally common summer resident.* *Range:* Breeds over most of North America to central Mexico; winters in central and southern South America.

388. Cave Swallow

Hirundo fulva (L—6 W—12)
See Cliff Swallow. *Voice:* Song is a rapid series of squeaks, softer than those of Cliff Swallow. *Similar species:* See Cliff Swallow. *Habitat:* Open areas, near water; nests in sinkholes, caves, and most recently, culverts. *Texas:* Historically a locally common summer resident* (Mar.–Sept.) in the cave and sinkhole region of the Edwards Plateau and Trans-Pecos, expanding east in recent years in South Texas to the Coast—nesting in culverts. *Range:* Breeds from New Mexico and Central Texas south through central and southern

Mexico, Greater Antilles, northern South America in Ecuador and Peru; winters in southern portion of breeding range.

389. Barn Swallow

Hirundo rustica (L—7 W—13)
Dark blue above; orange below with deeply forked tail. *Immature:* Paler with shorter tail. *Voice:* Song is a series of squeaks and twitters, some harsh, some melodic. *Habitat:* Savanna, prairie, open areas near water; like Cliff and Cave Swallows, it requires special sites for nesting, e.g., bridges, culverts, buildings. *Texas:* Locally common summer resident* (Mar.–Oct.) nearly throughout; rare in winter along central and lower coast. *Range:* Cosmopolitan—breeds over much of northern hemisphere; winters in South America, Africa, northern Australia, Micronesia.

Family Corvidae
Jays, Crows, and Ravens

Medium-sized to large songbirds; crows and ravens have generally dark plumages, jays are blues, greens, and grays. Most members are social, aggressive, and highly vocal.

390. Steller's Jay

Cyanocitta stelleri (L—12 W—18)
Blackish head, crest, and back with bluish belly; wings and tail blue barred with black; throat, forehead, and supraocular region streaked with white. *Voice:* A loud, harsh "shook shook shook," and various other harsh calls; song a softer series of warbles; imitates hawks. *Habitat:* Pine-oak and spruce-fir woodlands. *Texas:* Common permanent resident* of Guadalupe and Davis mountains (above 5,000 feet) of Trans-Pecos. *Range:* Mountains of western North America from Alaska south through the highlands of Middle America to Nicaragua.

391. Blue Jay

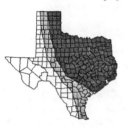

Cyanocitta cristata (L—11 W—16)
Blue above; dirty white below; blue crest; white wing bars and tip of tail; black necklace. *Voice:* A loud harsh cry, "jaaaay," repeated; a liquid gurgle; many other cries and calls; mimics hawks. *Habitat:* Oak woodlands, eastern deciduous forest, residential areas. *Texas:* Common permanent resident* in eastern third south to Calhoun Co., uncommon in north-central Texas and eastern Panhandle; rare and irregular in western Panhandle, western Edwards Plateau, Trans-Pecos, and South Texas. *Range:* Temperate and boreal North America east of the Rockies.

392. Green Jay

Cyanocorax yncas (L—13 W—15)
Bright green above; yellow below; throat black; head blue; outer tail feathers yellow; inner tail feathers blue. *Voice:* "Chik" repeated; "cleep" repeated; a two-tone rattle. *Habitat:* Thorn forest, savanna, riparian forest. *Texas:* Common permanent resident* from Nueces and Webb counties south. *Range:* South Texas through eastern and central Mexico south to Honduras; north-central South America.

393. Brown Jay

Cyanocorax morio (L—17 W—24)
Dark brown above; head and throat brown; belly whitish; bill yellowish in immature. *Voice:* A harsh scream, "aahh," repeated; various clicks and cries. *Habitat:* Riparian forest. *Texas:* Rare permanent resident* in Lower Rio Grande Valley. *Range:* South Texas through eastern and central Mexico to Panama.

394. Scrub Jay

Aphelocoma coerulescens (L—11 W—13)
Blue above; white throat; gray breast and belly with dark streaks on throat and breast; grayish back; black cheek and eye bordered by white above. *Voice:* A harsh "kuweeep"; "kay kay kay kay kay kay"; "keeaah"; other cries. *Similar species:* Gray-breasted Jay has gray throat, lacks black streaking on throat and breast. *Habitat:* Oak, juniper, pinyon woodlands. *Texas:* Common permanent resident* in Edwards Plateau and Trans-Pecos; uncommon to rare elsewhere in western third. *Range:* Western North America from Washington south to southern Mexico; Florida.

395. Gray-breasted Jay

Aphelocoma ultramarina (L—11 W—13)
Blue above; grayish below; grayish on back; black cheek and eyeline. *Voice:* "Chink," "kek, kek, kek, kek," other calls. *Similar species:* See Scrub Jay. *Habitat:* Pine-oak-juniper woodlands. *Texas:* Common permanent resident* in Chisos Mountains (Big Bend) of Trans-Pecos. *Range:* Central Arizona, New Mexico, and West Texas south in mountains to south-central Mexico.

396. Pinyon Jay

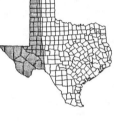

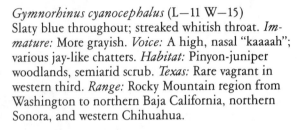

Gymnorhinus cyanocephalus (L—11 W—15)
Slaty blue throughout; streaked whitish throat. *Immature:* More grayish. *Voice:* A high, nasal "kaaaah"; various jay-like chatters. *Habitat:* Pinyon-juniper woodlands, semiarid scrub. *Texas:* Rare vagrant in western third. *Range:* Rocky Mountain region from Washington to northern Baja California, northern Sonora, and western Chihuahua.

397. Clark's Nut-cracker

Nucifraga columbiana (L—16 W—22)
Gray body; wings and central tail feathers black; speculum and outer tail feathers white. *Voice:* A nasal "kaaaaa." *Habitat:* Montane coniferous forests. *Texas:* Rare and irregular winter resident (Oct.–Mar.) of Trans-Pecos and Panhandle. *Range:* Mountains of western North America from central British Columbia south to southern Arizona and New Mexico.

398. Black-billed Magpie

Pica pica (L—19 W—24)
Striking pattern of black and white body and wings with very long, dark tail. *Voice:* A rapid series of "chek"s; a nasal "aaaah." *Habitat:* Open woodlands, savanna, grasslands, especially near rivers and streams. *Texas:* Casual winter visitor in western third. *Range:* Western Canada and U.S. from Alaska and British Columbia east to western Ontario, south to Oklahoma, New Mexico, Arizona, California; temperate and boreal Europe and Asia south to North Africa, Iran, northern India, Southeast Asia, eastern China, and Japan.

399. American Crow

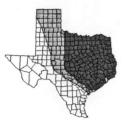

Corvus brachyrhynchos (L—18 W—36)
Black throughout. *Voice:* A series of variations on "caw"—fast, slow, high, low, and various combinations; nestlings and fledglings use an incessant, nasal "caah." *Habitat:* Nearly ubiquitous in woodlands, grasslands, farmlands, and residential areas. *Similar species:* Smaller Fish Crow is very similar, best distinguished by call. Fish Crow has a high, nasal "caah" compared to the American Crow's familiar "caw". Ravens croak, and have wedged-shaped rather than square tails of crows. *Texas:* Common permanent resident* in eastern half south to Calhoun and Kerr cos. Irregular winter resident in Edwards Plateau and Panhandle. *Range:* Temperate and boreal North America; migratory in northern portion of range.

400. Mexican Crow

Corvus imparatus (L—15 W—29)
Black throughout. *Voice:* A harsh "awwwwk." *Habitat:* Dumps, riparian woodland, farmland, urban areas, thorn forest. *Similar species:* Chihuahuan Raven is larger, has wedged-shaped rather than square tail. *Texas:* Rare permanent resident in the Lower Rio Grande Valley. *Range:* Texas-Mexico border and northern Sonora south to Colima and northern Veracruz.

401. Fish Crow

Corvus ossifragus (L—15 W—33)
Black throughout. *Voice:* A high, nasal "cah." *Habitat:* Flood plain forests, bayous, coastal waterways. *Similar species:* See American Crow. *Texas:* Uncommon resident* in extreme east (Orange, Jefferson, Newton, Harrison, Marion cos.). *Range:* Coastal plain of eastern U.S. from Massachusetts to East Texas.

402. Chihuahuan Raven

Corvus cryptoleucus (L—19 W—40)
Black throughout; feathers of neck are white basally (only show when ruffled). *Voice:* A croak. *Habitat:* Dry thorn forest, desert. *Similar species:* Common Raven is larger, has a lower croak; see Mexican Crow. *Texas:* Common permanent resident* over western half east to Kleberg Co. *Range:* Western Kansas, eastern Colorado south through Arizona, New Mexico, and Texas and central highlands of Mexico to Guanajuato, San Luis Potosí and southern Tamaulipas. Northern populations are at least partially migratory.

403. Common Raven

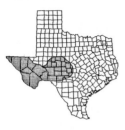

Corvus corax (L—24 W—48)
Black throughout; large heavy bill; shaggy appearance in facial region; wedge-shaped tail. *Voice:* A harsh, low croak; also some higher-pitched croaks. *Habitat:* Rugged crags, cliffs, canyons as well as a variety of forested and open lands. *Similar species:* See Chihuahuan Raven and American Crow. *Texas:* Rare permanent resident* in Trans-Pecos and Edwards Plateau. *Range:* Arctic and boreal regions of the northern hemisphere south through mountainous regions of the western hemisphere to Nicaragua, and in the eastern hemisphere to North Africa, Iran, the Himalayas, Manchuria, and Japan.

Family Paridae
Chickadees and Titmice

Small, perky, active birds with plumages of gray and white; generally these birds forage in small groups, feeding on arthropods and seeds.

404. Black-capped Chickadee

Parus atricapillus (L—5 W—8)
Black cap and throat contrasting with white cheek; dark gray back; grayish-white breast and belly; white edging to gray secondaries. *Voice:* Plaintive, whistled "fee bee"; buzzy "chicka dee dee." *Habitat:* Woodlands. *Similar species:* Carolina Chickadee has four-part song ("see dee see doo")—two-part song for Black-capped Chickadee; Carolina also lacks broad white edging to secondaries. *Texas:* Hypothetical (Phillips 1986:83). *Range:* Temperate and boreal North America south to California, New Mexico, Oklahoma, New Jersey; south in Appalachians to North Carolina.

405. Carolina Chickadee

Parus carolinensis (L—5 W—8)
Black cap and throat contrasting with white cheek, dark gray back, and grayish-white breast and belly. *Voice:* "See dee see doo"; "chick a dee dee dee." *Habitat:* Riparian forest, deciduous and mixed woodlands. *Similar species:* Mountain Chickadee has a white eyeline. See Black-capped Chickadee. *Texas:* Common permanent resident* in eastern half south to the Aransas River (San Patricio Co.). *Range:* East-

ern U.S. from Kansas east to New Jersey and south to Florida and Texas.

406. Mountain Chickadee

Parus gambeli (L—5 W—8)
Gray above; lighter gray below; black cap and bib; white eyeline. *Voice:* A rough "chick a dee a dee a dee"; "see dee dee" or "see dee see dee." *Habitat:* Montane coniferous forest. *Similar species:* See Carolina Chickadee. *Texas:* Common permanent resident* at high elevations of the Trans-Pecos. *Range:* Mountains of western North America from northern British Columbia and Alaska south to southern California, Arizona, New Mexico, and Texas.

407. Bridled Titmouse

Parus wollweberi (L—6 W—9)
Gray above; paler below; conspicuous crest; distinctive black and white face pattern. *Voice:* Song—"weeta weeta weeta"; call—a high, clipped "sik-a-dee-dee." *Habitat:* Montane oak and juniper woodlands. *Texas:* Hypothetical—sight records from Big Bend; questionable record from "the Rio Grande" in 1850. *Range:* Central Arizona and southwestern New Mexico south through the highlands of western and central Mexico.

408. Plain Titmouse

Parus inornatus (L—6 W—9)
Gray throughout; slight crest. *Voice:* Song—"weedee weedee weedee"; call—a harsh "chick a dee dee." *Habitat:* Oak, juniper, pine woodlands. *Similar species:* Immature Black-crested form of Tufted Titmouse is paler below and has buffy sides. *Texas:* Rare permanent resident* in Guadalupe Mountains of Trans-Pecos (Culberson Co.). *Range:* Western U.S. from southern Oregon, Idaho, and Wyoming south to southern California, New Mexico, and West Texas.

409. Tufted Titmouse

Parus bicolor (L—6 W—9)
This species is composed of two groups that are markedly different in song and appearance. Members of the "Tufted Titmouse" group are gray above and white below with buffy sides, gray crest, and black forehead. "Black-crested" group members have a black crest and white forehead. *Voice:* Black-crested group sings "peet

peet peet"; Tufted group sings "peter peter peter"; both groups give various chickadee-like calls. *Habitat:* Tufted group is found in temperate woodlands; Black-crested group is in thorn forest, oak, juniper, and riparian woodlands. *Similar species:* See Plain Titmouse. *Texas:* Tufted group — common permanent resident* in eastern Texas south to the San Antonio River in Calhoun Co. Black-crested group — common permanent resident* in western two-thirds, and from the Mission River (Refugio Co.) south. *Range:* Eastern U.S. west to Nebraska, Iowa, Oklahoma, and West Texas and in Mexico south to Hidalgo and northern Veracruz.

Family Remizidae
Verdin

As Phillips (1986:98) notes, this little bird has caused considerable taxonomic consternation, having been placed in Paridae (chickadees), Coerebinae (honey-creepers), and Polioptilinae (gnatcatchers) by different authors. Currently, it has been placed in its own family by the American Ornithologists' Union (1983).

410. Verdin *Auriparus flaviceps* (L— 5 W— 7)
Gray body above and below; yellowish head; chestnut shoulder. *Immature:* Uniformly grayish brown; somewhat paler below. *Voice:* A weak "tsee see see" or "tseeip" song; call is a series of rapid "tsip"s. *Habitat:* Thorn forest, oak-juniper, desert. *Similar species:* Immature is similar to Bushtit but lacks brown cheek patch and has tail shorter than body (Bushtit has tail equal to or longer than body). *Texas:* Uncommon permanent resident* in southern Panhandle, Edwards Plateau, Trans-Pecos, and South Texas. *Range:* Southwestern U.S. and Mexico south to Jalisco, Hidalgo, Tamaulipas.

Family Aegithalidae
Bushtit

This family is composed of a single species, as described below.

411. Bushtit

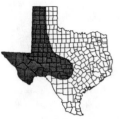

Psaltriparus minimus L— 5 W— 6)
Gray above; paler below; brown cheek patch; black eyes; elongate tail. Some males have black cheek patch. *Female:* Like male but with yellow eyes. *Voice:* Various "tsit"s and "tsee"s. *Habitat:* Oak-juniper, pine, thorn forest. *Similar species:* See Verdin. *Texas:* Uncommon permanent resident* in Panhandle, Edwards Plateau, and Trans-Pecos. *Range:* Western North America from southern British Columbia and southern Idaho east to Colorado, New Mexico, and Texas and south through central and western Mexico to Guatemala.

Family Sittidae
Nuthatches

Nuthatches are peculiar birds in both appearance and behavior. Long-billed, short-tailed, hunched little beasts, built for probing bark on tree trunks, they creep along the trunks, usually from the top down.

412. Red-breasted Nuthatch

Sitta canadensis (L— 5 W— 8)
Gray above; orange buff below; black cap with white line over eye. *Female and immature:* Paler buff below. *Voice:* A nasal, high-pitched series of "anh"s. *Habitat:* Coniferous and mixed woodlands, deciduous woodlands occasionally in winter. *Texas:* Uncommon winter resident over eastern third south to Calhoun Co.; irregular irruptions further south and west in winter. *Range:* Breeds in boreal, transitional, and montane forests of North America, from Alaska across the northern tier of Canada to Labrador, south to New Jersey, New York, Ohio, and Michigan; to North Carolina in Appalachians and to New Mexico, California, and Arizona in Rockies. Winters throughout breeding range and over much of U.S. south to Central Texas, northwestern Mexico, and northern Florida.

413. White-breasted Nuthatch

Sitta carolinensis (L—6 W—11)
Gray above; white below with black cap; buffy flanks. *Female:* Cap is gray or dull black. *Voice:* A series of "yank"s. *Habitat:* Deciduous and mixed woodlands, pinyon-juniper, coniferous forest. *Texas:* Rare permanent resident* in Trans-Pecos, Edwards Plateau, and eastern third south to Houston. *Range:* Southern tier of Canada and most of U.S.; local in Great Plains region; highlands of Mexico south to Oaxaca.

414. Pygmy Nuthatch

Sitta pygmaea (L—5 W—8)
Gray above, buff below; dark grayish-brown cap; white cheeks, throat, and nape. *Voice:* A rapid series of "peeep"s; also a two-note "weebee." *Similar species:* The closely related (conspecific?) Brown-headed Nuthatch of the southeastern U.S. has a chestnut brown cap. *Habitat:* Coniferous forest, especially ponderosa pine. *Texas:* Uncommon permanent resident* at high elevations (above 7,500 feet) in the Guadalupe and Davis mountains; rare to casual elsewhere in mountains of the Trans-Pecos. *Range:* Pine forest of western North America from central British Columbia and Montana south through western U.S. and highlands of Mexico to Jalisco, Morelos, and Veracruz.

415. Brown-headed Nuthatch

Sitta pusilla (L—5 W—8)
Gray above; buff below; brown cap; white cheeks, throat, and nape. *Voice:* "Ki tee"; also various "kit" calls. *Similar species:* See Pygmy Nuthatch. *Habitat:* Coniferous forest. *Texas:* Uncommon permanent resident* in extreme eastern Texas, south and west to Houston. *Range:* Southeastern U.S. from Delaware to eastern Texas.

Family Certhiidae
Creepers

Creepers, like nuthatches, are built for probing tree trunks. These no-necked bits of brown and white fluff have long, decurved bills and stiff tails for foraging over tree trunks, picking arthropod larvae from bark. They generally work from the bottom up, opposite from the way a nuthatch works a trunk.

416. Brown Creeper

Certhia americana (L— 5 W— 8)
Brown streaked and mottled with white above; white below; white eyeline; decurved bill. *Voice:* A high-pitched "tseeee." *Habitat:* Woodlands; breeds mainly in coniferous forests. *Texas:* Uncommon and irregular winter resident (Oct.–Mar.) over most of state, rare and irregular in South Texas; has bred* in Guadalupe Mountains. *Range:* Breeds in boreal, montane, and transitional zones of North America south through the highlands of Mexico and Central America to Nicaragua; winters nearly throughout in temperate, boreal, and montane regions of the continent.

Family Troglodytidae
Wrens

Wrens are a large, mostly tropical family of superb songsters. Most species have plumages of brown and white, sharp, decurved bills, and short, cocked tails. Nests are often built in a cavity or a completely closed structure of grasses.

417. Cactus Wren

Campylorhynchus brunneicapillus (L— 9 W— 11)
Mottled brown and white above; buff below heavily spotted and streaked with dark brown, especially on the throat; dark brown cap with white eyeline. *Voice:* A rolling series of "chrrr"s; Abbey (1973:22) calls it "a small bird with a big mouth and a song like the sound of a rusty adding machine"; also a series of "tschew"s. *Habitat:* Thorn forest, desert. *Texas:* A common permanent resident* of South Texas, the Trans-Pecos, southern plains, and western Edwards Plateau. *Range:* Southwestern U.S. south through arid and semiarid regions of Mexico to Michoacán.

418. Rock Wren

Salpinctes obsoletus (L— 6 W— 9)
Grayish-brown above; whitish below with faint streaks; rusty rump and tail with dark subterminal band. *Voice:* "Tik ear"; a mixture of buzzes, trills. *Habitat:* Rocky canyons, slopes, arroyos, cliffs and crags. *Texas:* Common permanent resident* in Edwards Plateau, Panhandle, and from Trans-Pecos south and east along the Rio Grande to Starr Co.; uncommon to rare winter resident over western half

(Sept.–Apr.). *Range:* Breeds in western North America from southwestern Canada to central Mexico; winters in southern half of breeding range and along Pacific coast.

419. Canyon Wren

Catherpes mexicanus (L— 6 W— 8)
Brownish above and below with contrasting white throat and gray cap. *Voice:* A limpid, descending "tuwee tuwee tuwee tuwee," voice of the western canyon lands; also a harsh "cheeeer." *Habitat:* Canyons, crags, cliffs, outcrops of arid and semiarid regions. *Texas:* Common permanent resident* in Edwards Plateau, north-central Texas, and Trans-Pecos; locally in central Panhandle. *Range:* Western North America from southern British Columbia, Idaho, and Montana south to the highlands of southern Mexico.

420. Carolina Wren

Thryothorus ludovicianus (L— 6 W— 8)
A rich brown above; buff below with prominent white eyeline and whitish throat. *Voice:* Song is a loud, clearly whistled "tea kettle tea kettle tea kettle" or variations on this theme; also a sharp trill call. *Habitat:* Thickets, tangles, and undergrowth of moist woodlands, riparian forest, swamps. *Texas:* Common permanent resident* over eastern half; rare in west. *Range:* Eastern North America from Iowa, Minnesota, New York, and Massachusetts south through southeastern states, eastern Mexico, and Central America along the Caribbean slope to Nicaragua.

421. Bewick's Wren

Thryomanes bewickii (L— 5 W— 7)
Brown (eastern forms) or grayish-brown (western) above; white below with prominent white eyeline; long, active tail is tipped in white. *Voice:* A series of buzzy whistles and warbles reminiscent of the Song Sparrow; also a harsh "churr." *Similar species:* No other small wren has the combination of prominent white eyeline, white underparts, and white-tipped tail. *Habitat:* Thorn forest, savanna, oak woodland, riparian forest, shrubby fields. *Texas:* Common permanent resident* over western two-thirds; common winter resident (Oct.–Apr.) throughout. *Range:* Breeds in most of temperate North America (except Atlantic coastal area and southern portions of Gulf

states) south in highlands to southern Mexico; eastern U.S. populations have become scarce in recent years; winters in southern portion of breeding range.

422. House Wren

Troglodytes aedon (L– 5 W– 7)
Brown above; buff below; buff eyeline; barred flanks (western races are grayer). *Voice:* A descending series, "chipy-chipy-chipy-chipy," with associated buzzes and churrs. *Habitat:* Thickets, undergrowth, and tangles in riparian forest, woodlands, and hedgerows. *Similar species:* Winter Wren is a richer brown below, has shorter tail, and more prominent barring on flanks and belly. Songs and calls are very different. *Texas:* Rare summer resident* in Panhandle and Trans-Pecos; common winter resident (Oct.–Mar.) over most of state. *Range:* Breeds (Northern House Wren group) in temperate North America from southern Canada south to south-central U.S.; winters from southern U.S. south to southern Mexico. The Southern House Wren group, now considered to be conspecific with the Northern, is resident over much of Mexico, Central and South America, and the Lesser Antilles.

423. Winter Wren

Troglodytes troglodytes (L– 4 W– 6)
Brown above; brownish-buff below; buffy eyeline; barred flanks and belly; short tail. *Voice:* Song– a rich, cascading series of trills and warbles; calls are staccato "chuck"s, "kip"s, "churr"s. *Habitat:* Thickets, tangles, undergrowth of fens, bogs, and swamps; riparian forest. *Similar species:* See House Wren. *Texas:* Uncommon winter resident (Oct.–Mar.) in eastern third south to San Patricio Co.; rare in Edwards Plateau, South Texas, and Trans-Pecos. *Range:* Most of Palearctic; breeds in boreal regions of North America from Alaska and British Columbia to Labrador, south along Pacific coast to central California and in the Appalachians to northern Georgia; winters in central and southern U.S. and northern Mexico.

424. Sedge Wren

Cistothorus platensis (L—4 W—6)
Crown and back brown streaked with white; pale buff below; indistinct white eyeline; short bill; short, cocked tail. *Voice:* Song—a weak series of gradually accelerating "tsip"s; call note is a sharp "chip" or "chip chip." *Similar species:* Marsh Wren has plain brown (unstreaked) crown, distinct white eyeline, and black and white streaking on back (no black in Sedge Wren). *Habitat:* Low, wet marshes, grasslands; estuaries. *Texas:* Common winter resident (Oct.–Mar.) along coast, uncommon elsewhere in eastern third, rare to casual in Edwards Plateau and Trans-Pecos. *Range:* Breeds across northeastern U.S. and southeastern Canada from southeastern Saskatchewan to New Brunswick, south to Virginia and Oklahoma; winters along Atlantic and Gulf coastal plain from New Jersey to northern Mexico. Scattered resident populations in Mexico and Central and South America.

425. Marsh Wren

Cistothorus palustris (L—5 W—7)
Brown above; black back prominently streaked with white; white eyeline and throat; buff underparts. *Voice:* Song—a rapid series of dry "tsik"s, like the sound of an old sewing machine; call is a sharp "tsuk." *Similar species:* See Sedge Wren. *Habitat:* Cattail and bulrush marshes, wet prairies. *Texas:* Common to uncommon transient throughout; uncommon to rare summer resident* along upper and north-central coast, and Rio Grande of Trans-Pecos; common to uncommon winter resident (Sept.–Apr.) in southern half. *Range:* Breeds across central and southern Canada and northern U.S., south along both coasts in northern Baja California and southeastern Texas; rare and local in inland U.S.; winters along both coasts, and southern U.S. to southern Mexico.

Family Cinclidae
Dippers

Dippers constitute a small family of drab, wren-like birds, highly specialized for foraging for aquatic arthropods on the bottom of mountain streams and rivers.

426. American Dipper

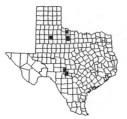

Cinclus mexicanus (L—7 W—12)
Blackish-gray throughout; short, stubby tail. *Immature:* Dark gray above, paler below; yellowish bill. *Habits:* Continual bobbing and habit of walking underwater in mountain streams are distinctive. *Voice:* Song—a boisterous series of trills and warbles; a sharp "zheet" call. *Habitat:* Cataracts, rushing mountain streams, tarns. *Texas:* Casual; scattered records from Edwards Plateau, north-central Texas, and southern Panhandle. *Range:* Breeds in mountains of western North America from Alaska to Panama; winters over most of breeding range except where waters are frozen.

Family Muscicapidae
Kinglets, Gnatcatchers, and Thrushes

This family is a large and diverse group of passerines within which there are two major New World subgroups: thrushes, and kinglets and gnatcatchers. The "kinglet and gnatcatcher" group includes several small, active birds of woodlands and scrub. The "thrush" group includes a number of our most familiar and beloved songbirds, such as the Eastern Bluebird, American Robin, and Wood Thrush.

427. Golden-crowned Kinglet

Regulus satrapa (L—4 W—7)
Greenish above, whitish below; white wing bars, white eyeline; orange crown bordered by yellow and black. *Female:* Yellow crown bordered in black. *Habits:* Continually flicks wings while foraging. *Voice:* Song is a series of "tsee"s, first rising then descending in pitch; call "tse tse tse." *Similar species:* Ruby-crowned has broken white eyering, which Golden-crowned lacks; Golden-crowned has white eyeline, which Ruby-crowned lacks. *Habitat:* Coniferous forest; a variety of woodland habitats in winter. *Texas:* Uncommon winter resident (Oct.–Mar.) in eastern half, rare west. *Range:* Breeds in boreal North America (except Great Plains), in Appalachians south to North Carolina; south in Rockies to Guatemala; winters in southern Canada, U.S., through highland breeding range in Mexico and Guatemala.

428. Ruby-crowned Kinglet

Regulus calendula (L–4 W–7)
Greenish above; whitish below; white wing bars; broken white eyering; scarlet crown. *Female and immature male:* Lack scarlet crown. *Habits:* Continually flicks wings while foraging. *Voice:* Song begins with a series of "tsee" notes followed by lower pitched "tew" notes and terminated by a series of "teedadee"s; distinctive "tsi tit" call. *Similar species:* See Bell's Vireo and Golden-crowned Kinglet. *Habitat:* Coniferous forest; a variety of woodlands during winter including riparian forest and thorn forest. *Texas:* Common winter resident (Oct.–Mar.) over most of state, uncommon to rare in Panhandle and Trans-Pecos. *Range:* Breeds in boreal North America from Alaska to Labrador, south to northern New York, Michigan, and Minnesota, and in Rockies south to New Mexico, and Arizona; winters over most of U.S., Mexico to Guatemala; resident population on Guadalupe Island (Baja California).

429. Blue-gray Gnatcatcher

Polioptila caerulea (L–5 W–7)
Bluish-gray above; white below; long tail black above with white outer feathers (tail appears white from below); white eyering; black forehead and eyeline. *Female and winter male:* Head is uniformly bluish-gray (no black on forehead or eyeline). *Voice:* Song is a barely audible string of high-pitched warbles and squeaks; "tsee" call note. *Similar species:* Tail of Black-tailed Gnatcatcher appears black (not white) from below; Black-tailed male has black cap in breeding plumage (Apr.–Aug.). *Habitat:* Broadleaf woodlands; thorn forest. *Texas:* Common to uncommon summer resident* (Mar.–Sept.) in eastern and north-central Texas, Edwards Plateau, and Trans-Pecos, rare to casual elsewhere; common transient (Aug.–Sept.), (Mar.–Apr.) throughout; common winter resident (Sept.–Apr.) in South Texas, uncommon to rare elsewhere. *Range:* Breeds in temperate U.S. through Mexico to Guatemala; winters in southern Atlantic (from Virginia south) and Gulf states, California, Arizona, New Mexico, throughout Mexico and Central America to Honduras; resident in Bahamas.

430. Black-tailed Gnatcatcher

Polioptila melanura (L— 5 W— 7)
Bluish-gray above; white below; long tail black above with white outer feathers, (appears black from below); indistinct white eyering; black cap. *Female and winter male:* Head bluish-gray (no black cap). *Voice:* Song a metallic "tsee dee dee dee dee"; call a repeated, mewing "chee." *Similar species:* See Blue-gray Gnatcatcher. *Habitat:* Dry thorn forest, desert. *Texas:* Uncommon permanent resident* in Trans-Pecos and western portions of South Texas, south and east to Rio Grande City (Starr Co.); uncommon winter resident in Lower Rio Grande Valley. *Range:* Southwestern U.S. to central Mexico.

431. Eastern Bluebird

Sialia sialis (L— 7 W— 12)
Blue above; brick red below with white belly. *Female:* Similar but paler. *Voice:* Song—a whistled "cheer cheerful farmer"; "tur lee" call. *Similar species:* Western Bluebird male has blue (not red) throat and rusty upper back (not blue); Western Bluebird female has gray (not reddish) throat and rusty upper back. *Habitat:* Open woodlands, savanna, oak, and pine-oak. *Texas:* Common to uncommon permanent resident* over eastern half, rare to casual in west. *Range:* Breeds in eastern North America from southern Saskatchewan to New Brunswick south to Florida and Texas; through highlands of Mexico and Central America to Nicaragua; Bermuda; winters in southern portion of breeding range (mideastern U.S. southward).

432. Western Bluebird

Sialia mexicana (L— 7 W— 12)
Head, throat, and upper parts deep blue; back and shoulders with some rusty color; breast brick red, belly white. *Female:* Similar but with head and back gray-blue; pale orange breast. *Voice:* Song—a whistled "pew pew pewee"; "pew" call note. *Similar species:* See Eastern Bluebird. *Habitat:* Open coniferous and broadleaf woodlands, savanna, juniper, pine-oak. *Texas:* Rare permanent resident* in Guadalupe and Davis mountains of Trans-Pecos; rare (most years) to common winter resident (Oct.–Apr.) over western half. *Range:* Breeds in western North America from southern British Columbia, Montana, and Wyoming south to the highlands of central Mexico.

433. Mountain Blue-bird

Sialia currucoides (L—7 W—13)
Blue above; paler blue below. *Female:* Grayish-blue above; bluish wings; grayish-white below. *Voice:* Song a whistled "tew lee"; call "tew." *Similar species:* Other bluebirds are more or less rusty below. *Habitat:* Highland meadows, open woodland, hedgerows, grasslands, agricultural areas. *Texas:* Uncommon permanent resident* in Guadalupe and Davis mountains of Trans-Pecos; uncommon winter resident (Nov.–Mar.) in western third; rare winter resident in north-central Texas, Edwards Plateau, and South Texas. *Range:* Breeds in western North America from Alaska, the Yukon, and northern Manitoba south to southern California, Arizona, and New Mexico; winters in southern portion of breeding range from southern British Columbia and Montana south through Texas and northern Mexico.

434. Townsend's Solitaire

Myadestes townsendi (L—9 W—14)
Gray body; black, notched tail with white outer tail feathers; buff wing patches; white eyering. *Voice:* Song—a long series of warbles; call—"eek." *Habitat:* Montane coniferous forest, juniper, arid and semiarid thorn forest. *Texas:* Uncommon winter resident (Oct.–Apr.) over western third, rare east through Edwards Plateau. *Range:* Breeds in western North America from Alaska and the Yukon south to New Mexico, Arizona, and southern California; winters in southern half of breeding range from southern British Columbia and Alberta to Texas, and in highlands to southern Mexico; resident population in highlands of northern and central Mexico.

435. Veery

Catharus fuscescens (L—7 W—12)
Russet above; throat buff with indistinct spotting; whitish belly. *Voice:* Song—a downward-spiraling "zheew zheew zhoo zhoo"; call—"zink." *Similar species:* Breast spotting more distinct in Swainson's and Gray-cheeked Thrush; Swainson's has distinct eyering; russet tail of Hermit Thrush contrasts with gray-brown back. *Habitat:* Moist forest, riparian forest, oak woodland. *Texas:* Common spring transient (Apr.–May), rare in fall (Sept.) over eastern third. *Range:* Breeds across southern Canada and northern U.S., south in

mountains to Georgia in the east and Colorado in the west; winters in northern South America.

436. Gray-cheeked Thrush

Catharus minimus (L—8 W—12)
Grayish-brown above; whitish below; heavy dark spotting at throat diminishing to smudges at belly and flanks. *Voice:* Song—"zhee zheeoo titi zhee"; call—"zheep." *Similar species:* The Gray-cheeked is distinguished from the other *Catharus* more by what it does not have than what it does. It does not have a rich buff eyering and underparts (Swainson's); it does not have a rusty tail (Hermit) or a rusty back and head (Veery). *Habitat:* Breeding—coniferous forest and shrubby taiga; migration and winter—riparian forest, deciduous and mixed woodlands and scrub. *Texas:* Common to uncommon spring transient (Apr.–May), rare in fall (Sept.) over eastern third. *Range:* Breeds from northeastern Siberia across Alaska and the northern tier of Canada, south along the Atlantic coast to New York and Massachusetts; winters in northern South America; resident in Hispaniola?

437. Swainson's Thrush

Catharus ustulatus (L—7 W—12)
Brown or grayish-brown above; buffy below with dark spotting; lores and eyering buffy (whitish in some races). *Voice:* Song—"zhoo zhoo zhee zhee" with rising pitch; call—"zheep." *Similar species:* See Gray-cheeked Thrush. *Habitat:* Breeding—coniferous forest, bogs, alder swamps and thickets; migration and winter—moist woodlands. *Texas:* Common spring transient (Apr.–May), uncommon in fall (Sept.–Oct.) over eastern half, scarcer in west. *Range:* Breeds in boreal North America from Alaska across Canada to Labrador south to northern U.S., south in mountains to central California, northern New Mexico; winters in southern Mexico, Central America, and the highlands of northern South America.

438. Hermit Thrush

Catharus guttatus (L—7 W—12)
Grayish-brown above; whitish below with dark spotting; rusty tail, often flicked. *Voice:* Song is in distinct phrases, each beginning with a long, whistled note followed by a trill; trills of different phrases have different inflection; call is "tuk tuk tuk" or a raspy "zhay." *Similar species:* See Gray-cheeked Thrush. *Habitat:* Coniferous and mixed forest, riparian forest, broadleaf woodlands, thorn forest. *Texas:* Uncommon summer resident* in Guadalupe Mountains, Culberson Co.; common to uncommon winter resident (Oct.–Mar.) over most of state, rare in Panhandle and western portions of north-central Texas. *Range:* Breeds in boreal Canada and northern U.S., south in mountains to central California, northern New Mexico, western Texas. Winters from southern U.S., north along coasts to southern British Columbia and New Jersey; Mexico (excluding Yucatán Peninsula) to Guatemala and El Salvador; resident population in Baja California.

439. Wood Thrush

Hylocichla mustelina (L—8 W—13)
Russet above; white below with distinct black spots; reddish-brown crown and nape. *Voice:* Song—distinct phrases of buzzy trills separated by pauses; call—"bup bup bup" *Similar species:* None of the *Catharus* thrushes has the clear white underparts and distinct, black spots. *Habitat:* Moist broadleaf or mixed forest, riparian woodland. *Texas:* Common summer resident* in northeastern Texas, scarcer west to Bastrop Co.; common spring transient (Apr.–May), uncommon in fall (Sept.–Oct.) over eastern third. *Range:* Breeds in eastern U.S. and southeastern Canada; winters from southern Mexico to Panama and northwestern Colombia.

440. Clay-colored Robin

Turdus grayi (L—9 W—16)
Brown above; tawny below; light streaking on throat; pale bill. *Voice:* Song is a sequence of melodious, whistled phrases similar in quality to the American Robin; call, a whiney "queeert." *Habitat:* Lowland wet, tropical forest, open tropical woodlands and riparian forest, gardens. *Texas:* Casual permanent resident* along lower Rio Grande River. *Range:* Mexico to northern South America (Colombia).

441. Rufous-backed Robin

Turdus rufopalliatus (L—9 W—16)
Gray head, wings, lower back and tail; rufous upper back, breast and belly; white throat with dark streaks. *Voice:* A "weak hesitant series of musical notes and phrases" (Edwards 1972:187). *Habitat:* Woodland and woodland edge, arid scrub, riparian forest. *Texas:* Casual (Sept.–Dec.) along Rio Grande. *Range:* Mexico from Sonora to Oaxaca and central highlands.

442. American Robin

Turdus migratorius (L—10 W—17)
Dark gray above; orange-brown below; white lower belly; white throat with dark streaks; partial white eyering. *Voice:* Song is a varied series of whistled phrases, "cheerily cheerup cheerio," etc. call, "tut tut." *Habitat:* Broadleaf and mixed forest, scrub, parkland, riparian forest, oak woodlands. *Texas:* Common summer resident* in the northeast, rare and local west of San Antonio, absent from South Texas; common winter resident (Nov.–Mar.) throughout. *Range:* Breeds nearly throughout Canada and U.S. and south through central highlands of Mexico; winters in southern half of breeding range into Guatemala, western Cuba, Bahamas; resident population in Baja California.

443. Varied Thrush

Ixoreus naevius (L—9 W—16)
Slate blue or gray above; brick red below; black breast band; black face patch; brick red eyeline and wing bars. *Female:* Patterned like male but brownish above; brownish breast band and cheek. *Voice:* Song—a series of long, wavering whistles and trills of different pitches; call—"tsook." *Habitat:* Breeds in wet, coniferous forest of the Pacific Northwest; winters in a variety of woodland, scrub and thorn forest habitats. *Texas:* Casual in winter, records from many different areas (e.g., Lubbock, El Paso, Houston). *Range:* Breeds in northwestern North America from Alaska through the Yukon and British Columbia to northern California; winters from southern British Columbia to southern California.

444. Aztec Thrush

Ridgwayia pinicola (L—8 W—15)
Dark brown streaked with buff above; dark brown throat and breast; belly white; white wing, rump, and terminal tail band. *Female:* Buffier. *Voice:* "A rolling tr-r-r; also a shrill, rising 'whiny' whistle" (Edwards 1972:189). *Habitat:* Pine, oak, fir forests of Mexican highlands. *Texas:* Casual—Brewster Co.; sightings from Aransas, Nueces and Val Verde cos. *Range:* Northern and central highlands of Mexico to Oaxaca.

Family Mimidae
Thrashers and Mockingbirds

This family of robin-sized birds or slightly smaller is characterized by long-tailed, aggressive birds with complex songs that often involve phrases borrowed from other bird species.

445. Gray Catbird

Dumetella carolinensis (L—9 W—12)
Slate gray throughout; black cap and tail; rusty undertail coverts. *Voice:* Song—a stream of whistles, mews, squeaks; sometimes mimics other species; call—a nasal, catlike mew. *Habitat:* Thickets, tangles, heavy undergrowth in coniferous and broadleaf woodlands; second growth, hedgerows. *Texas:* Uncommon summer resident* in northeast corner; common spring (Apr.–May) and fall (Sept.–Oct.) transient in eastern third, rare to casual west; rare winter resident along coast. *Range:* Breeds throughout eastern, central, and northwestern U.S. and southern Canada; winters along central and southern Atlantic and Gulf coasts south through Gulf and Caribbean lowlands of Mexico and Central America to Panama; Bahamas, Greater Antilles; resident in Bermuda.

446. Black Catbird

Melanoptila glabrirostris (L—8 W—11)
Entirely glossy black. *Habitat:* Thickets, scrub, deciduous woodlands. *Texas:* Accidental—Cameron Co. *Range:* Western Caribbean coast from Yucatán to northern Honduras.

447. Northern Mockingbird

Mimus polyglottos (L—10 W—14)
Gray body; paler below; long black tail with white outer tail feathers; white wing bars and white patches on wings. *Voice:* Song—a variety of whistled phrases, repeated several times and including pieces of other bird songs; call—a harsh "chert." *Similar species:* Loggerhead Shrike has heavy, hooked bill, short tail, and black mask. *Habitat:* Arid and semiarid thorn forest, savanna, old fields, hedgerows, residential areas, agricultural areas. *Texas:* Common permanent resident* throughout. *Range:* Resident in central and southern U.S. and Mexico to Oaxaca; Bahamas, Greater Antilles.

448. Sage Thrasher

Oreoscoptes montanus (L—9 W—13)
Grayish-brown above; whitish below with dark streaking; yellowish eye; white wing bars and tail tips. *Voice:* Song—a continuous series of warbles and trills; call—"chuk." *Habitat:* Sagebrush plains, semiarid and arid scrub, thorn forest. *Texas:* Uncommon to rare winter resident (Oct.–Apr.) over western half, southern Edwards Plateau, and South Texas. *Range:* Breeds in deserts of western North America from southern British Columbia, Montana, and southern South Dakota to northern New Mexico and southern California; winters from southern California, Arizona, New Mexico, and Texas south to north-central Mexico.

449. Brown Thrasher

Toxostoma rufum (L—11 W—13)
Rufous above; buff below with dark streaking; yellowish eye. *Voice:* Song—a long sequence of brief phrases of squeaky warbles, each phrase given twice. *Similar species:* Long-billed Thrasher has grayish rather than rufous face (especially note forehead and cheek) and is generally more grayish throughout; orange eye (not yellow). *Habitat:* Tangles, undergrowth, and thickets of forests, old fields, hedgerows, riparian forest, thorn forest. *Texas:* Common permanent resident* in eastern third south and west to Lavaca Co., scarcer westward to eastern Panhandle; common winter resident (Oct.–Mar.) over eastern half south to Calhoun Co., uncommon to rare over western half, and in South Texas. *Range:* Breeds across eastern and central North America from southern Canada west to Alberta,

south to east Texas and southern Florida; winters in southern portion of breeding range.

450. Long-billed Thrasher

Toxostoma longirostre (L—11 W—13)
Tawny brown above; whitish below with dark streaking; two whitish wing bars; grayish face and neck; orange-red eye. *Voice:* Similar to that of Brown Thrasher. *Similar species:* See Brown Thrasher. *Habitat:* Mesquite thorn forest, dry thorn forest, oak savannah. *Texas:* Common permanent resident* in South Texas. *Range:* South Texas through eastern Mexico to central Veracruz.

451. Bendire's Thrasher

Toxostoma bendirei (L—10 W—12)
Gray above; pale gray below with distinct arrowhead-shaped spotting; yellow eye; bill only slightly decurved and whitish at base; no wing bars. *Voice:* Song—a continuous warble of repeated phrases. *Similar species:* See Curve-billed Thrasher. *Habitat:* Desert scrub, cactus, creosote bush, yucca. *Texas:* Hypothetical—Randall Co., Palo Duro Canyon. *Range:* Breeds from southeastern California, southern Nevada, southern Utah, and New Mexico south to west-central Mexico; winters from southern Arizona and New Mexico to southwestern Mexico.

452. Curve-billed Thrasher

Toxostoma curvirostre (L—11 W—13)
Gray above; pale gray below with indistinct spotting; orange-red eye; bill solid black, sharply decurved; whitish wing bars and tail corners. *Voice:* Song is a series of musical warbles with the call notes, "whit" and "whit wheet," interspersed; some mimicking of other species. *Similar species:* Bendire's Thrasher is smaller, has a nearly straight bill that is whitish on the lower mandible, yellow rather than orange eye, no wing bars, and distinct arrowhead-shaped spots on breast (indistinct in Curve-billed). *Habitat:* Dry thorn forest, arid scrub, mesquite thorn forest. *Texas:* Common permanent resident* in West Central, and South Texas. *Range:* Southern Arizona, New Mexico, Colorado, western Oklahoma, and Texas south in arid areas to southern Mexico.

453. Crissal Thrasher

Toxostoma dorsale (L—12 W—13)
Gray above; paler below; whitish throat; black mustache; rusty undertail coverts; long, sharply decurved bill. *Voice:* Song is similar to Curve-billed Thrasher's but less hurried; "pitchoree," "tscha," and "tuwit" call notes. *Similar species:* Curve-billed and Bendire's Thrashers lack rusty undertail coverts and black mustache; have spotted breasts. *Habitat:* Riparian thickets in desert regions, pinyon-juniper. *Texas:* Uncommon permanent resident* in Trans-Pecos; further east in winter. *Range:* Southwestern U.S. and western Mexico.

Family Motacillidae
Pipits

Chaff-colored, long-tailed birds of open country. Like larks, they have an extremely long hind claw, and generally call and sing on the wing. They pump their tails with each step as they walk along the ground in search of seeds and insects.

454. American Pipit

Anthus rubescens (L—7 W—11)
Sparrow-like in size and coloration but sleek and erect in posture; walks rather than hops, and has thin bill; grayish-brown above; buffy below streaked with brown; whitish throat and eyeline; white outer tail feathers; dark legs; wags tail as it walks; undulating flight. *Voice:* flight song a sibilant "chwee," repeated; call—a thin "tsee-eet." *Similar species:* Sprague's Pipit has streaked back and pinkish-beige legs; Vesper Sparrow has cone-shaped bill, hops rather than walks. *Habitat:* Shortgrass prairie, plowed fields, ponds, swales, mud flats, roadsides. *Texas:* Common migrant and winter resident over most of state (Oct.–Apr.); rare in winter in northern Panhandle. *Range:* Breeds in arctic regions of Old and New World and in mountainous areas and high plateaus of temperate regions; winters in temperate regions and high, arid portions of the tropics.

455. Sprague's Pipit

Anthus spragueii (L—7 W—11)
Streaked brown above; whitish below streaked with brown; pale legs; white outer tail feathers; walks rather than hops; bobs tail. *Voice:* flight song—a series of high, sweet notes, descending in pitch; call—a hoarse "tsip." *Similar species:* See American Pipit. *Habitat:* Shortgrass prairie, dunes, pastures. *Texas:* Uncommon to rare migrant and winter resident over most of state (Oct.–Apr.); rare to casual in Panhandle and Trans-Pecos. *Range:* Breeds north-central Alberta east to southern Manitoba and into Montana, South Dakota, North Dakota, and western Minnesota; winters in southern Arizona, New Mexico, Texas, Arkansas, Louisiana, Mississippi and Mexico to southern Veracruz, Puebla, and Michoacán.

Family Bombycillidae
Waxwings

Waxwings are a small family of sleek, brown, crested birds with bright waxy tips on their secondaries. They are highly social during the non-breeding portion of the year, feeding mostly in flocks on tree fruits and berries.

456. Bohemian Waxwing

Bombycilla garrulus (L—8 W—14)
Dapper grayish-brown above and below with a sharp crest; black mask and throat; tail black with yellow tip; rusty undertail coverts; primaries black with white and yellow markings; secondaries with waxy red tips. *Immature:* Faint streaking below; whitish face and throat. *Voice:* High, thin, wavering "tseeeeet," louder and rougher than in Cedar Waxwing. *Similar species:* Cedar Waxwing has whitish rather than chestnut undertail coverts and lacks yellow and white markings on wings. *Habitat:* Orchards and fruiting trees: apples, juniper, hawthorn, mountain ash. *Texas:* Rare winter visitor (Nov.–Apr.) to the Panhandle. *Range:* Breeds in North America from Alaska and northwestern Canada to northwestern U.S.; winters northwestern U.S. and western Canada irregularly south and east across temperate U.S. Eurasian populations breed in boreal regions and winter in southern boreal and temperate areas of the Old World.

457. Cedar Waxwing

Bombycilla cedrorum (L—7 W—11)
Natty brown above and below with sharp crest; black face and throat; yellow wash on belly; tail tipped with yellow; red waxy tips to secondaries. *Immature:* Brown above; paler below with faint streaking; lacks waxy tips. *Voice:* A thin, gurgling "tseee." *Similar species:* See Bohemian Waxwing. *Habitat:* Open coniferous and deciduous woodlands, bogs, swamps, and old fields; winter flocks frequent fruiting trees (e.g., mountain ash, mulberry, pyracantha, crabapple, juniper). *Texas:* Common winter resident (Oct.–May) throughout. *Range:* Breeds across southern Canada and northern U.S. south to northern California, Kansas, and New York; winters from temperate U.S. through Mexico and Central America to Panama and Greater Antilles.

Family Ptilogonatidae
Silky-Flycatchers

This family is a small, tropical group of trim, crested birds; mostly frugivorous.

458. Gray Silky-Flycatcher

Ptilogonys cinereus (L—8 W—11)
A slender, gray, crested bird with yellow undertail coverts; white patch on central underside of long, black tail. *Female:* Similar but brownish. *Voice:* A sharp "kitick"; a whistled "chert." *Habitat:* Pine-oak, juniper. *Texas:* Accidental—Cameron Co. *Range:* Resident in the highlands of central Mexico.

459. Phainopepla

Phainopepla nitens (L—8 W—12)
Entirely black except for white primaries (visible in flight) and red eye; ragged crest; long tail. *Female and immature male:* Brownish-gray; grayish primaries and undertail coverts. *Habits:* Solitary birds sally for insects from exposed perch; small flocks feed on mistletoe and other berries. *Voice:* Song a thin warble; call a low, softly whistled "wirrp." *Habitat:* Desert scrub and riparian thickets; juniper-oak woodland. *Texas:* Common permanent resident* in Trans-Pecos, rare on western edge of Edwards Plateau. *Range:* Breeds in southwestern U.S., western and central

Mexico; winters in all but extreme northern portions
of breeding range.

Family Laniidae
Shrikes

The New World species in this group are medium-
sized, stocky, predominantly gray and white birds
with hooked beaks and strong feet for grasping and
killing insects, small mammals, birds, reptiles, and
amphibians.

460. Northern Shrike

Lanius excubitor (L—10 W—14)
Pearl gray above; faintly barred below; black mask,
primaries, and tail; white wing patch and outer tail
feathers; heavy, hooked bill. *Habits:* Sits on high, exposed perches; pumps tail; sometimes hovers while
hunting; larders prey on thorns and barbs. *Voice:*
Song of trills and buzzes; harsh chatter call is given
infrequently. *Similar species:* Loggerhead Shrike
doesn't hover or pump tail, is smaller and grayer with
black rather than whitish forehead, grayish rather
than whitish rump, and black rather than whitish
lower mandible. *Habitat:* Open woodlands, savanna,
farmland. *Texas:* Casual winter visitor (Nov.–Feb.) to
Panhandle. *Range:* Breeds across boreal regions of
Old and New World; winters in northern temperate
and southern boreal regions.

**461. Loggerhead
Shrike**

Lanius ludovicianus (L—9 W—13)
Gray above; paler below; black mask, wings, and tail;
white outer tail feathers and wing patch. *Habits:*
Hunts from exposed perches; wary, flees observer with
rapid wing beats; larders prey on thorns and barbs.
Voice: Song a series of weak warbles and squeaks; call
is a harsh "chaaa," often repeated three to four times.
Similar species: Mockingbird is slighter, lacks heavy,
hooked bill, has longer tail, and has no black mask.
See also Northern Shrike. *Habitat:* Savanna, tallgrass
prairie, farmland. *Texas:* Common permanent resident* over most of state; uncommon to rare in summer in Southern Texas. *Range:* Breeds locally over
most of U.S. and southern Canada south through

highlands of Mexico to Oaxaca; winters in all but northernmost portions of breeding range.

Family Sturnidae
Starlings

Starlings are an Old World family of birds with no members native to the New World. They are medium-sized, relatively long-billed songbirds, often with iridescent plumage. Many of the species mimic the songs of other birds.

462. European Starling

Sturnus vulgaris (L—9 W—15)
Plump, short-tailed, and glossy black with iridescent purple and green highlights; long, yellow bill. *Winter:* Dark bill; dark body plumage heavily speckled with white. *Habits:* Erect waddling gait when foraging on ground; forms large roosting flocks during nonbreeding season. *Voice:* Song includes various squeaks, harsh "churr"s, whistles, and imitations of other bird songs—often with repeated phrases; call is a high pitched, rising "tseee." *Similar species:* Other black songbirds are shorter billed, longer tailed; winter bird is speckled; summer bird has yellow bill. *Habitat:* Towns, savanna, farmland. *Texas:* Common permanent resident* nearly throughout; uncommon to rare breeding in West and South Texas. *Range:* New World—resident from southern Canada to northern Mexico, Bahamas, and Greater Antilles; Old World—breeds in temperate and boreal regions of Eurasia, and winters in southern portions of breeding range into North Africa, the Middle East, and southern Asia.

Family Vireonidae
Vireos

A predominantly tropical group of small, feisty birds, most of which are patterned in greens, yellows, grays, and browns. The relatively thick bill has a small, terminal hook. Most are woodland or scrub species that deliberately glean twigs, leaves, and branches for insect larvae.

463. White-eyed Vireo

Vireo griseus (L— 5 W— 8)
Greenish-gray above; whitish washed with yellow below; white eye, yellow eyering and forehead ("spectacles"); white wing bars. *Immature:* Has brown eye until Sept.–Oct. of hatching year. *Habits:* Solitary and retiring; both sexes sing occasionally in winter. *Voice:* Song—"tstlik tstlit-a-lur tslik" or variations; call a whiney "churr," repeated. *Similar species: Empidonax* flycatchers have erect posture, whiskers, and flattened bill; lack "spectacles" and white eye. *Habitat:* Deciduous woodland, thorn forest. *Texas:* Common summer resident* (Mar.–Oct.) in eastern half; common permanent resident* along coast and in South Texas; rare transient (Mar.–May, Aug.–Oct.) in Panhandle and western Edwards Plateau. *Range:* Breeds in eastern U.S. from southern Minnesota to Massachusetts, south to Florida and eastern Mexico to Veracruz; winters from southeastern U.S. south through eastern Mexico and Central America to northern Nicaragua; Bahamas and Greater Antilles.

464. Bell's Vireo

Vireo bellii (L— 5 W— 7)
Grayish-green above; whitish with yellowish flanks below; white "spectacles" (lores, eyering, forehead); two faint whitish wing bars. *Habits:* Normally forages in dense thickets. *Voice:* Song—a mixture of "tsitl tsitl tsee" and "tsitl tsitl tsoo" with pauses between phrases; call—a raspy "tsoo weea tsi." *Similar species:* Hutton's Vireo has grayish (not white) throat and incomplete eyering; Gray Vireo is gray (not green) above, lacks spectacles and yellow on flanks; Ruby-crowned Kinglet lacks spectacles, has thin bill, and yellow-green outer webs on primaries. *Habitat:* Thorn forest, savanna, deciduous woodlands; often near water. *Texas:* Locally common summer resident* (Mar.–Sept.) over most of state, rare (east) to casual (west) in Panhandle, rare in southeastern Texas. *Range:* Breeds in central and southwestern U.S. from Minnesota, South Dakota, Nevada, and southern California south through northern Mexico; winters from southern Mexico to Honduras.

465. Black-capped Vireo

Vireo atricapillus (L—5 W—7) **Endangered**
Grayish-green above; white below; black head with white "spectacles" (lores, forehead, eyering); red eye; whitish wing bars. *Female:* Buffier. *Habits:* Unusually active for a vireo; often hangs head downward during foraging. *Voice:* Song—a series of hurried, raspy phrases; call—a high-pitched, scratchy "tsee-itch." *Similar species:* Larger Solitary Vireo has black (not red) eye, prominent white wing bars, gray rump. *Habitat:* Oak scrub and juniper woodlands. *Texas:* Uncommon summer resident* (Mar.–Sept.) in Palo Pinto and Comanche cos., Edwards Plateau, and Terrell and Brewster cos. of Trans-Pecos. *Range:* Breeds in Central Texas and central Oklahoma to central Coahuila, Mexico; winters in southwestern Mexico.

466. Gray Vireo

Vireo vicinior (L—6 W—8)
Gray above; whitish below with narrow white eyering and single, faint wing bar. *Habits:* Active for a vireo; bobs tail; females sing. *Voice:* Song a series of varied, musical phrases—"che wee, che wit, chi wur, chi wit," etc., similar to that of Solitary Vireo but more rapid; call a harsh chatter. *Similar species:* See Bell's Vireo; Rocky Mountain race of Solitary Vireo has two prominent, white wing bars and white spectacles. *Habitat:* Desert thorn scrub, oak-pinyon-juniper woodlands. *Texas:* Rare summer resident* (Apr.–Sept.) in mountains of Trans-Pecos (2,400–6,000 feet). *Range:* Breeds in southwestern U.S. and northwestern Mexico; winters in western Mexico.

467. Solitary Vireo

Vireo solitarius (L—6 W—10)
Eastern race greenish on the back with a gray rump; whitish below with yellow flanks; two prominent, white wing bars; gray head and white "spectacles" (lores, forehead, eyering); Rocky Mountain race is uniformly gray above. *Habits:* A deliberate forager like most vireos but in contrast to warblers. *Voice:* Song is a rich series of "chu wit, chu wee, cheerio," etc., similar to that of Red-eyed Vireo but with longer pauses between phrases; call is a whiney "cheeer." *Similar species:* See Gray Vireo. *Habitat:* Coniferous and mixed woodlands, riparian forest, oak thickets. *Texas:* Uncommon summer resident* (Apr.–Nov.) in mountains of Trans-Pecos; common transient over eastern

third (Apr.–May, Sept.–Nov.), rare west; uncommon to rare winter resident (Sept.–May) in eastern third. *Range:* Breeds across central and southern Canada, northern and western U.S.; winters from southern U.S. through Mexico and Central America to Costa Rica; Cuba.

468. Yellow-throated Vireo

Vireo flavifrons (L– 6 W–10)
Greenish above with gray rump; yellow throat, breast, and "spectacles" (lores, forehead, eyering); white belly and wing bars. *Voice:* Like a hoarse, slow Red-eyed Vireo, "chearee (pause) chewia, (pause) tsuweet," etc. *Similar species:* The smaller, slimmer, more active Pine Warbler has yellow-green rump (not gray), white tail spots, and thin bill. *Habitat:* Deciduous forest, riparian and oak woodland. *Texas:* Uncommon spring (Mar.–Apr.) and rare fall transient (Aug.–Sept.) over eastern third; uncommon summer resident* in Central and East Texas. *Range:* Breeds in eastern U.S.; winters in southern Mexico, Central America, and northern South America; Bahamas; Greater Antilles.

469. Hutton's Vireo

Vireo huttoni (L– 5 W– 8)
Grayish-green above; buff below; white lores, incomplete eyering, and wing bars. *Habits:* A rather tame, deliberate forager. *Voice:* Song—"chew wit," often repeated; call—a raspy "za zee zee." *Similar species:* See Bell's Vireo. *Habitat:* Pine-oak, juniper woodlands. *Texas:* Uncommon permanent resident* in Presidio and Brewster cos.; uncommon transient (Apr.–May, Sept.–Oct.) elsewhere in Trans-Pecos. *Range:* Resident along west coast of North America from southern British Columbia to northern Baja California; southern Arizona, southwestern New Mexico, and West Texas through western and central Mexico to Guatemala.

470. Warbling Vireo

Vireo gilvus (L– 6 W–9)
Grayish-green above; whitish washed with yellow below; white eye stripe; no wing bars. *Voice:* Song is a long wandering series of warbles almost always ending with an upward inflection; call, a hoarse "tswee." *Similar species:* Can be difficult to separate from some pale Philadelphia Vireos, most of which are

yellower below and have a dark loral spot. *Habitat:* Deciduous and mixed forest, riparian and oak woodland. *Texas:* Uncommon summer resident* (Apr.–Oct.) in Trans-Pecos, East Texas, and the northeastern Panhandle; uncommon spring (Apr.–May) and rare fall (Sept.–Oct.) transient over eastern half, scarcer in west. *Range:* Breeds across North America south of arctic region to central Mexico; winters from Guatemala to Panama.

471. Philadelphia Vireo

Vireo philadelphicus (L— 5 W— 8) Grayish-green above; variably yellowish below; white eye stripe and dark loral spot; no wing bars. *Habits:* Deliberate foraging movements with much peering and poking in outer clumps of leaves and twigs; even hanging occasionally like a chickadee. *Voice:* Song is similar to the Red-eyed Vireo's but higher and slower. *Similar species:* See Warbling Vireo. Could be mistaken for immature Tennessee Warbler or Orange-crowned Warbler but note yellow throat, thick vireo bill, and deliberate foraging behavior. *Habitat:* Deciduous and mixed forest, riparian and oak woodland. *Texas:* Uncommon spring (Apr.–May) and rare fall (Sept.–Oct.) transient over eastern third. *Range:* Breeds in eastern and central boreal North America in Canada and northern U.S.; winters from Guatemala to Panama.

472. Red-eyed Vireo

Vireo olivaceus (L— 6 W— 10) Olive above; whitish below; gray cap; white eyeline; red eye (brown in juvenile). *Voice:* Song — a leisurely, seemingly endless series of phrases, "cheerup, cherio, chewit, chewee," etc. through the middle of long summer days. Male sometimes sings from nest. Call — a harsh "cheear." *Similar species:* This is the only gray-capped vireo without wing bars. *Habitat:* Deciduous and mixed forest, riparian and oak woodland. *Texas:* Common summer resident* in eastern Texas south to Refugio Co.; common spring (Apr.–May) and uncommon fall (Sept.–Oct.) transient over eastern half, scarcer in west. *Range:* Breeds over much of North America (not in western U.S., Alaska, or northern Canada); winters in northern South America.

473. Yellow-green Vireo

Vireo flavoviridis (L—6 W—10)
Olive above; yellowish below; gray cap; white eyeline; red eye (brown in juvenile). *Voice:* Similar to Red-eyed Vireo but with more abrupt phrases and longer pauses between phrases. *Similar species:* Very similar to the closely related (conspecific?) Red-eyed Vireo but yellowish below (not white), greenish on flanks, and has yellow undertail coverts (not white). *Habitat:* Lowland tropical forest, scrub, mangroves, second growth. *Texas:* Rare summer resident* in the Lower Rio Grande Valley. *Range:* Breeds from South Texas to Panama; winters in Amazon Basin of northern South America.

474. Black-whiskered Vireo

Vireo altiloquus (L—6 W—10)
Olive above; whitish below; gray cap; white eyeline; black whisker; red eye (brown in juvenile). *Voice:* Song—similar to Red-eyed Vireo but with repeated phrases. *Habitat:* Mangroves, coastal scrub. *Texas:* Casual transient (Apr.–May), Galveston Co. *Range:* Southern Florida, Bahamas, West Indies, northern Venezuela.

475. Yucatán Vireo

Vireo magister (L—6 W—10)
Olive above; grayish-white below; yellowish-white eye stripe and forehead; dark eyeline. *Voice:* Song—similar to Red-eyed Vireo's but with long pauses between phrases. *Habitat:* Coastal scrub, mangroves. *Texas:* Accidental—Galveston Co. *Range:* Caribbean coast and coastal islands of Yucatán, Belize, and Honduras; Grand Cayman Island.

Family Emberizidae
Wood Warblers, Tanagers, Sparrows, Blackbirds, Orioles, and Emberizine Finches

This is a large, diverse family of mostly tropical species. Most species are small to medium in size and highly colorful in plumage.

476. Bachman's Warbler

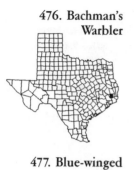

Vermivora bachmanii (L—5 W—8) **Endangered**
Olive above; yellow below; black cap and bib; yellow forehead and throat; white undertail coverts and tail spots. *Female:* Grayish crown; yellowish breast. *Habitat:* Swampy thickets. *Texas:* Hypothetical, may have occurred in Big Thicket area (extreme East Texas). *Range:* Breeds in southeastern U.S.; winters in Cuba and Isle of Pines.

477. Blue-winged Warbler

Vermivora pinus (L—5 W—8)
Greenish-yellow above; yellow below; head yellow with black line through eye; bluish-gray wings and tail with white wing bars and tail spots. *Female and immature male:* More greenish on head. *Voice:* Song—a dry, buzzy "beee bizzz." *Habitat:* Deciduous scrub, riparian and oak woodland, thorn forest. *Texas:* Common spring (Apr.–May), uncommon fall (Sept.–Oct.) transient in eastern third, scarcer elsewhere in eastern half. *Range:* Breeds in eastern U.S.; winters from southern Mexico to Panama. Interbreeds with Golden-winged Warbler to produce hybrid Brewster's Warbler (patterned like Blue-wing but with whitish underparts) and Lawrence's Warbler (patterned like Golden-wing but yellow below).

478. Golden-winged Warbler

Vermivora chrysoptera (L—5 W—8)
Gray above; whitish below; golden crown and epaulets; black throat and ear patch; white tail spots. *Female and immature male:* Patterned like male but with gray throat and ear patch. *Voice:* Song—"bee biz biz biz." *Habitat:* Deciduous scrub, riparian and oak woodland, thorn forest. *Texas:* Common spring (Apr.–May), uncommon fall (Sept.–Oct.) transient in eastern third, rare elsewhere in eastern half. *Range:* Breeds northeastern and north-central U.S.; winters from southern Mexico to Colombia and Venezuela; see Blue-winged Warbler for discussion of hybrids.

479. Tennessee Warbler

Vermivora peregrina (L—5 W—8)
Olive above; white below with gray cap, white eye stripe and dark line through eye. *Immature:* Tinged with yellow. *Voice:* Song—a series of rapid "tsip"s followed by a series of rapid "tsi"s; call—a strong "tsip." *Similar species:* The immature Tennessee is similar to the Orange-crowned Warbler, but lacks faint streaking on breast and yellow undertail coverts (white in Tennessee); Tennessee is greener above than Orange-crowned, and has a more prominent eye stripe. *Habitat:* Coniferous and deciduous woodlands; riparian, oak, and thorn forest. *Texas:* Common spring (Apr.–May) and uncommon fall (Sept.–Oct.) transient over eastern third. Breeds across boreal North America; winters from southern Mexico to northern South America.

480. Orange-crowned Warbler

Vermivora celata (L—5 W—8)
Greenish-gray above; dingy yellow faintly streaked with gray below; grayish head with faint yellowish eye stripe and eyering; orange crown visible on some birds at close range. *Voice:* Song—a weak, fading trill; call—a strong "cheet." *Similar species:* See Tennessee Warbler; immatures of some Yellow Warblers are similar but have yellow (not gray) undertail lining. *Habitat:* Deciduous, mixed, and coniferous woodlands, thickets, thorn forest. *Texas:* Uncommon summer resident* in pine-oak of Guadalupe Mountains, Culberson Co.; common to uncommon winter resident (Oct.–Mar.) elsewhere except Panhandle where rare. *Range:* Breeds in western and northern North America; winters in southern U.S., Mexico, Belize, and Guatemala.

481. Nashville Warbler

Vermivora ruficapilla (L—4 W—7)
Olive above; yellow below; gray head; white eyering; rufous cap. *Female and immature male:* Dingier, lack reddish cap. *Voice:* Song—"tsepit tsepit tsepit" followed by a trilled "tseeeeeeeeeeee"; call—"tsip." *Habitat:* Bog forest, coniferous, mixed and deciduous woodlands, riparian, oak, and thorn forest. *Texas:* Common transient (Apr.–May, Sept.–Oct.) except in West Texas and Panhandle where rarer; rare winter resident (Oct.–Mar.) in coastal Texas. *Range:* Breeds across extreme north-central and northeastern U.S.,

south-central and southeastern Canada, and north-western U.S.; winters in South Texas, Mexico, and Central America to Honduras.

482. Virginia's Warbler

Vermivora virginiae (L—5 W—8)
Gray above; white below with yellow breast; greenish-yellow rump, and undertail coverts; rufous crown patch; white eyering. *Female and immature male:* Dingier breast; no rufous crown. *Habits:* Wags tail while foraging. *Voice:* Song—"tsip tsip tsip tsip tsip tsweet tsweet," rising inflection at the end; call— "tsip." *Similar species:* See Colima Warbler. *Habitat:* Desert scrub, oak-pinyon-juniper. *Texas:* Rare transient (Apr.–May, Aug.–Sept.) in Trans-Pecos; casual summer resident* in the Guadalupe Mountains (Culberson Co.). *Range:* Breeds in southwestern U.S.; winters in western Mexico.

483. Colima Warbler

Vermivora crissalis (L—5 W—8)
Brownish-gray above; grayish-white below with buffy brown flanks; gray head; rufous crown patch; white eyering; orange-yellow rump and undertail coverts. *Habits:* Deliberate, vireo-like forager. *Voice:* Song—a trill concluding with two lower notes; call—a sharp "tsit." *Similar species:* Virginia's Warbler has greenish-yellow rump and undertail coverts; Lucy's Warbler has rufous rump and white undertail coverts. *Habitat:* Oak-juniper. *Texas:* Rare summer resident* in Chisos Mountains (Presidio and Brewster cos.). *Range:* Breeds in Big Bend region of Texas and neighboring mountains of northeastern Mexico; winters in southwestern Mexico.

484. Lucy's Warbler

Vermivora luciae (L—4 W—7)
Gray above; white below; white eyering and cheek; rufous crown patch and rump. *Voice:* Song—"tsweeta tsweeta tsweeta chee chee chee chee" and variations. *Similar species:* See Colima Warbler. *Habitat:* Arid scrub, desert riparian thickets. *Texas:* Rare to casual summer resident* (Apr.–Aug.) in Hudspeth, Presidio, and Brewster cos. of Trans-Pecos. *Range:* Breeds in southwestern U.S.; winters in southwestern Mexico.

485. Northern Parula

Parula americana (L— 5 W— 8)
Bluish above; yellow throat and breast; black collar rimmed below with rust; broken white eyering; white belly and wing bars; greenish-yellow on back. *Female and immature male:* Lack collar. *Voice:* Song "brrrrrzzeeit," like a running a thumbnail up a comb; also a slower, rising "zhe zhe zhe zeeeeit." *Similar species:* Male Tropical Parula has black face mask (just a touch of black on the forehead in Northern Parula) and no eyering. *Habitat:* Swampy deciduous and mixed forest, riparian and oak woodlands. *Texas:* Common summer resident* (Mar.–Oct.) in eastern third and southern edge of Edwards Plateau; common spring (Mar.–Apr.) and rare fall (Aug.–Oct.) transient across eastern third, scarcer in west; rare winter resident in Lower Rio Grande Valley. *Range:* Breeds in eastern U.S. and southeastern Canada; winters from southern Mexico to Panama; West Indies.

486. Tropical Parula

Parula pitiayumi (L— 5 W— 8)
Bluish above; yellow throat and breast; black face, white belly and wing bars; greenish-yellow on back. *Female and immature male:* Lack mask. *Voice:* Song "brrrrrzzeeit," like running a thumbnail up a comb; also a slower, rising "zhe zhe zhe zeeet." *Similar species:* See Northern Parula. *Habitat:* Riparian forest and oak woodlands. *Texas:* Casual permanent resident* in Lower Rio Grande Valley north to Kenedy Co. *Range:* Resident from northern Mexico to northern Argentina.

487. Yellow Warbler

Dendroica petechia (L— 5 W— 8)
Yellow throughout, somewhat dingier on the back; yellow tail spots; streaked below with reddish. *Female and immature male:* Reddish streaking faint or absent. *Voice:* Song—"tseet tseet tseet tsitsitsi tseet"; call—"chip." *Similar species:* Some immature Yellow Warblers are similar to immature Orange-crowned or Wilson's warblers, but have yellow (not gray) undertail lining. *Habitat:* Riparian thickets, scrub, second growth forest, hedgerows. *Texas:* Common spring (Apr.–May) and fall (Aug.–Sept.) transient throughout; rare summer resident* in Trans-Pecos, Edwards Plateau, northeastern Panhandle, and East Texas; Rare winter resident in Lower Rio Grande

Valley. *Range:* Breeds across most of North America; winters from extreme southern U.S. through Mexico and Central America to northern and central South America; resident races in mangroves of West Indies and Central and South America.

488. Chestnut-sided Warbler

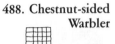

Dendroica pensylvanica (L—5 W—8)
Greenish streaked with black above; white below with chestnut sides; yellow cap; white cheek and wing bars; black facial markings. *Immature:* Spring green above; white below with whitish-yellow eyering, wing bars and tail spots. *Voice:* Song—"pleased pleased pleased ta meetcha" and variations; call—"tsip." *Similar species:* Bright yellow-green back and cap, yellowish wing bars, and white underparts separate the immature from other immature warblers. *Habitat:* Scrub, thickets, second growth, hedgerows. *Texas:* Common spring (Apr.–May) and rare fall (Sept.–Oct.) transient in eastern third, scarcer in west. *Range:* Breeds in northeastern U.S. and southeastern Canada; winters from southern Mexico to Panama.

489. Magnolia Warbler

Dendroica magnolia (L—5 W—8)
Black back; gray cap; yellow below broadly streaked with black; yellow rump; white wing and tail patch. *Female and winter male:* Brownish above; lack most of breast streaking. *Habits:* Continually fans tail, showing white band; often sallies for insects during foraging. *Voice:* Song—"tsweeta tsweeta tsweetee"; call is a hoarse, vireo-like "eeeeeh," very different from that of most other warblers. *Similar species:* No other warbler has a white band across the middle of the tail. *Habitat:* Coniferous, mixed, and deciduous forest; riparian and oak woodland; thickets and second growth. *Texas:* Common spring (Apr.–May) and uncommon fall (Sept.–Oct.) transient in eastern third, scarcer in west. *Range:* Breeds across much of boreal Canada and northeastern U.S.; winters from central Mexico to Panama; West Indies.

490. Cape May Warbler

Dendroica tigrina (L— 5 W— 8)
Greenish with black streakings above; yellow breast with black streaks; yellow rump; chestnut ear patch; white undertail coverts, wing patch, and tail spots. *Female and immature male:* Dingier; yellow or gray ear patch; sometimes lack white wing patch. *Voice:* Song— a weak, high-pitched "tsee tsee tsee tsee." *Similar species:* Female Yellow-rumped Warbler lacks distinct streaking on throat and breast; Palm Warbler has yellow (not white) undertail coverts, and wags tail. *Habitat:* Coniferous, mixed, and deciduous forest; riparian and oak woodland. *Texas:* Rare spring transient (Apr.–May) along coast. *Range:* Breeds in boreal regions of central and eastern Canada and northeastern U.S.; winters in the West Indies.

491. Black-throated Blue Warbler

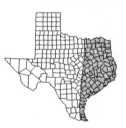

Dendroica caerulescens (L— 5 W— 8)
Blue-black above; black face, throat, and sides; white breast, belly, and spot on primaries. *Female:* Brownish above; dingy white below; whitish eye stripe; dark ear patch; white patch on primaries (usually). *Voice:* Song— a rising "tsee tsee tsee tsuree"; call—"tsik." *Similar species:* Female resembles Philadelphia Vireo and Tennessee Warbler, but dark cheek patch and white wing patch (when present) are distinctive. *Habitat:* Mixed and deciduous forest; riparian and oak woodland. *Texas:* Rare spring (Apr.–May) transient along coast. *Range:* Breeds in southeastern Canada and northeastern U.S. to northern Georgia; winters in Caribbean basin.

492. Yellow-rumped Warbler

Dendroica coronata (L— 5 W— 8)
Blue-gray above; black breast and sides; white belly; yellow cap, rump and shoulder patch. Breeding males of the eastern and northern race (Myrtle Warbler) have white throat and white wingbars; western race (Audubon's Warbler) has yellow throat and white wing patch. *Female and winter male:* Brownish above; dingy below with faint streaking; yellow rump. *Voice:* Song— a weak trill, rising at the end "tsitsitsitsitsitsee"; "chit" call note often given in flight. *Similar species:* See Cape May Warbler; female Magnolia Warbler is yellow (not dingy white) below. *Habitat:* A variety of forested and open areas. *Texas:* Common summer resident* in Guadalupe mountains above 8,000 feet

(Audubon's Warbler and Myrtle Warbler); common transient throughout; common winter resident (Nov.–Mar.) except in Panhandle where rare. *Range:* Breeds across northern boreal North America and in mountains of the west south to southern Mexico; winters from central and southern North America to Panama and West Indies.

493. Black-throated Gray Warbler

Dendroica nigrescens (L— 5 W— 8)
Dark gray above; whitish below with white wing bars; distinct facial pattern of black crown, white eye stripe, black eyeline and ear stripe, white chin stripe, and yellow loral spot; black throat and breast. *Female and immature male:* Throat and breast whitish. *Voice:* Song—"tseta tseta tseta tseeet cha" with rising inflection on penultimate syllable. *Similar species:* Female Cerulean Warbler has bluish cap and buffy (not gray) cheek patch; female Black-and-White Warbler has whitish (not dark) cheek and whitish throat. *Habitat:* Arid pinyon, oak, and juniper scrub. *Texas:* Rare to casual transient and winter resident (Nov.–Mar.) in West Texas, Edwards Plateau, and coastal South Texas; rare transient in Panhandle; may breed in Guadalupe Mountains (Culberson Co.). *Range:* Breeds in western U.S. and northwestern Mexico; winters from southwestern U.S. to southern Mexico.

494. Townsend's Warbler

Dendroica townsendi (L— 5 W— 8)
Greenish above; yellow breast; white wing bars and belly; distinct facial pattern of black crown, yellow eye stripe, black eyeline and ear stripe, yellow chin stripe; black throat. *Female and immature male:* Yellow throat. *Voice:* Song—a high-pitched, buzzy "zee zee zee tseetsee"; call—"tseet." *Similar species:* See Hermit Warbler. *Habitat:* Pine and oak forest. *Texas:* Uncommon transient (Apr.–May, Sept.–Oct.) in western third, scarcer in east. *Range:* Breeds in mountains of northwestern North America from Alaska to Oregon and Wyoming; winters in western coastal regions of U.S. and western highlands of Middle America from Mexico to Costa Rica.

495. Hermit Warbler

Dendroica occidentalis (L— 5 W— 8)
Gray above; white below; yellow head with black
throat and nape. *Female and immature male:* Dark
green nape and crown; throat grayish or white. *Voice:*
Song—a high-pitched "tseetl tseetl tseetl tseee";
call—"tseet." *Similar species:* Female Hermit has
yellow face and forecrown, and blackish or grayish
throat; female Black-throated Green has green crown,
with yellow face and throat; female Golden-cheeked
has dark cap, eyeline and throat; female Townsend's
has dark cap and cheek patch, and yellow throat.
Habitat: Pine, pine-oak, juniper. *Texas:* Rare transient
(Apr.–May, Aug.–Sept.) in Trans-Pecos. *Range:*
Breeds in coastal ranges of northwestern U.S.; winters
in coastal California and highlands of western Mexico
and Central America to Nicaragua.

**496. Black-throated
Green Warbler**

Dendroica virens (L— 5 W— 8)
Green above; black bib; green crown; golden face;
white belly. *Female and immature male:* Usually have
some gray or black across breast. *Voice:* Song—a lazy,
insect-like "zee zee zee zoo zee" or "zoo zee zeezee
zoo"; call—"chip." *Similar species:* See Hermit
Warbler. *Habitat:* Coniferous and mixed forest,
riparian and oak woodland, thorn forest. *Texas:* Common spring (Apr.–May) and uncommon fall (Sept.–
Oct.) transient across eastern third. *Range:* Breeds
across central and southern Canada and north-central
and northeastern U.S., also south in Appalachians
and along coastal plain to Georgia; winters from
southern Texas and southern Florida through Mexico
and Central America to Panama and West Indies.

**497. Golden-cheeked
Warbler**

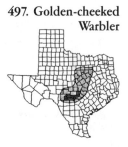

Dendroica chrysoparia (L— 5 W— 8)
Black above; black bib; golden cheek with black eyeline; white belly. *Female and immature male:* Greenish above and on crown; golden cheek; dark eyeline;
black bib is restricted or lacking; throat yellowish.
Voice: Song—"tweah tweah tweesy" (Pulich 1976);
call—"tsik." *Similar species:* See Hermit Warbler. *Habitat:* Oak-juniper, pine-oak. *Texas:* Uncommon summer
resident* (Mar.–Aug.) in Edwards Plateau, especially
the southeastern edge (Real, Kerr, Bandera, Kendall,
Blanco cos.). *Range:* Breeds in Central Texas; winters in
highlands of Guatemala, Honduras, and Nicaragua.

498. Blackburnian Warbler

Dendroica fusca (L—5 W—8)
Black above; white below; orange bib; black and orange facial pattern. *Female and immature male:* Patterned like adult male but black areas of male are grayish, orange areas are yellowish. *Voice:* Song—very high-pitched, rising "tsip tsip tsip tsip tsitsi tseeee"; call—"tsip." *Similar species:* Female Black-throated Green is greenish or mottled black and green on the back, female Blackburnian has pale striping on dark back. *Habitat:* Coniferous and mixed forest, riparian and oak woodland, thorn forest. *Texas:* Common spring (Apr.–May), rare fall (Sept.–Oct.) transient in eastern third. *Range:* Breeds in northeastern U.S. and southeastern Canada; winters in Costa Rica, Panama, and northern South America.

499. Yellow-throated Warbler

Dendroica dominica (L—5 W—8)
Dark gray above; white below with yellow bib; black mask; white eye stripe (yellow in some individuals); black streaks on sides. *Habits:* Often forages by creeping along tree branches. *Voice:* Song—a strong, slurred series of notes ending with an upward inflection, "tew tew tew tew teweesee." *Similar species:* White patch on side of neck distinguishes this bird from Grace's Warbler (gray neck). *Habitat:* Conifers, cypress, sycamores, riparian and oak woodland. *Texas:* Common spring (Mar.–Apr.), rare fall (Aug.–Sept.) transient in eastern half; locally common summer resident* in northeastern Texas and eastern portions of Edwards Plateau; rare to casual winter resident along coastal plain. *Range:* Breeds in eastern U.S.; winters along Gulf coast of U.S., Middle America to Costa Rica; Bahamas and Greater Antilles.

500. Grace's Warbler

Dendroica graciae (L—5 W—8)
Dark gray above; white below with yellow bib; black lores; gray cheek; yellow eye stripe; black streaks on sides. *Habits:* Forages by creeping along branches, occasionally sallying after insects. *Voice:* Song—a weak trill; two or three introductory notes followed by a trill; call "snip." *Similar species:* See Yellow-throated Warbler. *Habitat:* Pine, pine-oak. *Texas:* Uncommon summer resident* (Apr.–Sept.) in Trans-Pecos. *Range:* Breeds in mountains of southwestern U.S.; also in highlands and lowland pine savanna of Mexico, and

Central America to Nicaragua; winters in breeding range from central Mexico southward.

501. Pine Warbler

Dendroica pinus (L— 6 W— 9)
Olive above; yellow below with faint, grayish streaking; whitish belly; yellow eye stripe; white wing bars. *Female and immature male:* Like male but more olive throughout. *Voice:* Song— a series of chips similar to the Chipping Sparrow but slower, each chip distinct. *Similar species:* See Yellow-throated Vireo; immature is similar to immature Blackpoll and Bay-breasted but has an unstreaked back. *Habitat:* Pine, riparian forest, oak woodland. *Texas:* Common to uncommon permanent resident* in eastern quarter and southeastern Edwards Plateau; uncommon winter resident over eastern third south to Corpus Christi; rare winter resident (Nov.–Mar.) in South Texas. *Range:* Breeds in eastern half of U.S. and south-central and southeastern Canada, Bahamas, Hispaniola; winters in southern portion of breeding range.

502. Prairie Warbler

Dendroica discolor (L— 5 W— 7)
Greenish-yellow above streaked with chestnut; yellow below with black markings on sides; yellow face with black eyeline and chin stripe; two faint wing bars. *Female and immature:* Similarly patterned but much dingier. *Habits:* Wags tail while foraging. *Voice:* Song— an upward series of buzzy "zee"s. *Similar species:* Tail wagging habit separates this species from all but the immature Palm Warbler, which is brownish (not green) above, and has grayish streaking on breast (not restricted to sides). *Habitat:* Scrubby coniferous and deciduous second growth, pine plantations; thorn, riparian, and oak forest; mangroves. *Texas:* Rare summer resident* in northeastern portion; rare transient (Apr.–May, Aug.–Oct.) over eastern third. *Range:* Breeds in eastern half of U.S.; winters in southern Florida and Caribbean Basin.

503. Palm Warbler

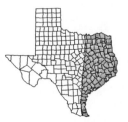

Dendroica palmarum (L—5 W—7)
Olive with dark streaks above; yellowish or creamy below with brownish streaks; yellow undertail coverts; chestnut cap in breeding plumage; yellow eye stripe. *Habits:* Wags tail while foraging; often forages low or on the ground. *Voice:* Song—a weak series of buzzy notes on the same pitch. *Similar species:* See Prairie Warbler. *Habitat:* Spruce bogs on breeding ground; marshes, swampy thickets, mangroves. *Texas:* Rare winter resident (Oct.–Apr.) across eastern third. *Range:* Breeds across central and eastern Canada and extreme north-central and northeastern U.S.; winters along Atlantic and Gulf coastal plain; northern Caribbean Basin.

504. Bay-breasted Warbler

Dendroica castanea (L—6 W—9)
Gray above with dark streaking; chestnut cap, throat and sides; black mask; beige neck patch. *Female and immature male:* Olive above; beige below, often with some chestnut on sides. *Voice:* Song—a very high-pitched "wesee wesee wesee." *Similar species:* Immature Blackpoll has faintly streaked breast and back (not plain), and pale legs (not dark). *Habitat:* Coniferous forest, riparian and oak woodland, thorn forest. *Texas:* Common spring (Apr.–May), rare fall (Sept.–Oct.) transient in eastern third, scarcer in west. *Range:* Breeds across central and eastern Canada and extreme north-central and northeastern U.S.; winters in Panama, Colombia, and northwestern Venezuela.

505. Blackpoll Warbler

Dendroica striata (L—6 W—9)
Grayish-green streaked with black above; white below; black cap; white cheek; black chin stripe and streakings on side; pale legs. *Female and immature male:* Olive cap streaked with black; faint white eye stripe; greenish cheek; whitish below with variable amounts of gray streaking. *Voice:* Song—a weak series of "tsi"s, building in volume and then trailing off; call—a soft "chuk." *Similar species:* Black-and-White Warbler crown has white median stripe (not solid black); see also Bay-breasted Warbler. *Habitat:* Coniferous forest, various forest and scrub sites. *Texas:* Rare spring (Apr.–May) transient, most often found on coastal barrier islands (especially High Island, Galveston Co.) following periods of strong north or east

winds. *Range:* Breeds in northern boreal regions of North America; winters in South America to northern Argentina.

506. Cerulean Warbler

Dendroica cerulea (L— 5 W— 8)
A delicate bluish-gray above; white below; black bar across chest and streakings down side; white wing bars. *Female and immature male:* Olive tinged with blue above; whitish below with grayish streakings; blue-gray crown; creamy eye stripe. *Voice:* Song— "chew chew sipisipisipi zeee"; "sippi zee"; call— "tsip." *Similar species:* Black throat band is distinctive for male; female resembles female Blackpoll but has unstreaked back, prominent eye stripe, and dark legs (not yellowish). *Habitat:* Deciduous forest, riparian and oak woodlands. *Texas:* Rare summer resident* in extreme northeastern Texas; uncommon spring (Apr.– May) transient in eastern third. *Range:* Breeds in eastern U.S. except southeastern coastal plain; winters in northern South America.

507. Black-and-White Warbler

Mniotilta varia (L— 5 W— 9)
Boldly striped with black and white above and below. *Female:* Faint grayish streaking below. *Habits:* Clambers up and down tree trunks and branches, nuthatch fashion. *Voice:* Song—a weak "wesee wesee wesee"; call—"pit." *Similar species:* This is the only species with white median stripe in black cap, and peculiar trunk-foraging behavior. *Habitat:* Deciduous and mixed forest, riparian and oak woodlands, thorn forest. *Texas:* Uncommon summer resident* in southeastern Edwards Plateau and northeastern Texas west to Cooke Co.; common transient (Mar.–Apr., Aug.–Sept.) across eastern third, rare in west; rare winter resident (Dec.–Mar.) along coastal plain. *Range:* Breeds across Canada east of the mountains and in eastern half of U.S.; winters in extreme southern U.S., eastern Mexico, and Central America to northern South America; West Indies.

508. American Redstart

Setophaga ruticilla (L—5 W—9)
Black above and below with brilliant orange patches on tail, wings, and sides of breast; white undertail coverts. *Female:* Grayish-brown above; whitish below with yellow patches on tail, wings and sides of breast. *Immature male:* Salmon-colored patches on sides of breast. *Habits:* This species catches much of its prey on the wing in brief sallies; often fans tail and droops wings while foraging. *Voice:* One individual will often have three or four different songs, even alternating song types from one phrase to the next. Some common phrases are "tsee tsee tsee tsee tseet," "tsee tsee tsee tsee tsee-o," "teetsa teetsa teeetsa teetsa teet" (Peterson 1960:227); call—a strong "chip." *Habitat:* Deciduous forest, riparian and oak woodland, thorn forest. *Texas:* Common spring (Apr.–May), uncommon fall (Sept.–Oct.) transient over eastern third, rare in west; uncommon summer resident* in eastern quarter, rare along southeastern edge of Edwards Plateau and in Trans-Pecos. *Range:* Breeds across Canada south of arctic region and in eastern half of U.S. except southeastern coastal plain; winters from central Mexico south to northern South America; West Indies.

509. Prothonotary Warbler

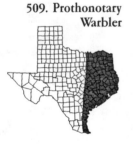

Protonotaria citrea (L—6 W—9)
Orange head and breast; yellow-green back; blue-gray wings; white belly and undertail coverts. *Female:* Similar but yellow rather than orange. *Voice:* Song—a loud, ringing "peeet weeet weeet weeet weeet weeet weeet"; call—"tsip." *Similar species:* Female Wilson's Warbler has brownish-green (not gray) wings, and yellow (not white) undertail coverts; Yellow Warbler has yellow wing bars (none on Prothonotary). *Habitat:* Wooded swamps, mangroves, riparian forest. *Texas:* Locally common summer resident* (Apr.– Sept.) in eastern quarter, rare south along coastal plain to Calhoun Co.; uncommon spring (Apr.), rare fall (Sept.) transient over eastern third. *Range:* Breeds in eastern half of U.S.; winters in southeastern Mexico and Caribbean Basin.

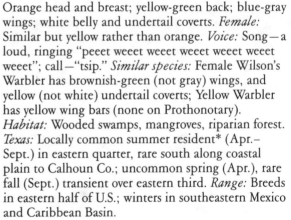

510. Worm-eating Warbler

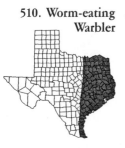

Helmitheros vermivorus (L−6 W−9)
Olive above; buffy below; crown striped with black and buff. *Habits:* Forages in dead leaf clumps in trees or on the ground. *Voice:* Song—an insect-like, buzzy trill; call—a strong "chip." *Habitat:* Deciduous forest, riparian forest, oak woodland. *Texas:* Common spring (Mar.–Apr.), uncommon fall (Aug.–Sept.) transient across eastern third; rare summer resident* in East Texas. *Range:* Breeds in eastern U.S.; winters from southern Mexico to Panama; West Indies.

511. Swainson's Warbler

Limnothlypis swainsonii (L−6 W−9)
Brown above; buff below with chestnut cap; whitish eye stripe. *Habits:* Feeds mainly on the ground. *Voice:* Song—a loud, clear "whee whee whitoo whee"; call—a ringing "chip." *Habitat:* Canebrakes, swampy thickets, riparian forest, mangroves. *Texas:* Uncommon spring (Apr.), rare fall (Sept.) transient along coastal plain; uncommon summer resident* in eastern quarter, rare south to Aransas Co. *Range:* Breeds in southeastern U.S.; winters in Bahamas, Greater Antilles, eastern Mexico, and Yucatán.

512. Ovenbird

Seiurus aurocapillus (L−6 W−10)
Olive above; white below with heavy dark streaks; orange crown stripe bordered in black; white eyering. *Habits:* Walks on forest floor, flicking leaves and duff while foraging for invertebrates. *Voice:* Song—a loud "teacher teacher teacher teacher," etc. *Similar species:* Northern and Louisiana waterthrushes have a prominent white or yellowish eye stripe; also, this species does not bob while walking as the waterthrushes do. *Habitat:* Deciduous forest, riparian and oak woodland. *Texas:* Common spring (Apr.–May), uncommon fall (Sept.–Oct.) transient over eastern third; rare winter resident (Nov.–Mar.) along coastal plain. *Range:* Central and eastern Canada and central and eastern U.S. south to Atlantic and Gulf coastal plain; winters in southern Florida, southern Mexico to northern Venezuela; West Indies.

513. Northern Water-thrush

Seiurus noveboracensis (L—6 W—10)
Brown above; white or yellowish below with dark streaking on throat and breast; prominent creamy or yellowish eye stripe. *Habits:* Forages on the ground, bobbing as it walks, usually in boggy or wet areas. *Voice:* Song—"chi chi chi chewy chewy will will"; call—"chink." *Similar species:* Louisiana Waterthrush has clear white throat (not streaked) and buffy flanks; see Ovenbird. *Habitat:* Swamps, bogs, swales, ponds, rivers, lakes, mangroves, usually near stagnant water. *Texas:* Common spring (Mar.–May), uncommon fall (Aug.–Sept.) transient over eastern third, rare in west; rare winter resident (Oct.–Mar.) along coastal plain. *Range:* Breeds in boreal North America south of the arctic circle; winters from central Mexico to northern South America; Caribbean Basin.

514. Louisiana Water-thrush

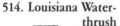
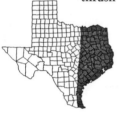

Seiurus motacilla (L—6 W—10)
Brown above; creamy below with dark streaking on breast; prominent white eye stripe. *Habits:* Forages on the ground, bobbing as it walks, usually near running water. *Voice:* Song—"tsee tsee tsee tsawit tsawit tseyo"; call—"chink." *Similar species:* See Northern Waterthrush. *Habitat:* Streams, rivers, swales, ponds, riparian forest. *Texas:* Uncommon summer resident* (Mar.–Sept.) in eastern quarter; common spring (Mar.–Apr.) and uncommon fall (Aug.–Sept.) transient over eastern third. *Range:* Breeds in eastern U.S.; winters from Mexico to northern South America; West Indies.

515. Kentucky Warbler

Oporornis formosus (L—5 W—8)
Green above; yellow below; yellow spectacles (forehead, eye stripe, eyering); black crown, lores, ear patch. *Female:* Black more or less replaced by green. *Habits:* Forages by hopping (not walking) on the ground, picking insects from overhanging vegetation. *Voice:* Song—a clear, loud "choree choree choree choree choree"; call—a series of "chip"s, repeated as the bird hops, rising and falling in volume as the bird turns one way and then another. *Similar species:* Male Common Yellowthroat has a black mask—no yellow spectacles. *Habitat:* Moist, lowland forest. *Texas:* Common summer resident* in East Texas and southeast portions of Edwards Plateau; common spring

(Mar.–Apr.), uncommon fall (Aug.–Sept.) transient in eastern third. *Range:* Breeds in eastern U.S.; winters from southern Mexico to northern Colombia and northwestern Venezuela.

516. Connecticut Warbler

Oporornis agilis (L– 6 W– 9)
Olive above; yellow below; gray hood; complete, white eyering; undertail coverts extend almost to tip of short tail. *Female and immature male:* Brownish-yellow head. *Habits:* Forages low and on the ground with a peculiar bobbing stride. *Voice:* Song– a loud, clear "chipychip chipychip chipychipchipit"; call note–"chink." *Similar species:* Spring male has a complete eyering (incomplete in MacGillivray's, lacking in Mourning), and gray breast (blackish in both MacGillivray's and Mourning); females and immatures of these three species are safely separable only in the hand (Lanyon and Bull 1967). *Habitat:* Bogs, dense thickets. *Texas:* Casual transient (Apr.–May, Sept.–Oct.) in eastern third. *Range:* Breeds in central Canada and extreme north-central U.S.; winters in northern South America.

517. Mourning Warbler

Oporornis philadelphia (L– 6 W– 9)
Olive above; yellow below; gray hood with black on breast. *Female and immature male:* Brownish-yellow head and partial eyering. *Habits:* Forages low and on the ground. *Voice:* Song– a loud, clear "chewy chewy chewy chewy chewit"; call– a dry "chit." *Similar species:* See Connecticut Warbler. *Habitat:* Dense thickets, riparian forest, oak woodlands. *Texas:* Common spring (Apr.–May) and fall (Aug.–Oct.) transient in eastern third. *Range:* Breeds in central and eastern Canada and extreme north-central and northeastern U.S.; winters from Nicaragua to northern South America.

518. MacGillivray's Warbler

Oporornis tolmiei (L– 5 W– 8)
Olive above; yellow below; gray hood with black on breast; incomplete white eyering. *Female and immature male:* Brownish-yellow head and partial eyering. *Habits:* Forages low and on the ground. *Voice:* Song– a loud, clear "chewy chewy chewy chewit chewit." *Similar species:* See Connecticut Warbler.

Habitat: Dense thickets, riparian forest, oak wood-lands. *Texas:* Uncommon spring (Apr.–May) and fall (Aug.–Oct.) transient in western half, scarcer in east. *Range:* Breeds in western U.S. and southwestern Canada; winters in highlands of Mexico and Central America to Panama.

519. Common Yellowthroat

Geothlypis trichas (L— 5 W— 7)
Olive above; yellow below with black mask. *Female:* Brownish above; yellow to buff throat fading to whitish on belly; brownish on sides. *Habits:* Skulks in low marsh vegetation. *Voice:* Song—"wichity wichity wichit"; call—a harsh "chuk." *Similar species:* See Kentucky Warbler. Lack of eyeline, eyering and wing bars plus whitish belly separates female from other warblers. *Habitat:* Marshes, streams, estuaries, wet meadows. *Texas:* Common transient (Apr.–May, Sept.–Oct.) throughout; common summer resident* (Mar.–Sept.) in eastern third south to Aransas Co. and along Rio Grande in Trans-Pecos, uncommon to rare in Panhandle; rare permanent resident* along Lower Rio Grande; common winter resident (Oct.–Apr.) in eastern third, scarcer in Edwards Plateau and Trans-Pecos. *Range:* Breeds from central Canada south throughout the continent to the southern U.S. and in highlands to southern Mexico; winters from southern U.S. to Costa Rica; Bahamas, Greater Antilles.

520. Gray-crowned Yellowthroat

Geothlypis poliocephala (L— 6 W— 9)
Olive above; yellow below; gray cap; white eyering; black lores and forehead. *Habits:* Frequently flicks tail while skulking in low vegetation. *Voice:* Song—"twe twe twe weechy weechy wit a twit weechy a weech" (Peterson and Chalif 1973:211). *Similar species:* Smaller Common Yellowthroat does not flick tail, lacks gray cap. *Habitat:* Marshes, wet meadows, overgrown pastures. *Texas:* Rare permanent resident* in the Lower Rio Grande Valley. *Range:* Resident from South Texas to Panama.

521. Hooded Warbler

Wilsonia citrina (L—5 W—8)
Olive above; yellow below with black hood, yellow forehead and face; white tail spots. *Female:* Usually lacks hood but has greenish cap, yellow forehead and eye stripe. *Habits:* Sallies from low perches for insects; often fans tail exposing white spots. *Voice:* Song—"sweeta wee teeoo"; call—a clear musical "chip," usually given repeatedly for up to a minute. *Similar species:* Female Wilson's Warbler lacks white tail marks and does not fan tail. *Habitat:* Dense thickets, tree falls in lowland deciduous forest, swamp and riparian forest, oak woodland. *Texas:* Locally common summer resident* in eastern Texas south to Matagorda Co., rare south to Aransas Co.; common spring (Mar.–Apr.), rare fall (Aug.–Sept.) transient over eastern third. *Range:* Breeds in eastern U.S.; winters from southern Mexico to Panama.

522. Wilson's Warbler

Wilsonia pusilla (L—5 W—7)
Olive above; yellow below with a black cap. *Female:* Often has only a partially black or completely greenish-yellow crown. *Habits:* Flycatches at mid- to upper canopy level, using short, sallying flights. *Voice:* Song—"Chee chee chee chee chipy-chipy-chipy-chipy" (almost a trill); call—a wheezy "ship." *Similar species:* See Hooded Warbler; female differs from female Yellow Warbler by brownish tail lacking yellow spots. *Habitat:* Riparian forest, thorn forest, oak woodlands, thickets. *Texas:* Common transient throughout (Apr.–May, Sept.–Oct.); rare winter resident (Nov.–Mar.) along coastal plain. *Range:* Breeds in boreal regions of northern and western North America; winters from southern California and Texas through low to middle elevations of Mexico and Central America to western Panama.

523. Canada Warbler

Wilsonia canadensis (L—5 W—8)
Slate gray above; yellow below with black "necklace" across breast; yellow lores and eyering. *Female and immature male:* Similar but necklace is usually fainter. *Voice:* Song—a high, thin, slurred series of notes "tsi tsi tsi tsewy tsi," etc. *Habitat:* A variety of forests and thickets. *Texas:* Common transient. (Apr.–May, Sept.–Oct.) in eastern half. *Range:* Breeds in eastern and central Canada from Labrador to north-

eastern British Columbia and in boreal U.S. from Minnesota to New England; south in Appalachians to northern Georgia.

524. Red-faced Warbler

Cardellina rubrifrons (L— 5 W— 8)
Gray above; red face and breast; black crown and ear; white nape, rump, and belly. *Immature:* Similar but paler. *Habitat:* Often feeds by hanging at the tips of branches, chickadee fashion. *Voice:* A high, thin series of "tseeit"s. *Habitat:* Montane fir, spruce, and pine forests. *Texas:* Casual in summer (May–Aug.), mainly in Big Bend. *Range:* Breeds from Arizona south to west-central Mexico; winters in highlands from western Mexico to Honduras.

525. Painted Redstart

Myioborus pictus (L— 6 W— 9)
Black back, head, and breast; red belly; white wing patch and outer tail feathers. *Immature:* Paler with blackish belly. *Habitat:* Flicks wings and fans tail while foraging. *Voice:* Song — a warbled "wetew-wetew-wetew-weet"; call — a clear "peep." *Habitat:* Pine-oak, juniper, pinyon. *Texas:* Uncommon summer resident* (Apr.–Aug.) in Big Bend region, rare elsewhere in West Texas. *Range:* Breeds from southwestern U.S. and mountains of western Mexico to Nicaragua; winters in southern portion of breeding range.

526. Golden-crowned Warbler

Basileuterus culicivorus (L— 5 W— 8)
Slaty gray above; yellow below; golden stripe through crown bordered by black. *Voice:* Song — "weetee weetee weetew"; call — "tik." *Habitat:* Wet, lowland forest. *Texas:* Casual fall and winter visitor (Sept.–Feb.) to Lower Rio Grande Valley. *Range:* Central Mexico to southern South America.

527. Rufous-capped Warbler

Basileuterus rufifrons (L— 5 W— 7)
Greenish above; rufous cap and cheeks; white eyeline; yellow breast; belly whitish or yellowish. *Habits:* Often cocks long tail in wren-like fashion. *Voice:* A variable, twittering series of high-pitched chips and trills. *Habitat:* Brushy fields and thickets. *Texas:* Rare visitor, mainly in Big Bend. *Range:* Northern Mexico to Honduras.

528. Yellow-breasted Chat

Icteria virens (L—7 W—10)
A nearly thrush-sized warbler; brown above; yellow throat and breast; white belly and undertail coverts; white eyering and supraloral stripe; lores black or grayish. *Habits:* Very shy; sings in flight. *Voice:* A varied series of clear whistles and harsh, scolding "chak"s and "jeer"s. *Habitat:* Dense thickets, brushy pastures, riparian and oak forest undergrowth, thorn forest. *Texas:* Common summer resident* (Apr.–Sept.) and transient over much of the state except north-central region and Panhandle where uncommon to rare or absent; rare in winter along coast. *Range:* Breeds locally nearly throughout the U.S. and southern Canada south to central Mexico; winters from central Mexico to Panama.

529. Olive Warbler

Peucedramus taeniatus (L—5 W—7)
Gray above; rusty hood; black mask; white below; two white wing bars; white outer tail feathers. *Female and immature male:* Tawny or yellowish hood but still show dark mask. *Voice:* Song—a whistled "weeta" repeated; call—"tew." *Habitat:* Montane pine and pine-oak woodlands. *Texas:* Hypothetical—Big Bend. *Range:* Breeds from Arizona and southwestern New Mexico through the highlands of Mexico and Central America to Nicaragua; winters through all except northernmost portions of breeding range.

530. Hepatic Tanager

Piranga flava (L—8 W—13)
Red body; gray cheek patch; grayish tinge on back and flanks; dark bill. *Female and immature male:* Grayish-brown above; yellowish below; gray cheek patch; yellowish crown. *Voice:* Song consists of rough, robin-like phrases; call—"tshup." *Similar species:* Summer Tanager lacks contrasting cheek patch and usually (during breeding season) has a brownish bill (black in Hepatic). *Habitat:* Montane pine and pine-oak forest. *Texas:* Uncommon summer resident* in mountains of the Trans-Pecos. *Range:* Breeds from southwestern U.S. through the mountains of Mexico, Central America, and South America to northern Argentina; winters in all but northernmost parts of range.

531. Summer Tanager

Piranga rubra (L—8 W—13)
Entirely red. *Female and immature male:* Tawny brown above; yellowish below; second-year males and some females are blotched with red. *Voice:* Song consists of slurred, robin-like phrases; call—"pit-a-chuk." *Similar species:* See Hepatic Tanager. *Habitat:* Deciduous and mixed woodlands, riparian and oak forest. *Texas:* Common summer resident* (Mar.–Oct.) over much of the state, rare in South Texas, nearly absent from north-central Texas and Panhandle; rare winter resident (Nov.–Mar.) along coastal plain. *Range:* Breeds across eastern and southern portions of U.S. and northern Mexico; winters from southern Mexico through Central America to northern South America.

532. Scarlet Tanager

Piranga olivacea (L—8 W—13)
Red with black wings. *Winter:* Greenish above; black wings and tail—splotched with red during molt. *Female and immature male:* Olive above; yellowish below. *Voice:* Song—hoarse, loud, robin-like phrases; call—"chik-burr." *Similar species:* Female is distinguished from other female tanagers by whitish (not greenish or yellowish) wing linings and greenish (rather than brownish or grayish) cast to plumage. *Habitat:* Deciduous and mixed forest, oak and riparian woodland. *Texas:* Uncommon spring (Apr.–May) and rare fall (Sept.–Oct.) transient in eastern third. *Range:* Breeds in northeastern U.S. and southeastern Canada; winters in northern South America.

533. Western Tanager

Piranga ludoviciana (L—8 W—13)
Red head; yellow below; yellow rump, neck and shoulder; black back, wings and tail; two white wing bars. *Winter:* Lacks red on head. *Female and immature male:* Similar to winter male but duller. *Voice:* Song—hoarse and robin-like with pauses between phrases; call—"chit-it" or "chit-a-chit." *Similar species:* Female resembles some female orioles but has heavy tanager bill, and yellowish rump and nape contrast with olive back. *Habitat:* Montane fir, pine, and pine-oak forest; nonbreeders in arid thorn and riparian forest. *Texas:* Uncommon summer resident* (Apr.–Oct.) in the mountains of the Trans-Pecos; rare transient (Apr.–May, Aug.–Oct.) elsewhere; rare

winter resident in Lower Rio Grande Valley. *Range:* Breeds in mountains of western North America from Alaska to northwestern Mexico; winters from central Mexico through Central America to Costa Rica.

534. Crimson-collared Grosbeak

Rhodothraupis celaeno (L—8 W—13)
Black body and face; red hood; rump and eyering red. *Female and immature male:* Similar in pattern but yellowish green rather than red. *Voice:* Song—two or three whistled phrases followed by a descending series of warbled notes; call—"peek." *Habitat:* Thickets in humid forest, riparian woodland, and brushy pastures. *Texas:* Casual in the Lower Rio Grande Valley. *Range:* Eastern Mexico from central Tamaulipas to Veracruz and Puebla.

535. Northern Cardinal

Cardinalis cardinalis (L—9 W—12)
Red with crest; black face patch at base of red bill. *Female and immature male:* Crested like male but greenish-brown; paler below; bill brownish or reddish. *Voice:* Song—loud, ringing whistle "whit-chew," repeated; call—a sharp "peak." *Similar species:* Female and immature cardinal have sharp, orange or brown, conical bill as compared with the snubbed, pale bill of the grayer Pyrrhuloxia. *Habitat:* Deciduous and mixed forest, oak and riparian woodland, mesquite thorn forest. *Texas:* Common permanent resident* in eastern two-thirds; scattered local populations in west. *Range:* Eastern U.S. and southeastern Canada; southwestern U.S., Mexico, Guatemala, and Belize.

536. Pyrrhuloxia

Cardinalis sinuatus (L—9 W—12)
Dusty gray body; red crest, face, belly, wings, and tail. *Female:* Similar but red on face mostly lacking. *Voice:* Similar to Northern Cardinal—"whit whit whit whit." *Similar species:* See Northern Cardinal. *Habitat:* Arid thorn forest. *Texas:* Common but local permanent resident* in South Texas, southern and western portions of Edwards Plateau, Trans-Pecos, and southern Panhandle. *Range:* Arid regions of southern Arizona, New Mexico, and Texas south to central Mexico.

537. Rose-breasted Grosbeak

Pheucticus ludovicianus (L— 8 W—13)
Black head, back, wings, and tail; red breast; white belly, rump, wing patches, and tail spots; red underwing. *Female:* Mottled brown above; buffy below heavily streaked with dark brown; white eyebrow and wing bars; yellow underwing. *First-year male:* Like female but shows rose tints on breast and underwing coverts. *Second-year male:* Patterned much like adult male but splotched brown and black on head and back. *Voice:* Song— rapid, robin-like phrases; call—a sharp "keek" or "kik." *Similar species:* Female Black-headed Grosbeak is only faintly streaked below and has yellowish rather than pale buff breast. *Habitat:* Deciduous forest, riparian and oak woodlands, thorn forest, savanna. *Texas:* Common spring (Apr.–May) and uncommon fall (Oct.) transient in eastern third, scarcer in west. *Range:* Breeds in northeastern U.S., central and southeastern Canada; winters from southern Mexico to northern South America; western Cuba.

538. Black-headed Grosbeak

Pheucticus melanocephalus (L— 8 W—13)
Black head; body a rich orange buff streaked with black on the back; wings black; two white wing bars. *Female and immature male:* Brown head; white eyebrow; brown streaked with buff above; buffy below with faint brownish streaks; white wing bars on brown wings; yellow underwing. *Voice:* Song— rapid robin-like phrases, slightly hoarser and lower pitched than the Rose-breasted Grosbeak; call—"kik." *Similar species:* See Rose-breasted Grosbeak. *Habitat:* Open deciduous, pinyon, pine, and pine-oak woodlands; riparian and thorn forest. *Texas:* Common summer resident* (Mar.–Oct.) in mountains of the Trans-Pecos; rare transient (Mar.–Apr., Aug.–Oct.) in western half; rare winter resident (Oct.–May) along Rio Grande River and coastal plain. *Range:* Breeds from southwestern Canada through western U.S. and highlands of northern and central Mexico; winters in central Mexico.

539. Blue Bunting

Cyanocompsa parellina (L— 6 W— 9)
Dark blue; light blue face, rump, flanks, and bend of wing. *Female:* Mahogany; paler below. *Voice:* Song—a warbling series of "chewy"s; call—"tink." *Habitat:* Thickets along streams, brushy pastures, second-growth woodland. *Texas:* Casual winter visitor (Oct.–Mar.) to Lower Rio Grande Valley. *Range:* Northern Mexico to Nicaragua.

540. Blue Grosbeak

Guiraca caerulea (L— 7 W—11)
Dark blue; two rusty wing bars. *Female and immature male:* Brownish above; paler below; tawny wing bars; often has a blush of blue on shoulder or rump. *Habits:* Flicks and fans tail. *Voice:* Song—a rapid series of up and down warbles, some notes harsh, some slurred; call—"chink." *Similar species:* Male and female Indigo Bunting resemble corresponding sex of Blue Grosbeak but are smaller, and lack tawny wing bars and massive grosbeak bill. *Habitat:* Savanna, scrub, brushy pastures, hedgerows. *Texas:* Uncommon to rare summer resident* (Apr.–Oct.) nearly throughout. *Range:* Breeds from central and southern U.S. through Mexico and Central America to Costa Rica; winters from northern Mexico to Panama, rarely Cuba.

541. Lazuli Bunting

Passerina amoena (L— 6 W— 9)
Turquoise head, back and rump; rusty breast and buffy belly; two white wing bars. *Female:* Brown above; paler below; two buffy wing bars; often has blue cast on rump. *Voice:* Song—three- to four-second phrases of rough, slurred warbles; call—"tsik." *Similar species:* Female Indigo Bunting lacks bluish rump, and wing bars are indistinct. However, these two species (subspecies?) interbreed in areas of overlap in central and southwestern U.S., producing hybrids with mixed plumage characters. *Habitat:* Willow thickets, hedgerows, savanna, thorn forest. *Texas:* Rare spring transient (Apr.–May) nearly throughout, casual in East Texas; rare summer resident (Apr.–Oct.) in Panhandle and Trans-Pecos; has bred* (1903) on Edwards Plateau (Kerr Co.). *Range:* Breeds in southwestern Canada and western U.S.; winters in western Mexico.

542. Indigo Bunting

Passerina cyanea (L— 6 W— 9)
Entirely indigo blue. *Female and immature male:*
Brown above; paler below; faint streaking on breast.
Winter adult and second-year males: Bluish with
variable amounts of brown on back and wings. *Voice:*
Song—warbled phrases of paired or triplet notes;
call—"tsink." *Similar species:* See Blue Grosbeak and
Lazuli Bunting. *Habitat:* Thickets, hedgerows, brushy
fields, savanna, thorn forest. *Texas:* Common spring
(Apr.–May) and fall (Sept.–Oct.) transient over
eastern third, scarcer in west; uncommon summer
resident* (Apr.–Oct.) in eastern quarter, southeastern
edge of Edwards Plateau, and northeastern Panhandle;
rare winter resident (Oct.–Apr.) along coastal plain.
Range: Breeds from extreme southeastern and south-
central Canada south through eastern and southwestern U.S.; winters from central Mexico to Panama;
West Indies.

543. Varied Bunting

Passerina versicolor (L— 6 W— 8)
Blue head and rump; rose below and on back; red
nape; black face. *Winter:* Rose areas brownish. *Female
and immature male:* Grayish-brown. *Voice:* Song—
three to four weakly warbled phrases; call—"tink."
Similar species: Female Varied is the only gray Texas
bunting with unstreaked breast. *Habitat:* Riparian
thickets, thorn forest, hedgerows, oak scrub. *Texas:*
Uncommon to rare summer resident* (Apr.–Aug.)
along the Rio Grande and southern edge of Edwards
Plateau. *Range:* Breeds from U.S.–Mexico border to
Guatemala; winters in southern half of breeding
range.

544. Orange-breasted Bunting

Passerina leclancherii (L— 5 W— 8)
Sky blue above; yellow below, tinged with orange on
breast. *Female:* Greenish-gray above; yellow below.
Voice: Song—"a warbling series of tinkling musical
notes" (Edwards 1972:249). *Habitat:* Arid scrub.
Texas: Accidental in Lower Rio Grande Valley (pos-
sibly an escaped cage bird). *Range:* Southwestern
Mexico.

545. Painted Bunting

Passerina ciris (L—6 W—9)
Purple head; red underparts and rump; green back; dark wings and tail. *Female and immature male:* Bright green above, paler below; dark wings and tail. *Voice:* Song—a prolonged series of rapid warbles; call—"tsip." *Similar species:* Other female buntings are brownish or grayish, not green. *Habitat:* Riparian and thorn forest, oak woodlands, savanna, brushy pastures, hedgerows. *Texas:* Common summer resident* (Apr.–Oct.) throughout except western and northern Panhandle where rare or absent; rare winter resident (Nov.–Mar.) in Lower Rio Grande Valley. *Range:* Breeds in coastal Georgia and South Carolina, south-central U.S., and northeastern Mexico; winters from northern Mexico to western Panama; also southern Florida, Bahamas, and Cuba.

546. Dickcissel

Spiza americana (L—6 W—9)
Patterned like a miniature meadowlark—black bib (gray in winter) and yellow breast; streaked brown above; grayish head with creamy eyebrow; rusty red wing patch. *Female and immature male:* Patterned like male but paler yellow below and without black bib. *Voice:* Song—a dry "chik sizzzle"; also a "brrrzeet" given in flight. *Similar species:* Pale females and immatures resemble House Sparrow female but usually have traces of yellow on pale white (not dirty white) breast, a clear, whitish or yellowish eyebrow, and some chestnut on shoulder. *Habitat:* Prairies, savannas, agricultural fields. *Texas:* Common to uncommon summer resident* (Apr.–Oct.) over most of state, rare in Trans-Pecos; rare in winter along coast. *Range:* Breeds across eastern and central U.S. and south-central Canada; winters mainly in northern South America.

547. Olive Sparrow

Arremonops rufivirgatus (L—6 W—9)
Olive above; buff below with rufous stripes on crown; a touch of yellow at bend of wing. *Voice:* Song—an accelerating series of "chip"s; call—"tsee." *Similar species:* Green-tailed Towhee has whitish throat with black whiskers and solid brownish or rusty crown; Olive Sparrow has grayish median crown stripe and grayish throat with no well-defined black whiskers; Canyon Towhee has brown crown and grayish throat

with dark streaks. *Habitat:* Thorn forest. *Texas:* Common permanent resident* in South Texas. *Range:* South Texas, lowlands of Mexico and Central America to northern Costa Rica.

548. Green-tailed Towhee

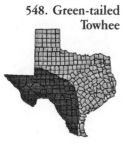

Pipilo chlorurus (L—7 W—10)
Green above; gray below; rufous crown; white throat; long, rounded tail. *Habits:* Like other towhees, this bird spends most of its time on the ground using backward kick-hops to scatter duff and expose seeds and invertebrate prey. *Voice:* Song—opens with a few melodic whistles followed by a dry trill; calls—"chink," and a nasal "eyew." *Similar species:* See Olive Sparrow. *Habitat:* Thickets in arid scrub, thorn forest, brushy pastures, hedgerows. *Texas:* Uncommon to rare winter visitor (Sept.–May) throughout except Panhandle, north-central Texas, and forests of East Texas; rare summer resident* (May–Aug.) in mountains of Trans-Pecos. *Range:* Breeds in western U.S., mostly in montane regions; winters from southern California, southern Arizona, southern New Mexico, and Texas south to central Mexico.

549. Rufous-sided Towhee

Pipilo erythrophthalmus (L—8 W—11)
Eastern race (*P. e. erythrophthalmus*): Red eye; black head, breast and back; rufous sides; white belly; tail black and rounded with white corners. *Female:* Patterned similarly but brown instead of black. *Western races:* White spotting on back and white wing bars in both sexes. *Habits:* See Green-tailed Towhee. *Voice:* Song—"drink your teeee" (eastern race); "tsip tsip tsip tseeee" and variations in western races; call—"chewink," "shrrinnk." *Habitat:* Undergrowth and thickets of deciduous woodlands; riparian, oak, and thorn forest. *Texas:* Common to uncommon winter resident over most of the state (Nov.–Mar.); common permanent resident* (western race) in Trans-Pecos. *Range:* Breeds from extreme southern Canada across U.S. (except most of Texas) and in the highlands of Mexico and Guatemala; winters in central and southern U.S., Mexico, and Guatemala.

550. Canyon Towhee

Pipilo fuscus (L—9 W—12)
Grayish-brown above; paler below; rusty crown; buffy throat with brown necklace across breast and dark brown central breast spot; rusty undertail coverts; long, rounded tail. *Habits:* See Green-tailed Towhee. *Voice:* Song—an accelerating series of "chipi"s ending in a dry trill; call—"chap." *Similar species:* See Olive Sparrow. *Habitat:* Arid scrub. *Texas:* Locally common to rare resident* in Edwards Plateau, southern Panhandle (Palo Duro Canyon), and Trans-Pecos. *Range:* Southern Oregon, California, southwestern U.S., and western and central Mexico.

551. Abert's Towhee

Pipilo aberti (L—9 W—11)
Brown above; paler below with black face; rufous undertail coverts; long, rounded tail. *Habits:* See Green-tailed Towhee. *Voice:* Song—two trills at different pitches; call—"eek." *Similar species:* Other towhees lack black face. *Habitat:* Desert riparian scrub. *Texas:* Hypothetical—collected in El Paso Co. but specimen lost. *Range:* Southern California, southern Nevada, Arizona, extreme northwestern Mexico, and southwestern New Mexico.

552. White-collared Seedeater

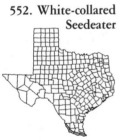

Sporophila torqueola (L—5 W—7)
Brown above; buffy below; white to buffy collar; two white wing bars—plumage characters variable. *Female:* Brown above; buffy below with buffy wing bars; tiny size (smaller than Chipping Sparrow), buffy eyering and thick, snubbed finch bill separate this from other Texas species. *Habits:* Almost always occurs in flocks. *Voice:* Song—a strong, whistled "wee wee wee" followed by a dry trill; call—"tik." *Habitat:* Savanna, pastures, brushy fields. *Texas:* Rare (formerly common? [Oberholser 1974:880]) resident in Lower Rio Grande Valley. *Range:* Mexico through Central America to western Panama.

553. Yellow-faced Grassquit

Tiaris olivacea (L—5 W—7)
Olive body; yellow forehead, eye stripe, and throat; black bib. *Female:* Similar pattern but duller. *Voice:* Song—an insect-like buzz, "tsi-tsi-tsi-tsi-tsi"; call—"tzzip" (Peterson and Chalif 1973:241). *Habitat:* Savanna, grasslands, brushy pastures, roadsides. *Texas:* Accidental—Hidalgo Co. *Range:* Caribbean slope of Mexico (southern Tamaulipas to Yucatán), Central America, and northern South America east to Venezuela; Greater Antilles and Puerto Rico.

554. Bachman's Sparrow

Aimophila aestivalis (L—6 W—8)
Grayish streaked with brown above; pale gray below; dark malar stripe; gray cheek; central crown stripe bordered by brown. *Habits:* Secretive. *Voice:* Song—"tseeee chi chi chi," "tsoooo chew chew chew," and other variations on a similar theme. *Similar species:* Field Sparrow is more rusty with pinkish bill (brown in Bachman's); Grasshopper Sparrow is yellowish-buff with creamy central crown stripe (not gray). *Habitat:* Mature longleaf pine–palmetto savannas; open pine woods; brushy, overgrown fields. *Texas:* Uncommon permanent resident* in East Texas. *Range:* Southeastern U.S.

555. Botteri's Sparrow

Aimophila botterii (L—6 W—9)
Gray streaked with brown above; dirty white below; crown gray, finely streaked with brown. *Voice:* Song—one or two introductory "tsip" notes followed by an accelerating trill; call—a dry "tik." *Similar species:* Cassin's Sparrow has white corners at tip of tail; also Cassin's Sparrow song starts with trill and ends with lone whistle notes. *Habitat:* Cordgrass (*Spartina*) prairies, savanna, grasslands, pastures. *Texas:* Uncommon local permanent resident* in central and lower coastal counties. *Range:* Southeastern Arizona and South Texas south locally through Mexico and Central America to northwestern Costa Rica; northern populations may be migratory although nonsinging birds are extremely difficult to locate and identify. As Phillips et al. (1964:200) state, ". . . its winter range is almost wholly a matter of conjecture!"

556. Cassin's Sparrow

Aimophila cassinii (L—6 W—8)
Grayish streaked with brown above, dirty white below; white corners on rounded tail. *Voice:* Song—a tinkling trill followed by two notes, "tse-tse-tse-tse-tse chik cheek"—usually given in a flight display. *Similar species:* See Botteri's Sparrow. *Habitat:* Thorn forest, brushy fields, arid grasslands and scrub. *Texas:* Locally common summer resident* over western two-thirds; apparently withdraws from Panhandle in winter. *Range:* Breeds in dry grasslands of Great Plains from Colorado and Nebraska south to northern and central Mexico; winter distribution is poorly known, but apparently the bird migrates from northern portion of range.

557. Rufous-crowned Sparrow

Aimophila ruficeps (L—6 W—8)
Grayish streaked with brown above; dirty white below; rusty crown and dark malar stripe ("whisker"); whitish supraloral stripe. *Habits:* Not particularly secretive. *Voice:* Song—a trill; call—characteristic "teer teer teer." *Similar species:* Other rufous-capped sparrows lack black whisker. *Habitat:* Rocky, arid scrub; oak-juniper and pine-oak. *Texas:* Uncommon local permanent resident* in Edwards Plateau, southern Panhandle, and Trans-Pecos, rare in northern Panhandle and north-central Texas; rare winter resident (Nov.–Apr.) in rocky, arid portions of South Texas. *Range:* Southwestern and south-central U.S. to southern Mexico; apparently migratory in northeastern portions of range.

558. American Tree Sparrow

Spizella arborea (L—6 W—9)
Streaked brownish above; dingy white below with dark breast spot; rufous crown; two white wing bars. *Voice:* Song—a rapid, high-pitched series of notes, "tse tse tse tsetl tse" and similar variations; call—"tsetl-de." *Similar species:* This is the largest rufous-capped sparrow, and the only one with a dark spot on an unstreaked breast. *Habitat:* Weedy fields, overgrown pastures, prairies. *Texas:* Uncommon to rare and irregular winter visitor (Nov.–Feb.) in northern third; scattered records elsewhere. *Range:* Breeds in bog, tundra, and willow thickets of northern North America; winters in southern Canada, northern and central U.S.

559. Chipping Sparrow

Spizella passerina (L— 5 W— 8)
A small sparrow; streaked rusty brown above; dingy white below; two white wing bars; rufous cap (somewhat streaked in winter); white eyebrow; black eyeline. *Immature:* Streaked crown; gray or buffy eyebrow; brown cheek patch. *Voice:* Song—a rapid, metallic trill; call—"tsip." *Similar species:* Adult facial pattern is distinctive; immature is similar to Clay-colored Sparrow but has grayish rather than buffy rump, and is gray (not buffy) below. *Habitat:* Open pine, pine-oak, and oak woodlands; orchards, parks, suburbs and cemeteries with scattered coniferous trees. *Texas:* Locally common permanent resident* in Trans-Pecos, Edwards Plateau, and East Texas; common winter resident (Nov.–Apr.) in most other parts of state (except Panhandle where scarce). *Range:* Breeds over most of North America south of the tundra, south through Mexico and Central America to Nicaragua; winters along coast and in southern portions of breeding range.

560. Clay-colored Sparrow

Spizella pallida (L— 5 W— 8)
Streaked brown above; buffy below; streaked crown with central gray stripe; grayish eyebrow; buffy cheek patch outlined in dark brown; gray nape; two white wing bars. *Immature:* Buffier throughout. *Voice:* Song—a buzzy "zee zee zee," the number and speed of the zees varying; call—"sip." *Similar species:* See Chipping Sparrow. *Habitat:* Dry grasslands, savanna, dry thorn forest, low, brushy pastures. *Texas:* Locally common winter resident (Nov.–Apr.) over western two-thirds except Panhandle where it occurs only as a transient (Apr.–May, Oct.–Nov.); rare transient in eastern quarter. *Range:* Breeds in central Canada and north-central U.S.; winters from Texas south through the highlands of central Mexico to Guatemala.

561. Brewer's Sparrow

Spizella breweri (L— 6 W— 8)
Streaked brownish above; buff below; crown buff finely streaked with dark brown; buffy eyebrow; white eyering; tawny cheek patch; buffy rump; two buffy wing bars. *Voice:* Song—trills at different pitches; call—"chip." *Similar species:* White eyering and finely streaked crown (no central stripe) separate this desert species from Clay-colored Sparrow and immature

Chipping Sparrow. *Habitat:* Creosote bush (*Larea*) deserts, arid scrub, dry thorn forest, sagebrush (*Artemesia*). *Texas:* Common to uncommon winter resident (Oct.–Apr.) in Trans-Pecos and western Edwards Plateau; uncommon transient (Mar.–May, Sept.–Oct.) in Panhandle, formerly bred.* *Range:* Breeds in desert regions of western North America; winters from southwestern U.S. to central Mexico.

562. Field Sparrow

Spizella pusilla (L—6 W—8)
Pink bill; streaked brown above; buff below; crown with gray central stripe bordered by rusty stripes; two white wing bars. *Voice:* Song—a series of "tew"'s, beginning slowly and accelerating to a trill; call—"tsee." *Similar species:* No other plain-breasted sparrow has pink bill. *Habitat:* Savanna, old fields, brushy pastures, thorn scrub. *Texas:* Common winter resident (Nov.–Mar.) throughout; locally common summer resident* in eastern third. *Range:* Breeds across eastern half of U.S. and southeastern Canada; winters in southern half of breeding range and into Florida, South Texas, New Mexico, and northeastern Mexico.

563. Black-chinned Sparrow

Spizella atrogularis (L—6 W—8)
Black face and throat; pink bill; gray head, breast, belly, and rump; streaked brown back. *Female and immature male:* Black face nearly or completely lacking. *Voice:* Song—a series of "tsweet"'s accelerating into a trill; call—"sip." *Similar species:* "Gray-headed" form of the Dark-eyed Junco has white outer tail feathers (dark in Black-chinned Sparrow), unstreaked back and gray (not brown) wings. *Habitat:* Montane desert scrub. *Texas:* Uncommon permanent resident* at higher elevations of Trans-Pecos. *Range:* Mountains of southwestern U.S. to western and central Mexico; northern populations (California, Arizona, New Mexico, Utah) are migratory.

564. Vesper Sparrow

Pooecetes gramineus (L— 6 W—10)
Grayish streaked with brown above; white with brown streaks below; rusty shoulder patch; white outer tail feathers; whitish or yellowish eyering. *Voice:* Song— "chew chew chew chi-chi-chi titititi," etc.; call—"chip." *Similar species:* Savannah Sparrow has yellow lores and brown (not white) outer tail feathers. *Habitat:* Shortgrass prairie, savanna, arid scrub, agricultural fields. *Texas:* Common winter resident (Oct.–Apr.) over most of state except Panhandle where found as a transient (Mar.–Apr., Oct.–Nov.); has bred* in Tom Green Co. *Range:* Breeds across much of northern North America to central U.S.; winters in southern U.S. and Mexico.

565. Lark Sparrow

Chondestes grammacus (L— 7 W—11)
Streaked brown above; dingy below; distinctive chestnut, white, and black face pattern; white throat; black breast spot; white corners on dark, rounded tail. *Voice:* Song— towhee-like with two or three whistled introductory notes followed by various trills; call—"tseek." *Habitat:* Prairie, savanna, thorn forest, agricultural fields. *Texas:* Common to uncommon permanent resident* over most of state except Panhandle where common to uncommon in summer (Mar.–Oct.) but absent in winter. *Range:* Breeds in Canadian prairie states and across most of the U.S. except eastern, forested regions, south into northern Mexico; winters from southern U.S. to southern Mexico.

566. Black-throated Sparrow

Amphispiza bilineata (L— 6 W— 9)
Dark gray above; whitish below; black throat and breast; gray and white face pattern; white outer tail feathers. *Immature:* Similar to adult but breast faintly streaked rather than black. *Voice:* Song— two introductory "weet"s followed by a trill on a different pitch. *Similar species:* Immatures can resemble Sage Sparrow but lack black breast spot. *Habitat:* Dry thorn forest, desert scrub, juniper. *Texas:* Common permanent resident* in Trans-Pecos, Edwards Plateau, parts of north-central Texas, and South Texas; rare summer resident in Panhandle (Armstrong Co.). *Range:* Breeds in western U.S. from southern Oregon, Idaho, and Wyoming south to central Mexico; winters in southern half of breeding range.

567. Sage Sparrow

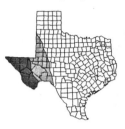

Amphispiza belli (L—6 W—10)
Grayish streaked with brown above; whitish below
with streaking on flanks; black, central, breast spot;
distinctive gray and white face pattern; black tail with
white corners. *Habits:* flicks and cocks tail; often
scurries—tail cocked—along the ground instead of
flying to cover. *Voice:* Song—a few clear, whistled
notes; first ascending, then descending. *Similar species:* See Black-throated Sparrow. *Habitat:* Desert
scrub, sagebrush (*Artemesia*), creosote bush (*Larea*),
arid grasslands. *Texas:* Uncommon to rare winter resident (Nov.–Mar.) in western quarter. *Range:* Breeds in
deserts and arid grasslands of western U.S.; winters in
southwestern U.S. and northwestern Mexico.

568. Lark Bunting

Calamospiza melanocorys (L—7 W—11)
A stocky, black finch with white wing patches; white
undertip of tail. *Female:* Streaked brown and gray
above; whitish below with brown streaks; white or
buffy wing patch and undertail tip. *Winter male:* like
female but with black chin and heavier breast streaking. *Habits:* Often in flocks. *Voice:* Song—"chik chik
chik chik tse-e-e-e-e tik-tik-tik-tik"; variable but
usually in this pattern of introductory whistles followed by a trill on a different pitch and a second trill
at a third pitch; call—"tsoo wee." *Similar species:* Immature Harris' Sparrow has pink (not brown) bill and
two white wing bars rather than a wing patch. *Habitat:* Shortgrass prairie, desert scrub, agricultural fields.
Texas: Common winter resident (Nov.–Mar.) in
western half, scarcer in east; common to uncommon
summer resident* in Panhandle. *Range:* Breeds in
Great Plains from southern Canada to northern Texas;
winters from southern Arizona, New Mexico, and
West Texas south to northern Mexico.

569. Savannah Sparrow

Passerculus sandwichensis (L—6 W—9)
Buff striped with brown above; whitish variously
streaked with brown below; yellow or yellowish lores;
whitish or yellowish eyebrow; often with dark, central
breast spot; short, notched tail. Plumage is highly
variable in amount of yellow on face and streaking on
breast according to subspecies, several of which winter
in Texas. *Habits:* Often in flocks. *Voice:* Song—a
high-pitched, insect-like "tseet tsitit tsee tsoo"; call—

"tsee." *Similar species:* See Vesper Sparrow. *Habitat:* Grasslands, savanna, pastures, agricultural fields, coastal marshes. *Texas:* Common winter resident (Nov.–Mar.) throughout except Panhandle where irregular and scarce. This is the commonest winter sparrow over most of Texas. *Range:* Breeds throughout northern half of North America south to central U.S.; also breeds in central highlands of Mexico and Guatemala; winters in coastal and southern U.S., Mexico, Guatemala, Belize, and Honduras.

570. Baird's Sparrow

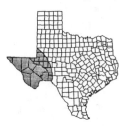

Ammodramus bairdii (L—6 W—9)
Streaked brownish above; buffy below with brown streaks across the breast forming a necklace; buffy crown and eyebrow stripes; buffy cheek patch; dark malar stripes. *Habits:* Secretive. *Voice:* Song—very high-pitched "tsit tsitleeeeeeee"; call—"tik" *Similar species:* Henslow's Sparrow has rusty (not brown) wings, and grayish-green (not buffy) head pattern. *Habitat:* Grasslands, savanna. *Texas:* Rare winter resident (Oct.–Apr.) in Trans-Pecos, western Edwards Plateau and southwestern Panhandle, scattered records elsewhere. *Range:* Breeds in northern Great Plains; winters in Texas, southern Arizona, and northwestern Mexico.

571. Grasshopper Sparrow

Ammodramus savannarum (L—5 W—8)
A stubby, short-tailed bird; streaked brown above; creamy buff below; buffy crown stripe; yellow at bend of wing; yellowish or buffy lores and eyebrow. *Voice:* Song—an insect-like "tsi-pi-ti-zzzzzzzzz"; call—a weak "kitik." *Similar species:* LeConte's Sparrow has streaking on sides, and buffy orange breast contrasting with white belly. *Habitat:* Shortgrass prairie, overgrazed pasture, savanna. *Texas:* Locally common permanent resident* in Edwards Plateau and South and north-central Texas; common to uncommon summer resident* (Apr.–Oct.) in Panhandle; uncommon to rare transient (Apr.–May, Sept.–Oct.) in Trans-Pecos. *Range:* Breeds across northern and central U.S., southern Mexico to northwestern South America, Bahamas, and Cuba; winters in southern U.S., Mexico, and elsewhere within its tropical breeding range.

Grasshopper   Baird's   Henslow's

Sharp-tailed   Seaside   LeConte's

Facial patterns of flat-headed sparrows

572. Henslow's Sparrow

Ammodramus henslowii (L—5 W—7) Streaked rusty brown above with rusty wings; buffy breast with dark streaks; whitish belly; grayish-green head with dark brown crown and malar stripes. *Voice:* Song—a high-pitched, repeated "tse-ik"; call—"tsip." *Similar species:* See Baird's Sparrow. *Habitat:* Tallgrass prairie, wet meadows, sedge marshes, weedy fields. *Texas:* Rare winter resident (Nov.–Apr.) in eastern third south to Nueces Co.; has bred* in Houston area. *Range:* Breeds in northeastern and north-central U.S. and southeastern Canada; winters in southeastern U.S.

573. LeConte's Sparrow

Ammodramus leconteii (L—5 W—7) Streaked brown above; whitish below with dark streaking on sides; whitish central crown stripe bordered by dark brown stripes; buffy yellow eyebrow stripe; gray cheek patch outlined by buffy yellow. *Voice:* Song—a high-pitched, insect-like buzz, "tsi tsi tzzzzz"; call—"tseak." *Similar species:* See Grasshopper Sparrow. Sharp-tailed Sparrow has gray nape (LeConte's is buffy). *Habitat:* Tallgrass prairies, wet meadows, salt marsh, rank fields. *Texas:* Uncommon to rare (hard to see?) winter resident (Oct.–Apr.) in eastern third. *Range:* Breeds in central Canada (British Columbia to Quebec) and extreme north-central U.S. (Montana to Michigan); winters in southeastern U.S.

574. Sharp-tailed Sparrow

Ammodramus caudacutus (L—6 W—8)
Streaked dark brown above; buffy orange breast; belly whitish; gray crown stripe bordered by dark brown crown stripes; buffy orange eyebrow; gray nape. *Voice:* Song—a hoarse, buzzy "chur-chur-aaaaa zee-zurr zee-zurr"; call—"tsuk." *Similar species:* See LeConte's Sparrow. *Habitat:* Wet grasslands, coastal and inland marshes. *Texas:* Rare transient (Oct.–Nov., Apr.–May) in eastern third; rare winter resident (Oct.–Apr.) along coast mainly north and east of Nueces Co. *Range:* Breeds in central Canada and north-central U.S. (North Dakota, Minnesota); resident population along coast of eastern Canada and northeastern U.S.; winters along coast of southeastern U.S. from North Carolina to Texas.

575. Seaside Sparrow

Ammodramus maritimus (L—6 W—8)
Yellow lores; white throat; grayish streaked with dark brown above; buffy breast and whitish belly streaked with brown; a stocky bird with longish bill and short tail. *Voice:* Song—"brrrt zee zzurr zee," reminiscent of Red-winged Blackbird; call—"kak." *Similar species:* LeConte's and Sharp-tailed sparrows lack yellow lores and clear, white throat of Seaside Sparrow. *Habitat:* Salt marshes. *Texas:* Common permanent resident* along upper and central coast, scarcer along lower coast. *Range:* Resident along coast of eastern U.S. from Massachusetts to Texas.

576. Fox Sparrow

Passerella iliaca (L—7 W—11)
Hefty, for a sparrow—nearly thrush-sized; streaked dark gray or rusty brown above; whitish below with heavy dark or rusty streakings that often coalesce as a blotch on the breast; rusty rump and tail. *Habits:* Forages in towhee fashion, jump-kicking its way through forest duff. *Voice:* Song—whistled, with long, varied phrases; call—"tshek." *Similar species:* See Song Sparrow; *Catharus* thrushes have long, pointed bills (not conical). *Habitat:* Thickets and un-

dergrowth of deciduous, mixed, and coniferous woodlands; thorn forest. *Texas:* Uncommon winter resident (Nov.-Apr.) in eastern third; rare to casual elsewhere. *Range:* Breeds across northern tier of North America and in mountains of the West; winters in coastal and southern U.S.

577. Song Sparrow

Melospiza melodia (L— 6 W— 9)
Streaked brown above; whitish below with heavy brown streaks and central breast spot; gray eyebrow; dark whisker and postorbital stripe. *Voice:* Song— "chik sik-i-sik choree k-sik-i-sik," with many variations; call—a nasal "chink." *Similar species:* Fox Sparrow head is unstriped and brownish or grayish—lacks light/dark striping of Song Sparrow. *Habitat:* Swamps, inland and coastal marshes, streamside thickets, brushy fields. *Texas:* Locally common winter resident (Oct.-Apr.) in eastern third south to Calhoun Co.; uncommon to rare elsewhere. *Range:* Breeds across temperate and boreal North America; winters in temperate breeding range, southern U.S., and northern Mexico; resident population in central Mexico.

578. Lincoln's Sparrow

Melospiza lincolnii (L— 6 W— 8)
Streaked brown above; patterned gray and brown face; white throat and belly; distinctive finely streaked, buffy breast band. *Voice:* Song—a series of brief trills at different pitches; call—"shuk." *Similar species:* Finely streaked, buffy breast band is unique. *Habitat:* Boggy thickets, riparian and oak woodlands, thorn forest, brushy fields, hedgerows. *Texas:* Common winter resident (Nov.-Apr.) in eastern half; uncommon to rare in west. *Range:* Breeds across northern tier of North America and in mountains of the West; winters in coastal and southern U.S. south through Mexico and Central America to Honduras.

579. Swamp Sparrow

Melospiza georgiana (L— 6 W— 8)
Rusty crown with central grayish stripe; gray face; streaked brown above with rusty wings; whitish throat but otherwise grayish below with tawny flanks— faintly streaked. *Voice:* Song—long "chipy-chipy-chipy" trills at various pitches and speeds; call— "chip." *Similar species:* Only the Swamp and Rufous-

crowned among rusty-crowned sparrows lack white wing bars. Rufous-crowned Sparrow, which lacks rusty wings and faint breast streaking of Swamp Sparrow, lives in desert scrub. *Habitat:* Bogs, coastal and inland marshes, wet grasslands, brushy pastures. *Texas:* Common winter resident (Nov.–Apr.) in eastern third; uncommon to rare in west—absent from Panhandle and western Trans-Pecos. *Range:* Breeds in central and eastern Canada and north central and northeastern U.S.; winters in eastern and south-central U.S. south to east and central Mexico.

580. White-throated Sparrow

Zonotrichia albicollis (L—7 W—9)
White throat; alternating black and white (or black and buff) crown stripes; yellow lores; streaked brown above; grayish below. *Voice:* Song—a thin, wavering whistle often heard in March thickets, "poor sam peabody peabody"; call—"seet." *Habitat:* Woodland thickets, brushy fields. *Texas:* Common winter resident (Dec.–Mar.) in eastern third; rare to casual in west. *Range:* Breeds across most of boreal Canada and northeastern and north-central U.S.; winters in eastern and southern U.S. and northern Mexico.

581. Golden-crowned Sparrow

Zonotrichia atricapilla (L—7 W—10)
Yellow crown bordered by blackish stripes; streaked gray and brown above; dingy white below; two white wing bars. *Immature:* Yellow crown somewhat dingy. *Voice:* Song—a whistled "oh dear" or "oh dear me"; call—"zink." *Habitat:* Bogs, thickets, scrub, brushy pastures and fields. *Texas:* Casual in winter (Oct.–Mar.), mainly in Panhandle. *Range:* Breeds along western coastal regions of Alaska and Canada; winters along western coastal areas of U.S.

582. White-crowned Sparrow

Zonotrichia leucophrys (L—7 W—10)
Black and white striped crown; gray neck, breast, and belly; streaked gray and brown back; pinkish bill. *Immature:* Crown stripes are brown and gray. *Voice:* Song—"tsee tsee tsee zzeech-i chi-i-i"; call—"chip." *Similar species:* White-throated Sparrow is also a large, plain-breasted, striped-crowned sparrow, but it has a white throat and yellow lores. *Habitat:* Thickets in coniferous and deciduous woodlands, brushy fields,

thorn forest. *Texas:* Common to uncommon winter resident (Nov.–Mar.) in western two-thirds, uncommon to rare in eastern third. *Range:* Breeds in northern and western North America; winters across most of U.S. south to central Mexico.

583. Harris' Sparrow

Zonotrichia querula (L–8 W–11)
A large sparrow with black breast, throat, and crown (gray cast in winter); gray face with black ear patch; pink bill; streaked brown and gray on back; white belly with black flanks. *Immature:* Crown mottled, throat white with dark malar stripe. *Voice:* Song–a clear, whistled "see see see" repeated at different pitches; also some "chipy" notes; call–"chik." *Similar species:* Immatures of other *Zonotrichia* sparrows lack black on breast. *Habitat:* Scrub, undergrowth in open woodlands and savanna, thickets, brushy fields, hedgerows. *Texas:* Common winter resident in northeastern and Central Texas; rare and irregular elsewhere. *Range:* Breeds in tundra of north-central Canada; winters in central and southern Great Plains of U.S.

584. Dark-eyed Junco

Junco hyemalis (L–6 W–10)
This species consists of three well-marked groups, formerly considered separate species, in which the plumage is quite distinct. *"Slate-colored" group:* Male is entirely dark gray except for white belly and outer tail feathers, and pinkish bill; the female is similar but brownish rather than gray. *"Oregon" group:* Male has black head, brown back and sides, gray rump, and white belly and outer tail feathers; the female is similar but has a grayish head. *"Gray-headed" group:* Gray head and underparts; black lores; brown back; white outer tail feathers. *Voice:* Song–"zrrr chipipipi-pipi tseee"; call–"tsik." *Habitat:* Open woodlands, grasslands, agricultural fields. *Texas:* Juncos are winter residents (Dec.–Apr.) in Texas: the Slate-colored form is common in the northeast, uncommon to rare elsewhere; the Oregon form is uncommon in Central and West Texas; the Gray-headed form is uncommon to rare in West Texas. *Range:* Breeds across northern North America and in eastern and western U.S. in the mountains; winters from southern Canada south through U.S. to northern Mexico.

585. Yellow-eyed Junco

Junco phaeonotus (L—6 W—9)
Yellow eye set off by gray head and black lores; brown back; grayish-white below; gray rump; white outer tail feathers. *Voice:* Song—three or four whistled, repeated phrases; call—"tsip." *Similar species:* Gray-headed form of Dark-eyed Junco has a black eye. *Habitat:* Montane fir, pine, and pine-oak forest. *Texas:* Casual in mountains of Trans-Pecos. *Range:* Montane forest from southern Arizona south through highlands of Mexico to western Guatemala.

586. McCown's Longspur

Calcarius mccownii (L—6 W—11)
Black cap, whisker, and breast; white throat and belly; streaked brown above; chestnut wing patch; tail black in center and at tip, the rest white. *Winter male and female:* Brown rather than black cap, whisker, and breast. *Voice:* Song—a long, wandering series of warbles, given in flight; call—a short, metallic "ti-ti-ti-ti." *Similar species:* Large amount of white on base and sides of tail distinguish winter birds from Lapland and Smith's longspurs; chestnut wing patch of McCown's separates it from the Chestnut-collared Longspur; beak is larger and tail is shorter than in other longspurs. *Habitat:* Shortgrass prairie, plowed fields. *Texas:* Common winter resident (Oct.–Apr.) in Panhandle, rare to casual elsewhere; formerly more common throughout. *Range:* Breeds in northern and central Great Plains from southern Canada to Nebraska; winters in Kansas, Oklahoma, Texas, southern New Mexico, southern Arizona, and northwestern Mexico.

587. Lapland Longspur

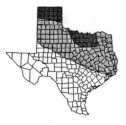

Calcarius lapponicus (L—6 W—11)
Black head and breast with white or buff face pattern; rusty nape; streaked brown above; white belly; tail is all dark except for outermost tail feathers. *Winter male and female:* Brownish crown; buffy eyebrow, nape, and throat with darker brown mottlings on breast and flanks; buffy cheek outlined by darker brown. *Voice:* Song—short phrases of squeaky, slurred notes, given in flight; call—"tseeu." *Similar species:* Mostly dark tail with white edgings distinguishes this bird from Chestnut-collared and McCown's longspurs; Smith's Longspur is uniformly buffy below, not white with streaks. *Habitat:* Shortgrass prairie, plowed

fields, overgrazed pasture. *Texas:* Common to uncommon and irregular winter visitor (Nov.–Feb.) in northern Panhandle and East Texas south to Harris Co. *Range:* Breeds in tundra of extreme northern North America and Eurasia; winters in temperate regions of Old and New World.

588. Smith's Longspur

Calcarius pictus (L—7 W—11)
Bold black and white face pattern; buffy nape and underparts; back streaked with brown and buff; white wing patch; tail dark with white outer feathers. *Winter male and female:* Streaked brownish above; buffy below; brown streaked crown; buffy eyebrow and brown cheek patch; white wing patch shows in some males. *Voice:* Song—a series of high-pitched, squeaky and buzzy notes and "brrreooo" trills; call—a dry "titititit." *Similar species:* See McCown's Longspur. *Habitat:* Shortgrass prairie, overgrazed pasture, plowed fields. *Texas:* Rare winter resident (Nov.–Apr.) in northeast corner west to Dallas. *Range:* Breeds in tundra of northernmost North America; winters in central Great Plains from Nebraska to Texas.

589. Chestnut-collared Longspur

Calcarius ornatus (L—6 W—11)
Black and white face pattern; chestnut nape; yellow throat; black breast and flanks; white belly; base and sides of tail white; center and tip of tail dark. *Winter male and female:* Streaked brown above and on crown; buffy below with various amounts of black on breast; male often has black and white shoulder patch. *Voice:* Song—"tsee tseeoo tseeoo tsee" and similar squeaky phrases, repeated; call "chi-pl." *Similar species:* See McCown's Longspur. *Habitat:* Shortgrass prairie, plowed fields, overgrazed pasture. *Texas:* Irregularly common to rare winter resident (Oct.–Apr.) in northern and western portions, scarcer south and east. *Range:* Breeds in Great Plains of south-central Canada and north-central U.S.; winters in south-central and southwestern U.S. and northwestern Mexico.

590. Snow Bunting

Plectrophenax nivalis (L—7 W—11)
White head, rump, and underparts; black back; wings white with black primaries. *Winter male and female:* White is tinged with buff and dark back is mottled with white. *Voice:* Song—repeated musical, whistled "tsee tsee chewee," and similar phrases; flight call—"tseoo." *Habitat:* Shortgrass prairie, fields, pastures, agricultural areas. *Texas:* Casual in winter in northern half. *Range:* Breeds circumpolar in tundra; winters in southern boreal and northern temperate regions of Old and New World.

591. Bobolink

Dolichonyx oryzivorus (L—7 W—12)
Black with creamy nape; white rump and shoulder patch. *Winter male and female:* Streaked brown and yellow buff above; yellow-buff below; crown with central buff stripe bordered by dark brown stripes; buff eyebrow. *Voice:* Song—twittering, bubbling series of squeaks, "cherk"s, ink"s, along with a few "bob-o-link"s and other, similar phrases thrown in, given in flight; call—"tink." *Similar species:* Blackbird size and bill separate this bird from sparrows and buntings. *Habitat:* Tallgrass prairie, grain and hay fields, brushy pastures, savanna, rice paddies. *Texas:* Rare spring transient (May) in eastern third. *Range:* Breeds in northern U.S. and southern Canada; winters in South America.

592. Red-winged Blackbird

Agelaius phoeniceus (L—8 W—14)
Entirely black; red epaulets bordered in orange. *Female and immature male:* Dark brown above, whitish below heavily streaked with dark brown; whitish eyebrow and malar stripes. *Second-year male:* Intermediate between female and male—black blotching, some orange on epaulet. *Voice:* Song—"konk-ka-ree"; call—a harsh "shek." *Similar species:* Blackbird size and bill separate females from female Purple and House finches, which are also heavily streaked. *Habitat:* Inland and coastal marshes, brushy fields, tallgrass prairie, grain and hay fields. *Texas:* Common permanent resident* throughout except Trans-Pecos where uncommon; numbers greatly increase in winter with arrival of migrants. *Range:* Breeds nearly throughout North America from the arctic circle south to Costa Rica; winters from temperate portions

of breeding range southward; resident populations in Bahamas and Cuba.

593. Eastern Meadowlark

Sturnella magna (L—10 W—15)
Streaked brown and white above; yellow below with a black or brownish "V" on the breast; crown striped with buff and dark brown; tail is dark in center, white on outer edges. *Voice:* Song—"see-ur see-ur," the second phrase at a lower pitch than the first; call—a rattling, harsh "ka-kak-kak-kak-kak." *Similar species:* Western Meadowlark is paler on the back; malar stripe is white in Eastern, yellow in Western. *Habitat:* Tallgrass prairie, savanna, grain and hay fields, overgrown pastures. *Texas:* Common summer resident* (Apr.–Aug.) over most of state (but only in mountains of Trans-Pecos, scarce inland in South Texas, and absent from western Panhandle); common winter resident (Sept.–Mar.) in eastern third, uncommon to rare in western two-thirds. *Range:* Breeds in southeastern Canada and east and south U.S. west to Arizona; Mexico through central and northern South America; Cuba; winters through most of breeding range except northernmost portions.

594. Western Meadowlark

Sturnella neglecta (L—10 W—15)
See Eastern Meadowlark. *Voice:* Song—"tsee chertelee chi chor," very different from the plaintive Eastern Meadowlark song; rattle given in flight is similar to that of Eastern Meadowlark. *Similar species:* See Eastern Meadowlark. *Habitat:* Shortgrass prairie, overgrazed pasture, savanna. *Texas:* Common summer resident* (Apr.–Sept.) in northwestern portion of state; common winter resident (Oct.–Apr.) nearly throughout except eastern quarter. *Range:* Breeds across southwestern and south-central Canada in prairies, and all except eastern third of U.S., south to central Mexico; winters in southern half of breeding range.

595. Yellow-headed Blackbird

Xanthocephalus xanthocephalus (L−10 W−16)
Black body with yellow head and breast; white wing patch. *Female and immature male:* Brown body; yellowish breast and throat; yellowish eyebrow. *Voice:* Song−"like a buzz saw biting a hard log" (Edwards in Oberholser 1974:808); call−a croak. *Similar species:* Female could be confused with female Boat- or Great-tailed grackle but Yellow-headed Blackbird has short, square tail (not long and wedge-shaped), and is usually yellowish, not buff, on breast. *Habitat:* Marshes, brushy pastures, agricultural fields. Favorite sites for these and several other blackbird species are cattle feedlots and grain elevators. *Texas:* Uncommon transient (May, Sept.) in western two-thirds, rare in east. *Range:* Breeds in south-central and southwestern Canada, north-central and northwestern U.S.; winters southern California, Arizona, and New Mexico south to central Mexico.

596. Rusty Blackbird

Euphagus carolinus (L−9 W−14)
Entirely black with creamy yellow eye. *Breeding female:* Grayer. *Winter male:* Black tinged with rusty; often shows a buffy eyebrow. *Winter female:* Rusty above; buffy below; prominent buffy eyebrow. *Voice:* Song−"curtl seee," repeated; call−"chik." *Similar species:* Prominent creamy eye separates this bird from female Brewer's Blackbird. The few fall male Brewer's that show some rusty are black (not rusty as in Rusty Blackbird) along the trailing edge (tertials) of the wing. *Habitat:* Deciduous and coniferous forests, marshes. *Texas:* Uncommon to rare winter resident (Nov.–Mar.) in eastern third south to Nueces Co. *Range:* Breeds in boreal coniferous forest and bogs across the northern tier of North America; winters in eastern U.S.

597. Brewer's Blackbird

Euphagus cyanocephalus (L−9 W−15)
Entirely black; purplish gloss on head (in proper light); yellow eye; some fall males are tinged rusty. *Female:* Dark brown above; dark brown eye; slightly paler below. *Voice:* Song−"chik-a-chik-a perzee chik-a-chik-a perzee," etc.; call−"chik." *Similar species:* See Rusty Blackbird; female resembles the smaller, female Brown-headed Cowbird, which is buffy below with faint gray streaking; all black males resemble

Bronzed Cowbirds but creamy eye (not orange-brown) is diagnostic. *Habitat:* Prairies, pastures, agricultural fields, feedlots, grain elevators. *Texas:* Common winter resident (Nov.–Mar.) throughout; has bred* (Wilbarger Co.). *Range:* Breeds in western and central U.S. and Canada; winters in southwestern Canada and western U.S. breeding range and southern U.S. south to central Mexico.

598. Great-tailed Grackle

Quiscalus mexicanus (Male L–18 W–24; Female L–14 W–18)
Entirely black; purplish gloss on head (in proper light); tail wedge-shaped and longer than body; creamy eye. *Female:* Brown above; paler below; buffy eyebrow; creamy eye; wedge-shaped tail not as long as male's. *Voice:* Song–"kak kak kak kak weeeooo weeeooo kik kik kik" with numerous variations, given by males while fluffing out and waving wings at a display perch; calls–several different ones including a strident "cheak" familiar to those with homes near their large roosts. *Similar species:* The Boat-tailed Grackle is very similar but has a brownish eye (in Texas). The two species overlap along the upper Texas coast. *Habitat:* Marshes, agricultural areas, roadsides, urban areas, pastures. *Texas:* Common permanent resident* in eastern third and South Texas (northern populations are partially migratory); locally common to rare summer resident* in northwestern portions–apparently increasing. *Range:* Southwestern U.S. south through Mexico and Central America to northern South America.

599. Boat-tailed Grackle

Quiscalus major (Male L–17 W–23;Female L–13 W–18)
Entirely black; purplish gloss on head (in proper light); tail wedge-shaped and longer than body; brown eye in Texas populations (creamy eye in Atlantic populations). *Female:* Brown above, paler below; buffy eyebrow; brown eye; wedge-shaped tail not as long as male's. *Voice:* Song–a series of harsh "eeek"s, "aaahhk"s, and similar squawks–very different from Great-tailed; calls–varied "chak"s and "cluk"s. *Similar species:* See Great-tailed Grackle. *Habitat:* Coastal marshes. *Texas:* Common permanent resident* along upper coast south to Calhoun Co. *Range:* Coastal eastern U.S. from New York to Texas.

600. Common Grackle

Quiscalus quiscula (L—12 W—17)
Entirely black; bronze gloss on head in proper light (purple-headed eastern form is casual in Texas); tail long and rounded; creamy eye. *Female:* Dull black; whitish eye; tail not as long as male's. *Voice:* Song—a repeated squeak, like a rusty hinge, with "chek"s interspersed; call—"chek." *Similar species:* Cowbirds and blackbirds have short, square tails. *Habitat:* Open woodlands, urban areas, agricultural fields, pastures. *Texas:* Common permanent resident* in northeastern portion west to Dallas and south to Calhoun Co.; uncommon summer resident* (Apr.–Sept.) in Panhandle; uncommon to rare and irregular in winter in south and west except Trans-Pecos where absent. *Range:* Breeds east of the Rockies in Canada and U.S.; winters in southern half of breeding range.

601. Bronzed Cowbird

Molothrus aeneus (L—9 W—14)
Entirely black with bronzy sheen in proper light; eye is red during the breeding season, orange-brown in winter; neck ruff gives male a hunch-backed appearance. *Female:* Dull black; orange-brown eye; little or no neck ruff. *Habits:* Male hovers in front of perched female as part of breeding display. Like the Brown-headed Cowbird, this species is a social parasite, laying its eggs in the nests of other species. *Voice:* Song—a squeaky, bubbly "gurgl eeee"; call—"shek." *Similar species:* See Brewer's Blackbird. *Habitat:* Thorn forest, savanna, agricultural fields, urban areas. feedlots, grain elevators. *Texas:* Common permanent resident* in South Texas, rare along Rio Grande in Trans-Pecos and in Edwards Plateau; uncommon to rare winter resident (Sept.–Mar.) along upper coast. *Range:* Borderlands of southwestern U.S. (isolated population in Louisiana) south through Mexico and Central America to central Panama.

602. Brown-headed Cowbird

Molothrus ater (L—7 W—13)
Black body; brown head. *Female:* Brown above; paler below with grayish streakings. *Habits:* A social parasite, laying its eggs in other birds' nests. *Voice:* Song—a series of high-pitched whistles ("tseee"), guttural chatters, and rising squeaks; call—"chek." *Similar species:* See Brewer's Blackbird. *Habitat:* Prairie, savanna, pastures, agricultural fields, feedlots, grain

elevators. *Texas:* Common permanent resident*
throughout; migrants from the north swell numbers
in winter. *Range:* Breeds across most of North
America south of the arctic south to central Mexico;
winters in southern half of breeding range.

**603. Black-vented
Oriole**

Icterus wagleri (L— 8 W—13)
Entirely black except for bright orange rump, belly,
and wing patch. *Immature:* Brownish above; orange-
yellow below with varying amounts of black on breast
and throat; orange wing patch. *Voice:* "Song, a complex rather rapid series of about a half-dozen notes. . . .
Call-note, a rather nasal, weak *rank*" (Edwards 1972:
228). *Similar species:* No other orange Texas oriole
lacks white on wing. *Habitat:* Thorn forest, pine-oak,
arid scrub, hedgerows. *Texas:* Accidental—Brewster,
Kleberg cos. *Range:* Western and central Mexico
south in dry highlands to Nicaragua.

604. Orchard Oriole

Icterus spurius (L— 7 W—10)
Black hood, wings, and tail; bright chestnut belly,
wing patch, lower back, and rump. *Female:* Greenish-
yellow above; yellow below with two white wing bars;
blue-gray legs. *Second-year male:* Like female but
with black throat and breast. *Voice:* Song—"tsee tso
tsee tsoo tewit tewit tewit tseerr" and similar wandering twitters; call—"kuk." *Similar species:* Female
Scott's Oriole has dark streaking on crown and back;
female Western Tenager has stubby bill (not long and
pointed) and dark legs (not blue-gray). *Habitat:* Savanna, open woodlands, orchards, brushy pastures.
Texas: Common summer resident* (Apr.–Sept.) in
East and Central Texas, uncommon to rare elsewhere;
common transient (Apr.–May, Aug.–Sept.) over
eastern two-thirds. *Range:* Breeds across eastern and
central U.S. south into central Mexico; winters from
central Mexico to northern South America.

605. Hooded Oriole

Icterus cucullatus (L—8 W—11)
Orange head, belly and rump; black face, throat, and center of breast; black upper back and tail; wings black with white wing bars and primary edgings. *Female:* Brownish-orange above; buffy orange below; white wing bars and primary edgings. *Immature male:* Like female but with black throat and upper breast. *Voice:* Song—a catbird-like series of rapidly warbled notes interspersed with harsher notes and trills; call—"cheek." *Similar species:* Grackle-sized Altamira Oriole has orange shoulder patch; female Bullock's form of Northern Oriole has pale belly (orange-yellow in Hooded). *Habitat:* Thorn forest, oak mottes, riparian forest, palms. *Texas:* Locally common summer resident* (Mar.–Oct.) along the coastal plain north to Kleberg Co. and along the Rio Grande west to Brewster Co. *Range:* Breeds from southwestern U.S. south to southern Mexico; winters in western, central, and southern Mexico.

606. Altamira Oriole

Icterus gularis (L—10 W—14)
Orange head, belly, and rump; black face, throat, and center of breast; black upper back and tail; wings black with orange shoulder patch and white wing bars and primary edgings. *Immature:* Brownish above; yellowish or orange-yellow below; blackish throat; yellowish rump; white wing bars. *Voice:* Song—composed of clear, individually whistled notes, varying in pitch; call—a whiney, jay-like "ehh ehh." *Similar species:* See Hooded Oriole. *Habitat:* Riparian and thorn forest, second growth, open woodlands. *Texas:* Common permanent resident* along the Rio Grande from the coast to Zapata Co. *Range:* South Texas, eastern and central Mexico south to Nicaragua.

607. Audubon's Oriole

Icterus graduacauda (L—10 W—13)
Body yellow; black hood, tail, and wings; yellow shoulder patch; wedge-shaped tail. *Voice:* Song—repeated, down-slurred whistles, each at a slightly different pitch. *Similar species:* Scott's Oriole has black back (not yellowish-green). *Habitat:* Thorn and riparian forest, pine-oak woodlands. *Texas:* Uncommon resident* in South Texas north to Nueces and Webb cos.; rare and local north to Kinney and Bee cos. *Range:* South Texas to southern Mexico.

608. Northern Oriole

Icterus galbula (L—8 W—12)
Formerly considered two species. *Eastern form* (Baltimore Oriole): Black hood, back, and wings; tail black at base and center but outer terminal portions orange; orange belly, rump, and shoulder patch. *Female and immature:* Orange-brown above; yellow-orange below; varying amounts of black on face and throat; white wing bars. *Western form* (Bullock's Oriole): Like eastern male but with orange cheeks and eyebrow; white shoulder patch. *Female and immature:* Like female eastern form but olive above and yellowish, not orange, below; whitish belly. *Voice:* Eastern form song—slurred, rapid series of easily imitated whistles; call—a chatter; also, "wheweee." Western form song—a sibilant "sip-pit ip-pert-seee-per-sip-pit-ip-pert-sip" with many variations; call—"tseeip." *Similar species:* The only other Texas oriole that has black on the crown is the accidental Black-vented Oriole, which has no white on wings; see Hooded Oriole. *Habitat:* Deciduous and thorn forest, oak woodlands, hedgerows, second growth. *Texas:* Eastern form—common transient (Apr.–May, Sept.–Oct.) in eastern half; uncommon and local summer* resident in northeastern portion and eastern third of Panhandle. Western form—Common transient (Apr.–May, Sept.–Oct.) through all but eastern quarter; locally common to rare summer resident* in western two-thirds; rare winter resident mainly along lower coast. *Range:* Breeds across U.S. and southern Canada south to northwestern and north-central Mexico; winters from northern Mexico to Guatemala; also in Greater Antilles.

609. Scott's Oriole

Icterus parisorum (L—9 W—13)
Body yellow; black hood extending to middle of back; tail and wings black; yellow shoulder patch; wedge-shaped tail. *Female and immature:* Streaked brownish and yellow on crown and back; yellowish below with various amounts of black on face, throat, and breast; white wing bars. *Voice:* Song—a whistled "chi-per-ti chi-per-ti cheep per-ti per-ti," etc.; call—"chek." *Similar species:* See Audubon's Oriole. *Habitat:* Desert scrub, oak chaparral, pinyon-juniper. *Texas:* Locally common summer resident* (Apr.–Oct.) in Trans-Pecos and southwestern Edwards Plateau, scarcer east to Comal Co. *Range:* Breeds from borderlands of

southwestern U.S. south to west-central Mexico; winters in southern portions of breeding range.

Family Fringillidae
Old World Finches

Small to medium-sized seedeaters with large, strong, conical bills. Many species are gregarious during the nonbreeding season, moving in large, vocal groups from one weed patch to the next with a characteristic, undulating flight.

610. Pine Grosbeak

Pinicola enucleator (L—9 W—14)
Rosy head, breast, and rump; gray flanks and belly; black back, wings, and tail; white wing bars; heavy, black grosbeak bill. *Female:* Gray body; head tinged with yellow; white line under eye; white wing bars. *Voice:* Song—a weak twitter, rising and falling; call—a faint "che chu." *Habitat:* Coniferous forest. *Texas:* Casual winter visitor to Panhandle, north-central Texas, and Trans-Pecos. *Range:* Breeds in boreal forest of Old and New Worlds, south to New Mexico in Rockies; winters in southern portions of breeding range south into northern temperate regions of Old and New World.

611. Purple Finch

Carpodacus purpureus (L—6 W—10)
Rosy head and breast; whitish belly; brown above suffused with rose; rose rump. *Female and immature male:* Brown above; white below heavily streaked with brown; brown head with white eyebrow and malar stripes. *Voice:* Song—a rapid, tumbling series of slurred notes and trills; flight call "chit." *Similar species:* See Cassin's Finch. *Habitat:* Coniferous forest, pine-oak and, occasionally, open deciduous woodlands. *Texas:* Uncommon visitor (Nov.–Apr.) in eastern third west to Wichita Co. and south to Calhoun Co., scarcer elsewhere. *Range:* Breeds across Canada, northern borderlands and western mountains of U.S. south into Baja California; winters throughout U.S. except Great Plains and western deserts.

612. Cassin's Finch

Carpodacus cassinii (L−7 W−11)
Brown above; red cap; rosy throat and breast; white belly with brown streaking on flanks. *Female and immature:* Brown above; buffy below with fine, brownish streaks; buffy postocular stripe. *Voice:* Song−a rapid series of twitters and squeaks; flight call−"keeyip." *Similar species:* Cassin's Finch has brown streaked undertail coverts and notched tail while Purple Finch has white undertail coverts and square tail (both sexes). House Finch male has brown (not red) cap; female has buffy postocular stripe while female House Finch has buffy preocular stripe or none. *Habitat:* Pine and pine-oak woodlands. *Texas:* Uncommon to rare winter visitor (Nov.–Mar.) in western third. *Range:* Resident in western mountains of North America from British Columbia to New Mexico; winters in southwestern and northwestern Mexico.

613. House Finch

Carpodacus mexicanus (L−6 W−10)
Brown above with red brow stripe; brown cheeks; rosy breast; whitish streaked with brown below. *Female and immature:* Brown above; buffy head and underparts finely streaked with brown; buffy preorbital stripe in some. *Voice:* Song−a very rapid twitter; call−a nasal "wink." *Similar species:* See Cassin's Finch. *Habitat:* Thorn forest, arid scrub, pine-oak, agricultural and urban areas. *Texas:* Common to uncommon permanent resident* in western two-thirds. *Range:* Resident in southwestern Canada and throughout much of U.S. except Great Plains, south to southern Mexico.

614. Red Crossbill

Loxia curvirostra (L−7 W−11)
Red with dark wings and tail; crossed bill. *Female and immature:* Yellowish body; dark wings and tail. *Voice:* Song−two-note "tsoo tee" repeated three or four times followed by a trill; call−repeated "kip" notes in flight. *Similar species:* Both sexes of White-winged Crossbill have broad, white wing bars. *Habitat:* Coniferous and mixed forest. *Texas:* Rare and irregular winter visitor across state; rare and irregular summer resident* in Guadalupe Mountains of Trans-Pecos. *Range:* Resident in boreal regions of Old and New World, south in the mountains of the West through Mexico and the highlands of Central America to

Nicaragua; winters in breeding range and irregularly south in northern temperate regions of the world.

615. White-winged Crossbill

Loxia leucoptera (L—7 W—11)
Rosy red body with dark band across back; black tail and wings with broad white wing bars; crossed bill. *Female and immature:* Brown tinged with yellow above; yellowish below; dark wings with white wing bars. *Voice:* Song—trilled phrases at various speeds and pitches; call—a raspy "chri-chri-chri-chri." *Similar species:* See Red Crossbill. *Habitat:* Coniferous and mixed forest. *Texas:* Casual—records from Lubbock and Amarillo. *Range:* Resident in boreal northern tier of North America ranging south in winter into northern temperate zone.

616. Common Redpoll

Carduelis flammea (L—5 W—9)
Front half of crown red; back of head and back streaked brown and white; black throat; white below tinged with rose on breast and flanks; brown streaks on flanks. *Female:* Like male but with little or no rose on breast. *Voice:* Song—a series of chips, churrs, and buzzy trills with whiney "tsewee" calls thrown in. *Similar species:* Hoary Redpoll is much paler with faint or no streaking below. *Habitat:* Tundra, agricultural fields, brushy pastures. *Texas:* Casual in winter (Nov.–Feb.) in Panhandle. *Range:* Breeds in the high arctic of both Old and New World; winters in boreal and northern temperate regions.

617. Pine Siskin

Carduelis pinus (L—5 W—9)
Streaked brown above; whitish below with brown streaks; yellow wing patch and at base of tail. *Voice:* Song—a sequence of "chipy chipy" notes interspersed with raspy, rising "zeeeech" calls. *Habitat:* Coniferous and mixed forest, riparian and oak woodlands, savanna. *Texas:* Irregular winter visitor (Nov.–Mar.) nearly throughout the state but mainly in northern two-thirds, common some years, absent others; rare and irregular summer resident* (May–July) in mountains of Trans-Pecos. *Range:* Breeds in boreal regions of northern North America and in western mountains south through the U.S. and highlands of Mexico to

Veracruz; winters in all except extreme north of breeding range and in most of temperate U.S.

618. Lesser Goldfinch

Carduelis psaltria (L— 5 W— 8)
Black above; yellow below; white patches on black primaries. *Female and immature:* Greenish above; yellow below; dark wings with white patches on primaries. *Voice:* Song— a long sequence of twitters, buzzes, and jeers; calls—"tseoo," also "tsoodoo." *Similar species:* American Goldfinch female is normally more brownish than green above and more whitish than yellow below; female Lesser normally has yellow undertail coverts (white in American Goldfinch). *Habitat:* Thorn forest, arid scrub, oak-juniper and pine-oak woodlands. *Texas:* Common to uncommon summer resident* in Trans-Pecos, southern Panhandle and Edwards Plateau, rare in Palo Duro Canyon region of Panhandle; uncommon and local permanent resident* in western portions of South Texas— east to the coast in Kenedy and Willacy cos., scarcer north and eastward. *Range:* Breeds in southwestern U.S. and Mexico south through Central America to central South America; winters in all but northernmost portions of breeding range.

619. Lawrence's Goldfinch

Carduelis lawrencei (L— 5 W— 8)
Grayish-brown above; black face; yellow breast and belly; yellow patches on dark wings; yellow lower back and rump. *Female and winter male:* Grayish-brown above; yellowish breast; belly grayish or buff; yellow patches on dark wings; yellow on rump. *Voice:* Song— a succession of squeaky, high-pitched twitters. *Similar species:* Other goldfinches lack yellow on wings and rump. *Habitat:* Oak chaparral, pinyon-juniper. *Texas:* Casual in winter (Nov.–Mar.) in Trans-Pecos. *Range:* Breeds in coastal central and southern California and northern Baja California; winters in breeding range and east to southern Arizona and northwestern Mexico.

**620. American
Goldfinch**

Carduelis tristis (L— 5 W— 9)
Yellow body; black cap, wings, and tail; white at base of tail and wing bar; yellow shoulder patch. *Female and winter male:* Brownish above; yellowish or buff breast; whitish belly; dark wings with white wing bars. *Habits:* Usually in flocks; dipping-soaring flight, like a roller coaster. *Voice:* Song—a sequence of trills, whiney "tsoowee"s, and "ker-chik"s; flight call—a characteristic and unmistakable "ker-chik ker-chik-chik-chik." *Similar species:* See Lesser Goldfinch. *Habitat:* Prairie, savanna, thorn forest, brushy pastures and fields. *Texas:* Common to uncommon winter resident (Nov.–Mar.) throughout. *Range:* Breeds across southern Canada and northern and central U.S. to southern California and northern Baja California in west; winters in central and southern U.S. and northern Mexico.

**621. Evening
Grosbeak**

Coccothraustes vespertinus (L— 8 W— 13)
A chubby bird with heavy, yellowish or whitish bill; yellow body; black crown and brownish head with yellow forehead and eyebrow; black tail and wings with white wing patch. *Female:* Grayish above; buffy below; dark malar stripe; white wing patch. *Habits:* Usually in flocks. *Voice:* Calls—a sharp "peak" and a hoarse "peer." *Habitat:* Coniferous and mixed forest; often at bird feeders in winter. *Texas:* Rare and irregular winter visitor (Nov.–Mar.) to northern half. *Range:* Breeds in boreal portions of central and southern Canada and northern and western U.S., south in western mountains to western and central Mexico; winters in breeding range and in temperate and southern U.S.

Family Passeridae
House Sparrows

Like fringillids, these birds have large, conical bills. The single species found in Texas is introduced from the Old World. These birds build large, woven nests.

622. House Sparrow

Passer domesticus (L—6 W—10)
A chunky, heavy-billed bird; brown above with heavy dark brown streaks; dingy gray below; gray cap; chestnut nape; black lores, chin, and bib. *Female:* Streaked buff and brown above; dingy gray below; pale buff postorbital stripe. *Voice:* Song—"chip cheap chip chip chi-chi-chi chip," etc; call—"cheap." *Similar species:* See Dickcissel. *Habitat:* Urban areas, pastures, agricultural fields, feedlots, farms, grain elevators. *Texas:* Common permanent resident* throughout. *Range:* Resident in boreal, temperate, and subtropical regions of Old and New World; currently expanding into tropical regions. Introduced into western hemisphere in 1850.

PHOTOGRAPHERS

EDWIN R. BOGUSCH: House Sparrow

VERNON GROVE: Acorn Woodpecker; Altamira Oriole; American Coot; Anhinga; Ash-throated Flycatcher; Bald Eagle; Barn Swallow; Black-bellied Plover; Black-crowned Night-Heron; Black-headed Grosbeak; Black Skimmer; Blue-footed Booby; Brown Booby; Burrowing Owl; Cactus Wren; Canyon Towhee; Cinnamon Teal; Common Barn-Owl; Common Nighthawk; Common Snipe; Curve-billed Thrasher; Eastern Kingbird; Eastern Meadowlark; European Starling; Golden-fronted Woodpecker; Greater Roadrunner; Greater White-fronted Goose; Great Horned Owl; Green Kingfisher; Green-tailed Towhee; Hook-billed Kite; Hudsonian Godwit; Killdeer; King Rail; Lesser Golden-Plover; Lesser Yellowlegs; Loggerhead Shrike; Long-billed Curlew; Long-eared Owl; McCown's Longspur; Magnificent Frigatebird; Mallard; Marbled Godwit; Montezuma Quail; Mountain Plover; Mourning Dove; Northern Bobwhite; Northern Jacana; Northern Pintail; Northern Shoveler; Osprey; Phainopepla; Pied-billed Grebe; Purple Gallinule; Pyrrhuloxia; Red-bellied Woodpecker; Red-billed Tropicbird; Red-footed Booby; Red Phalarope; Red-tailed Hawk; Ruddy Duck; Savannah Sparrow; Scissor-tailed Flycatcher; Semipalmated Plover; Short-eared Owl; Snowy Owl; Sora; Swainson's Hawk; Thick-billed Kingbird; Tricolored Heron; Trumpeter Swan; Tundra Swan; Turkey Vulture; Vermilion Flycatcher; Western Kingbird; Whimbrel; White-breasted Nuthatch; White Ibis; Whooping Crane; Wood Stork

JOSEPH A. GRZYBOWSKI: Black-capped Vireo; Black-throated Blue Warbler; Chestnut-collared Longspur; Broad-tailed Hummingbird; Great Black-backed Gull; Lesser Prairie-Chicken; Louisiana Waterthrush; Northern Goshawk; Rock Wren; Rufous-crowned Sparrow; Rufous Hummingbird; Short-billed Dowitcher; Smith's Longspur; Western Screech-Owl; Western Wood-Pewee; Yellow-billed Loon

TYRRELL HARVEY: Curlew Sandpiper

GREG W. LASLEY: Purple Sandpiper

WILLIAM A. PAFF: American Avocet; American Bittern; American Goldfinch; Audubon's Oriole; Barnacle Goose; Barred Owl; Black-capped Chickadee; Black Tern; Blue-throated Hummingbird; Bobolink; Brant; Brewer's Blackbird; Broad-billed Hummingbird; Buff-bellied Hummingbird; California Gull; Canyon Wren; Common Moorhen; Common Redpoll; Dark-eyed Junco; Double-crested Cormorant; Dunlin; Eastern Bluebird; Field Sparrow; Glossy Ibis; Gray Kingbird; Great Kiskadee; Green-backed Heron; Green Jay; House Wren; Lark Bunting; Least Sandpiper; Limpkin; Little Blue Heron; Magnificent Hummingbird; Marsh Wren; Pileated Woodpecker; Plain Chachalaca; Purple Martin; Red-breasted Nuthatch; Ruby-throated Hummingbird; Ruddy Turnstone; Smooth-billed Ani; Snowy Egret; Spotted Owl; Tree Swallow; Western Grebe; Western Gull; Yellow-crowned Night-Heron

DAVID PARMELEE: American Woodcock; Arctic Loon; Arctic Tern; Common Tern; Glaucous Gull; King Eider, Oldsquaw; Parasitic Jaeger; Pectoral Sandpiper; Pomarine Jaeger; Red Knot; Red-necked Phalarope; Sabine's Gull; Semipalmated Sandpiper; Snow Bunting; Stilt Sandpiper; Thayer's Gull

JOHN RAPPOLE: American Crow; American Oystercatcher; Black-bellied Whistling-Duck; Black-billed Magpie; Black-shouldered Kite; Black Vulture; Boat-tailed Grackle; Brown-headed Nuthatch; Buff-breasted Sandpiper; Caspian Tern; Cedar Waxwing; Chimney Swift; Chuck-will's-widow; Couch's Kingbird; Crested Caracara; Downy Woodpecker; Eastern Phoebe; Ferruginous Pygmy-Owl; Forster's Tern; Grasshopper Sparrow; Greater Prairie-Chicken; Great-tailed Grackle; Groove-billed Ani; Gull-billed Tern; Harris' Hawk; Horned Lark; Laughing Gull; Mottled Owl; Northern Mockingbird; Olivaceous Cormorant; Piping Plover; Purple Finch; Reddish Egret; Ring-billed Gull; Royal Tern; Royal Tern and Caspian Tern; Sanderling; Spotted Sandpiper; Steller's Jay; Upland Sandpiper; Western Sandpiper; White-tipped Dove; White-winged Dove; Wild Turkey; Willet; Yellow-headed Parrot

BARTH SCHORRE: Alder Flycatcher; American Redstart; American White Pelican; American Wigeon; Anna's Hummingbird; Barrow's Goldeneye; Bay-breasted Warbler; Bell's Vireo; Black-and-White Warbler; Black-chinned Hummingbird; Black-legged Kittiwake; Black-necked Stilt; Black-throated Green Warbler; Blue Grosbeak; Blue Jay; Blue-winged Warbler; Bonaparte's Gull; Bronzed Cowbird; Brown-headed Cowbird; Brown Pelican; Brown Thrasher; Canada Goose; Canada Warbler; Carolina Wren; Cattle Egret; Cerulean Warbler; Chestnut-sided Warbler; Chipping Sparrow; Clark's Nutcracker; Clay-colored Sparrow; Common Yellowthroat; Dickcissel; Eastern Screech-Owl; Emperor Goose; Evening Grosbeak; Golden-crowned Sparrow; Golden-winged Warbler; Gray Catbird; Gray-cheeked Thrush; Great Blue Heron; Greater Flamingo; Greater Yellowlegs; Green-winged Teal; Harris' Sparrow; Heermann's Gull; Hermit Thrush; Herring Gull; Hooded Merganser; Hooded Oriole; House Finch; Inca Dove; Indigo Bunting; Kentucky Warbler; Lark Sparrow; Least Tern; Lincoln's Sparrow; Long-billed Thrasher; MacGillivray's Warbler; Magnolia Warbler; Mountain Bluebird; Mourning Warbler; Nashville Warbler; Northern Cardinal; Northern Flicker; Northern Oriole; Northern Parula; Northern Waterthrush; Ovenbird; Painted Bunting; Pine Siskin; Prairie Warbler; Prothonotary Warbler; Red-eyed Vireo; Redhead; Red-headed Woodpecker; Red-winged Blackbird; Ring-necked Duck; Roseate Spoonbill; Ross' Goose; Rufous-sided Towhee; Scarlet Ibis; Scarlet Tanager; Snow Goose; Solitary Vireo; Summer Tanager; Swainson's Thrush; Tennessee Warbler; Tufted Titmouse; Veery; Warbling Vireo; Western Tanager; White-crowned Sparrow; White-eyed Vireo; White-faced Ibis; White-throated Sparrow; Wilson's Plover; Wilson's Warbler; Wood Duck; Wood Thrush; Worm-eating Warbler; Yellow-billed Cuckoo; Yellow-breasted Chat; Yellow-headed Blackbird; Yellow-rumped Warbler—eastern (Myrtle Warbler); Yellow-throated Warbler; Yellow Warbler

CLIFF STOGNER: Hermit Warbler

GEORGE WAGNER: Gray-crowned Yellowthroat

VIREO/P. ALDEN: Bridled Tern; Vaux's Swift; White-collared Swift

VIREO/K. ARNOLD: Mississippi Kite; Pine Grosbeak

VIREO/S. BAHRT: Black Scoter; Bohemian Waxwing; Eastern Wood-Pewee; Ring-necked Pheasant

VIREO/R. BEHRSTOCK: Flammulated Owl

VIREO/R. K. BOWERS: Allen's Hummingbird; Baird's Sparrow; Colima Warbler; Elf Owl; Mew Gull; Sprague's Pipit

VIREO/K. BRINK: Long-tailed Jaeger

VIREO/A. CAREY: Western Meadowlark

VIREO/R. J. CHANDLER: Ruff

VIREO/B. CHUDLEIGH: Great Knot; Sharp-tailed Sandpiper

VIREO/H. CLARKE: Black-chinned Sparrow; Black-throated Gray Warbler; Botteri's Sparrow; Cassin's Kingbird; Cordilleran Flycatcher; Grace's Warbler; Greater Scaup; Plain Titmouse; Red-faced Warbler; Sage Sparrow; Surf Scoter; Townsend's Solitaire; Townsend's Warbler; Violet-green Swallow; White-throated Swift

VIREO/A. CRUICKSHANK: Canvasback; Lesser Scaup; Red-breasted Merganser

VIREO/H. CRUICKSHANK: Brewer's Sparrow; Brown Noddy; Franklin's Gull; Hepatic Tanager; Lazuli Bunting; Least Bittern; Olive Sparrow; Orange-crowned Warbler; Painted Redstart; Red-necked Grebe; Roseate Tern; Rusty Blackbird; Scott's Oriole; Snail Kite; Whip-poor-will; Wilson's Phalarope

VIREO/B. CURTIS: Mangrove Cuckoo

VIREO/P. DAVEY: Fulvous Whistling-Duck

VIREO/J. H. DICK: Bachman's Warbler; Harlequin Duck

VIREO/G. DREMEAUX: American Black Duck; Black-throated Sparrow; Common Black-headed Gull; Gray Flycatcher

VIREO/J. DUNNING: Acadian Flycatcher; Black-billed Cuckoo; Black Phoebe; Black-whiskered Vireo; Blue Bunting; Blue Ground-Dove; Brown-crested Flycatcher; Common Pauraque; Connecticut Warbler; Fork-tailed Flycatcher; Golden-crowned Warbler; Gray-breasted Martin; Greenish Elaenia; Green Violet-ear; Least Flycatcher; Lesser Goldfinch; Roadside Hawk; Rose-throated Becard; Rufous-capped Warbler; Rufous-tailed Hummingbird; Spotted Rail; Sulphur-bellied Flycatcher; Tropical Parula; Violet-crowned Hummingbird; White-collared Seedeater; White-eared Hummingbird; Yellow-bellied Flycatcher; Yellow-throated Vireo; Yucatán Vireo

VIREO/T. FITZHARRIS: Eared Grebe

VIREO/A. FORBES-WATSON: Masked Booby; White-tailed Tropicbird

VIREO/SAM FRIED: Clapper Rail; Dusky-capped Flycatcher; Green Parakeet; Henslow's Sparrow; Lesser Black-backed Gull; Lesser Nighthawk; Mexican Crow; Ruddy Ground-Dove; Virginia Rail

VIREO/B. GADSBY: Bufflehead; Common Goldeneye; Eurasian Wigeon; Garganey

VIREO/W. GREENE: Yellow-bellied Sapsucker

VIREO/C. H. GREENEWALT: Carolina Chickadee; Green-breasted Mango; Horned Grebe; Red-throated Loon; Tropical Kingbird

VIREO/F. C. HAAS: Band-rumped Storm-Petrel

VIREO/R. & M. HANSEN: Greater Shearwater

VIREO/V. HASSELBLAD: Bank Swallow

VIREO/B. HENRY: Red Crossbill; White-winged Crossbill

VIREO/D. R. HERR: Merlin

VIREO/J. HOFFMAN: Black-tailed Gnatcatcher; Bridled Titmouse; Bushtit; Crissal Thrasher; Lucy's Warbler; Northern Beardless-Tyrannulet; Verdin

VIREO/STEVEN HOLT: Carolina Parakeet; Passenger Pigeon; Red-cockaded Woodpecker

VIREO/M. HYETT: Wilson's Storm-Petrel

VIREO/M. P. KAHL: Aplomado Falcon

VIREO/H. C. KYLLINGSTAD: Bristle-thighed Curlew

VIREO/S. LAFRANCE: Cory's Shearwater; Lapland Longspur; Little Gull; Red-crowned Parrot; Sooty Shearwater; White-winged Scoter

VIREO/S. J. LANG: Common Loon; Great Crested Flycatcher; Willow Flycatcher

VIREO/GREG W. LASLEY: Bachman's Sparrow; Cave Swallow; Clay-colored Robin; Golden-cheeked Warbler; Gray Vireo; LeConte's Sparrow; Lewis' Woodpecker

VIREO/P. LA TOURRETTE: Bewick's Wren; Hutton's Vireo; Lawrence's Goldfinch

VIREO/G. LEBARON: Ivory-billed Woodpecker; Leach's Storm-Petrel

VIREO/S. LIPSCHUTZ: Pine Warbler

VIREO/M. MARIN: Double-striped Thick-knee

VIREO/C. MOHR: American Kestrel

VIREO/A. MORRIS: Baird's Sandpiper; Elegant Tern; Fish Crow; Fox Sparrow; Golden-crowned Kinglet; Iceland Gull; Long-billed Dowitcher; Sandwich Tern; Seaside Sparrow; Surfbird; White-rumped Sandpiper; Winter Wren

VIREO/C. MUNN: Jabiru; Least Grebe

VIREO/J. P. MYERS: Red-legged Cormorant

VIREO/C. NEWELL: Mottled Duck

VIREO/J. M. PENHALLURICK: Yellow-nosed Albatross

VIREO/O. S. PETTINGILL, JR.: Red-shouldered Hawk; Sedge Wren; Vesper Sparrow; White-cheeked Pintail

VIREO/B. RANDALL: Brown Creeper; Dusky Flycatcher; Elegant Trogon; Mountain Chickadee; Pygmy Nuthatch; Western Bluebird; Williamson's Sapsucker

VIREO/M. J. RAUZON: Audubon's Shearwater; Manx Shearwater; Sooty Tern

VIREO/D. ROBY: Northern Shrike

VIREO/JANE RUFFIN: Snowy Plover

VIREO/A. M. SADA: Brown Jay; Common Raven: Crane Hawk; Olive Warbler; Orange-breasted Bunting; Red-billed Pigeon

VIREO/CARL R. SAMS: Yellow Rail

VIREO/F. K. SCHLEICHER: Hairy Woodpecker; Northern Harrier; Peregrine Falcon; Sharp-tailed Sparrow; Swamp Sparrow

VIREO/BARTH SCHORRE: American Robin; Blackburnian Warbler; Blackpoll Warbler; Common Grackle; Common Ground-Dove; Great Egret; Hooded Warbler; Orchard Oriole; Philadelphia Vireo; Rose-breasted Grosbeak

VIREO/J. SCHUMACHER: Belted Kingfisher; Blue-winged Teal; Gadwall; Palm Warbler; Song Sparrow

VIREO/C. SPEEGLE: Spotted Redshank

VIREO/J. STASZ: Common Merganser

VIREO/P. W. SYKES: Masked Duck; Northern Gannet

VIREO/T. J. ULRICH: Black Swift; Varied Bunting

VIREO/ROBERT VILLANI: American Dipper

VIREO/R. WEBSTER: Clark's Grebe

VIREO/D. WECHSLER: Rock Dove

VIREO/B. K. WHEELER: American Swallow-tailed Kite; Broad-winged Hawk; Ferruginous Hawk; Golden Eagle; Gray Hawk; Prairie Falcon; Ringed King-fisher; Rough-legged Hawk; Sharp-shinned Hawk; Short-tailed Hawk; White-tailed Hawk; Zone-tailed Hawk

VIREO/J. R. WOODWARD: American Tree Sparrow; Blue-gray Gnatcatcher; Solitary Sandpiper

VIREO/D. & M. ZIMMERMAN: Abert's Towhee; American Pipit; Aztec Thrush; Band-tailed Pigeon; Bendire's Thrasher; Calliope Hummingbird; Cape May Warbler; Cassin's Finch; Cassin's Sparrow; Chihuahuan Raven; Cliff Swallow; Common Black-Hawk; Common Poorwill; Cooper's Hawk; Costa's Hummingbird; Gambel's Quail; Greater Pewee; Hammond's Flycatcher; Ladder-backed Woodpecker; Lucifer Hummingbird; Northern Pygmy-Owl; Northern Rough-winged Swallow; Northern Saw-whet Owl; Olive-sided Flycatcher; Pinyon Jay; Ruby-crowned Kinglet; Sage Thrasher; Sandhill Crane; Say's Phoebe; Scaled Quail; Scrub Jay; Virginia's Warbler; Yellow-eyed Junco; Yellow-rumped Warbler—western (Audubon's Warbler)

VIREO/T. ZUROWSKI: Varied Thrush

REFERENCES

Abbey, E. 1973. *Cactus Country.* Time-Life Books, New York.

American Ornithologists' Union. 1983. *Check-list of North American Birds,* 6th ed. American Ornithologists' Union, Lawrence, Kansas.

American Ornithologists' Union. 1985. Thirty-fifth supplement to the American Ornithologists' Union *Check-list of North American Birds. Auk* 102: 680–86.

American Ornithologists' Union. 1987. Thirty-sixth supplement to the American Ornithologists' Union *Check-list of North American Birds. Auk* 104: 591–96.

American Ornithologists' Union. 1989. Thirty-seventh supplement to the American Ornithologists' Union *Check-list of North American Birds. Auk* 106: 532–38.

Clark, W. S., and B. K. Wheeler. 1987. *A Field Guide to the Hawks of North America.* Houghton Mifflin, Boston.

Dickens, C. A. 1843. *A Christmas Carol* (Everyman's Library ed., 1961), J. M. Dent and Sons, London.

Dunne, P., and C. Sutton. 1989. *Hawks in Flight: Flight Identification of North American Migrant Raptors.* Houghton Mifflin, Boston.

Edwards, E. P. 1972. *A Field Guide to the Birds of Mexico.* E. P. Edwards, Sweet Briar, Virginia.

Forshaw, J. M. 1973. *Parrots of the World.* Doubleday, New York.

Grant, P. J. 1982. *Gulls: A Guide to Identification.* Poyser, Calton, Stoke on Trent, United Kingdom.

Harrison, P. 1983. *Seabirds: An Identification Guide.* Houghton Mifflin, Boston.

Hines, R. W. 1985. *Ducks at a Distance: A Waterfowl Identification Guide.* U.S. Fish and Wildlife Service, Washington, D.C.

Howell, A. H. 1932. Florida Bird Life. Coward-McCann, New York.

Johnsgard, P. A. 1979. *A Guide to North American Waterfowl.* Indiana Univ. Press, Bloomington.

Kutac, E. A. 1982. *Texas Birds: Where They Are and How to Find Them.* Lone Star Books, Gulf Publ. Co., Houston, Texas.

Lanyon, W. E., and J. Bull. 1967. Identification of Connecticut, Mourning, and MacGillivray's warblers. *Bird-Banding* 38:187–94.

McCracken, K. H. 1986. *Connie Hagar: A Life History of a Texas Birdwatcher.* Texas A&M Univ. Press, College Station.

McMurtry, L. 1985. *Lonesome Dove*. Simon and Schuster, New York.

Marchant J., and T. Prater. 1986. *Shorebirds: An Identification Guide*. Houghton Mifflin, Boston.

Michener, J. A. 1985. *Texas*. Random House, New York.

National Geographic Society. 1983. *Field Guide to the Birds of North America*. National Geographic Society, Washington, D.C.

Oberholser, H. 1974. *The Bird Life of Texas*. Univ. Texas Press, Austin.

Peterson, R. T. 1960. *A Field Guide to the Birds of Texas*. Houghton Mifflin, Boston.

Peterson, R. T. 1961. *A Field Guide to Western Birds*. Houghton Mifflin, Boston.

Peterson, R. T. 1980. *A Field Guide to the Birds: A Completely New Guide to All the Birds of Eastern and Central North America*, 4th ed. Houghton Mifflin, Boston.

Peterson, R. T., and E. L. Chalif. 1973. *A Field Guide to Mexican Birds*. Houghton Mifflin, Boston.

Phillips, A. R. 1986. *The Known Birds of North and Middle America, part I*. A. R. Phillips, Denver, Colorado.

Phillips, A. R., M. A. Howe, and W. E. Lanyon. 1966. Identification of the flycatchers of eastern North America, with special emphasis on the genus *Empidonax*. *Bird-Banding* 37:153–71.

Phillips, A. R., and W. E. Lanyon. 1970. Additional notes on the flycatchers of eastern North America. *Bird-Banding* 41:190–97.

Phillips, A. R., J. T. Marshall, and G. Monson. 1964. *The Birds of Arizona*. Univ. Arizona Press, Tucson.

Pulich, W. M., Sr. 1976. *The Golden-cheeked Warbler: A Bioecological Study*. Texas Parks and Wildlife Dept., Austin.

Pulich, W. M., Sr. 1988. *The Birds of North Central Texas*. Texas A&M Univ. Press, College Station.

Rappole, J. H., and G. W. Blacklock. 1985. *Birds of the Texas Coastal Bend*. Texas A&M Univ. Press, College Station.

Seyffert, K. D. 1985. The breeding birds of the Texas Panhandle. *Bull. Texas Ornith. Soc.* 18:7–20.

Slud, P. 1964. The birds of Costa Rica. *Bull. Amer. Mus. Natur. Hist.* 128.

Stiles, G. 1972. Age and sex determination in Rufous and Allen hummingbirds. *Condor* 74:25–32.

Stiles, G., and A. F. Skutch. 1989. *A Field Guide to the Birds of Costa Rica*. Cornell Univ. Press, Ithaca, New York.

Texas Ornithological Society. 1984. *Checklist of the Birds of Texas,* 2nd ed. Texas Ornithological Society, Austin.

Wauer, R. H. 1973. *Birds of the Big Bend National Park and Vicinity*. Univ. Texas Press, Austin.

Wolfe, L. R., W. M. Pulich, Sr., and J. A. Tucker. 1975. *Checklist of the Birds of Texas*. Texas Ornithological Society, Waco.

Color Plates

Abbreviations for Color Plates

B   Breeding plumage (Alternate plumage)
W   Winter plumage (Basic plumage)
I   Immature plumage
IM   Immature male plumage
AM   Adult male plumage
AF   Adult female plumage

1. Red-throated Loon (B)

3. Pacific Loon (B)

4. Common Loon (B)

5. Yellow-billed Loon (AM/B)

6. Least Grebe (B)

7. Pied-billed Grebe (B)

8. Horned Grebe (B)

9. Red-necked Grebe (B)

10. Eared Grebe (B)

11. Western Grebe

12. Clark's Grebe

13. Yellow-nosed Albatross

14. Cory's Shearwater

15. Greater Shearwater

16. Sooty Shearwater

17. Manx Shearwater

18. Audubon's Shearwater

19. Wilson's Storm-Petrel

20. Leach's Storm-Petrel

22. White-tailed Tropicbird

23. Red-billed Tropicbird

24. Masked Booby

25. Blue-footed Booby

26. Brown Booby

27. Red-footed Booby

28. Northern Gannet

29. American White Pelican (B)

30. Brown Pelican

31. Double-crested Cormorant

32. Olivaceous Cormorant

33. Red-legged Cormorant

34. Anhinga (AM/B)

35. Magnificent Frigatebird (I)

36. American Bittern

37. Least Bittern (AM)

38. Great Blue Heron (B)

39. Great Egret (B)

40. Snowy Egret (B)

41. Little Blue Heron (W)

42. Tricolored Heron (B)

43. Reddish Egret (B)

44. Cattle Egret (B)

45. Green-backed Heron

46. Black-crowned Night-Heron (B)

47. Yellow-crowned Night-Heron (W)

48. White Ibis (B)

49. Scarlet Ibis

50. Glossy Ibis (B)

51. White-faced Ibis (B)

52. Roseate Spoonbill (B)

53. Jabiru

54. Wood Stork

55. Greater Flamingo

56. Fulvous Whistling-Duck

57. Black-bellied Whistling-Duck

58. Tundra Swan

59. Trumpeter Swan

60. Greater White-fronted Goose

61. Snow Goose (white phase)

62. Ross' Goose

63. Emperor Goose

64. Brant

65. Barnacle Goose

66. Canada Goose

68. Wood Duck (AM)

69. Green-winged Teal (AM)

70. American Black Duck

71. Mottled Duck

72. Mallard (AM)

73. White-cheeked Pintail

74. Northern Pintail (AM & AF)

75. Garganey (AM)

76. Blue-winged Teal (AM & AF)

77. Cinnamon Teal (AM)

78. Northern Shoveler (AM)

79. Gadwall (AM & AF)

80. Eurasian Wigeon (AM & AF)

81. American Wigeon (AM)

82. Canvasback (AM)

83. Redhead (AM)

84. Ring-necked Duck (AM)

85. Greater Scaup (AM)

86. Lesser Scaup (AM)

87. King Eider (AM & AF)

88. Harlequin Duck (AM & AF)

89. Oldsquaw (AM/B & AF/B)

90. Black Scoter (AM)

91. Surf Scoter (AM)

92. White-winged Scoter (AM)

93. Common Goldeneye (AM)

94. Barrow's Goldeneye (AM)

95. Bufflehead (AM & AF)

96. Hooded Merganser (AM)

97. Common Merganser (AM)

98. Red-breasted Merganser (AF)

99. Ruddy Duck (AF/B)

100. Masked Duck (AM/B)

101. Black Vulture

102. Turkey Vulture

103. Osprey

104. Hook-billed Kite (AM)

105. American Swallow-tailed Kite

106. Black-shouldered Kite

107. Snail Kite (I)

108. Mississippi Kite

109. Bald Eagle

110. Northern Harrier (I)

112. Cooper's Hawk (I)

113. Northern Goshawk (I)

113. Northern Goshawk

114. Crane Hawk

115. Common Black-Hawk

116. Harris' Hawk

117. Gray Hawk

118. Roadside Hawk

119. Red-shouldered Hawk

120. Broad-winged Hawk (I)

121. Short-tailed Hawk (dark phase)

122. Swainson's Hawk

123. White-tailed Hawk

124. Zone-tailed Hawk

125. Red-tailed Hawk

126. Ferruginous Hawk (I)

127. Rough-legged Hawk

128. Golden Eagle

129. Crested Caracara

130. American Kestrel (AM)

131. Merlin

132. Aplomado Falcon

133. Peregrine Falcon

134. Prairie Falcon

135. Plain Chachalaca (W)

136. Ring-necked Pheasant (AM)

137. Greater Prairie-Chicken (AM)

138. Lesser Prairie-Chicken (AM)

139. Wild Turkey (AM)

140. Montezuma Quail (AM)

141. Northern Bobwhite (AM)

142. Scaled Quail (AM & AF)

143. Gambel's Quail (AM)

144. Yellow Rail

146. Clapper Rail

147. King Rail

148. Virginia Rail

149. Sora (AM/B)

151. Spotted Rail

152. Purple Gallinule

153. Common Moorhen

154. American Coot

155. Limpkin

156. Sandhill Crane

157. Whooping Crane

158. Double-striped Thick-knee

159. Black-bellied Plover (B)

160. Lesser Golden-Plover (B)

161. Snowy Plover (B/AM)

162. Wilson's Plover (AM/B)

163. Semipalmated Plover (AM/B)

164. Piping Plover (W)

165. Killdeer

166. Mountain Plover (W)

167. American Oystercatcher

168. Black-necked Stilt (AM)

169. American Avocet (B)

170. Northern Jacana

171. Greater Yellowlegs (B)

172. Lesser Yellowlegs (B)

173. Spotted Redshank

174. Solitary Sandpiper (B)

175. Willet (W)

176. Spotted Sandpiper (B)

177. Upland Sandpiper

179. Whimbrel

180. Bristle-thighed Curlew

181. Long-billed Curlew

182. Hudsonian Godwit (B)

184. Marbled Godwit (W)

185. Ruddy Turnstone (W)

186. Surfbird (B)

187. Great Knot (W)

188. Red Knot (B)

189. Sanderling (W)

190. Semipalmated Sandpiper (B)

191. Western Sandpiper (W)

192. Least Sandpiper (B)

193. White-rumped Sandpiper (B)

194. Baird's Sandpiper (B)

195. Pectoral Sandpiper (B)

196. Sharp-tailed Sandpiper (B)

197. Purple Sandpiper (W)

198. Dunlin (B)

199. Curlew Sandpiper (B)

200. Stilt Sandpiper (B)

201. Buff-breasted Sandpiper

202. Ruff (W)

203. Short-billed Dowitcher (W)

204. Long-billed Dowitcher (W)

205. Common Snipe

206. American Woodcock

207. Wilson's Phalarope (AF/B & AM/B)

208. Red Phalarope (AM/B)

209. Red-necked Phalarope (AF/B)

210. Pomarine Jaeger (B)

211. Parasitic Jaeger

212. Long-tailed Jaeger

214. Laughing Gull (AM/B & AM/W)

215. Franklin's Gull (B)

216. Little Gull (W)

217. Common Black-headed Gull (B)

218. Bonaparte's Gull (W)

219. Heermann's Gull (W)

220. Mew Gull (B)

221. Ring-billed Gull (B)

222. California Gull (W)

223. Herring Gull (B)

224. Thayer's Gull (B)

225. Iceland Gull (W)

226. Lesser Black-backed Gull (W)

228. Western Gull (W)

229. Glaucous Gull (B)

230. Great Black-backed Gull (I)

231. Black-legged Kittiwake (W)

232. Sabine's Gull (B)

233. Gull-billed Tern (B)

234. Caspian Tern (B)

235. Royal Tern (I)

236. Elegant Tern (W)

237. Sandwich Tern (W)

238. Roseate Tern (B)

239. Common Tern (B)

240. Arctic Tern (B)

241. Forster's Tern (W)

242. Least Tern (B)

243. Bridled Tern

244. Sooty Tern

245. Black Tern (W)

246. Brown Noddy

248. Black Skimmer (B)

249. Rock Dove

251. Red-billed Pigeon

252. Band-tailed Pigeon

254. White-winged Dove (AM/B)

255. Mourning Dove

256. Passenger Pigeon

257. Inca Dove

258. Common Ground-Dove (AF)

259. Ruddy Ground-Dove (AF)

260. Blue Ground-Dove (AM)

261. White-tipped Dove

264. Carolina Parakeet

265. Green Parakeet

267. Red-crowned Parrot

270. Yellow-headed Parrot

271. Black-billed Cuckoo

272. Yellow-billed Cuckoo

273. Mangrove Cuckoo

274. Greater Roadrunner (AM)

275. Smooth-billed Ani

276. Groove-billed Ani

277. Common Barn-Owl

278. Flammulated Owl

279. Eastern Screech-Owl (gray phase)

280. Western Screech-Owl

281. Great Horned Owl

282. Snowy Owl

283. Northern Pygmy-Owl

284. Ferruginous Pygmy-Owl

285. Elf Owl

286. Burrowing Owl

287. Mottled Owl

288. Spotted Owl

289. Barred Owl

290. Long-eared Owl

291. Short-eared Owl

292. Northern Saw-whet Owl

293. Lesser Nighthawk

294. Common Nighthawk

295. Common Pauraque

296. Common Poorwill

297. Chuck-will's-widow

298. Whip-poor-will

299. Black Swift

300. White-collared Swift

301. Chimney Swift

302. Vaux's Swift

303. White-throated Swift

304. Green Violet-ear

305. Green-breasted Mango (AM)

308. Broad-billed Hummingbird (AM)

309. White-eared Hummingbird (AM)

310. Rufous-tailed Hummingbird

311. Buff-bellied Hummingbird (I)

312. Violet-crowned Hummingbird (AF)

313. Blue-throated Hummingbird (AF)

314. Magnificent Hummingbird (AM)

315. Lucifer Hummingbird (AM)

316. Ruby-throated Hummingbird (AM)

317. Black-chinned Hummingbird (AM)

318. Anna's Hummingbird (AM)

319. Costa's Hummingbird (AM)

320. Calliope Hummingbird (AM)

321. Broad-tailed Hummingbird (AM)

322. Rufous Hummingbird (AF)

323. Allen's Hummingbird (AF)

324. Elegant Trogon (AM)

325. Ringed Kingfisher (AM)

326. Belted Kingfisher (AM)

327. Green Kingfisher

328. Lewis' Woodpecker

329. Red-headed Woodpecker

330. Acorn Woodpecker (AM)

331. Golden-fronted Woodpecker (AM)

332. Red-bellied Woodpecker (AM)

333. Yellow-bellied Sapsucker (AM)

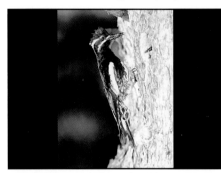

334. Williamson's Sapsucker (AM)

335. Ladder-backed Woodpecker (AM)

336. Downy Woodpecker (AF)

337. Hairy Woodpecker (AM)

338. Red-cockaded Woodpecker (AF)

339. Northern Flicker (western form) (AM)

340. Pileated Woodpecker (AF)

341. Ivory-billed Woodpecker (AM)

342. Northern Beardless-Tyrannulet

343. Greenish Elaenia

345. Olive-sided Flycatcher

346. Greater Pewee

347. Western Wood-Pewee

348. Eastern Wood-Pewee

349. Yellow-bellied Flycatcher (I)

350. Acadian Flycatcher

351. Alder Flycatcher

352. Willow Flycatcher

353. Least Flycatcher

354. Hammond's Flycatcher

355. Dusky Flycatcher

356. Gray Flycatcher

357. Cordilleran Flycatcher (I)

359. Plack Phoebe

360. Eastern Phoebe

361. Say's Phoebe

362. Vermilion Flycatcher (AM)

363. Dusky-capped Flycatcher

364. Ash-throated Flycatcher

365. Great Crested Flycatcher

366. Brown-crested Flycatcher

367. Great Kiskadee

368. Sulphur-bellied Flycatcher

369. Tropical Kingbird

370. Couch's Kingbird

371. Cassin's Kingbird

372. Thick-billed Kingbird

373. Western Kingbird

374. Eastern Kingbird

375. Gray Kingbird

376. Scissor-tailed Flycatcher

377. Fork-tailed Flycatcher

378. Rose-throated Becard (IM)

380. Horned Lark

381. Purple Martin (AF)

382. Gray-breasted Martin

383. Tree Swallow (AM)

384. Violet-green Swallow (AM)

385. Northern Rough-winged Swallow

386. Bank Swallow

387. Cliff Swallow

388. Cave Swallow

389. Barn Swallow

390. Steller's Jay

391. Blue Jay

392. Green Jay

393. Brown Jay (I)

394. Scrub Jay

396. Pinyon Jay

397. Clark's Nutcracker

398. Black-billed Magpie

399. American Crow

400. Mexican Crow

401. Fish Crow

402. Chihuahuan Raven

403. Common Raven

404. Black-capped Chickadee

405. Carolina Chickadee

406. Mountain Chickadee

407. Bridled Titmouse

408. Plain Titmouse

409. Tufted Titmouse (black crested)

410. Verdin

411. Bushtit

412. Red-breasted Nuthatch (AF)

413. White-breasted Nuthatch (AM)

414. Pygmy Nuthatch

415. Brown-headed Nuthatch

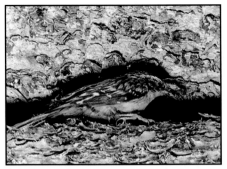

416. Brown Creeper

417. Cactus Wren

418. Rock Wren

419. Canyon Wren

420. Carolina Wren

421. Bewick's Wren

422. House Wren

423. Winter Wren

424. Sedge Wren

425. Marsh Wren

426. American Dipper (I)

427. Golden-crowned Kinglet (AF)

428. Ruby-crowned Kinglet (AF)

429. Blue-gray Gnatcatcher (AF)

430. Black-tailed Gnatcatcher (AF)

431. Eastern Bluebird (AM)

432. Western Bluebird (AM)

433. Mountain Bluebird (AM)

434. Townsend's Solitaire

435. Veery

436. Gray-cheeked Thrush

437. Swainson's Thrush

438. Hermit Thrush

439. Wood Thrush

440. Clay-colored Robin

442. American Robin (AM)

443. Varied Thrush (AM)

444. Aztec Thrush (AM)

445. Gray Catbird

447. Northern Mockingbird

448. Sage Thrasher

449. Brown Thrasher

450. Long-billed Thrasher

451. Bendire's Thrasher

452. Curve-billed Thrasher

453. Crissal Thrasher

454. American Pipit

455. Sprague's Pipit

456. Bohemian Waxwing

457. Cedar Waxwing

459. Phainopepla (AM)

460. Northern Shrike

461. Loggerhead Shrike

462. European Starling

463. White-eyed Vireo

464. Bell's Vireo

465. Black-capped Vireo (AM)

466. Gray Vireo

467. Solitary Vireo

468. Yellow-throated Vireo

469. Hutton's Vireo

470. Warbling Vireo

471. Philadelphia Vireo

472. Red-eyed Vireo (I)

474. Black-whiskered Vireo (I)

475. Yucatán Vireo

476. Bachman's Warbler (AM)

477. Blue-winged Warbler (AM)

478. Golden-winged Warbler (AM)

479. Tennessee Warbler (AM)

480. Orange-crowned Warbler

481. Nashville Warbler (AM)

482. Virginia's Warbler (AF)

483. Colima Warbler

484. Lucy's Warbler

485. Northern Parula (AF)

486. Tropical Parula (AM)

487. Yellow Warbler (AM)

488. Chestnut-sided Warbler (AM/B)

489. Magnolia Warbler (AM/B)

490. Cape May Warbler (AM/B)

491. Black-throated Blue Warbler (AM)

492a. Yellow-rumped Warbler (Myrtle Warbler) (W)   492b. Yellow-rumped Warbler (Audubon's Warbler) (AM/B)

493. Black-throated Gray Warbler (AM)   494. Townsend's Warbler (AM)

495. Hermit Warbler (AM)   496. Black-throated Green Warbler (AM)

497. Golden-cheeked Warbler (AM)   498. Blackburnian Warbler (AM)

499. Yellow-throated Warbler (AF)

500. Grace's Warbler (AM)

501. Pine Warbler (AM)

502. Prairie Warbler (AF)

503. Palm Warbler (B)

504. Bay-breasted Warbler (AM/B)

505. Blackpoll Warbler (AM/B)

506. Cerulean Warbler (AM)

507. Black-and-White Warbler (AM)

508. American Redstart (AM)

509. Prothonotary Warbler (AM)

510. Worm-eating Warbler

512. Ovenbird

513. Northern Waterthrush

514. Louisiana Waterthrush

515. Kentucky Warbler (AM)

516. Connecticut Warbler (AF)

517. Mourning Warbler (AM)

518. MacGillivray's Warbler (AM)

519. Common Yellowthroat (AM)

520. Gray-crowned Yellowthroat (AM)

521. Hooded Warbler (AM)

522. Wilson's Warbler (AM)

523. Canada Warbler (AM)

524. Red-faced Warbler

525. Painted Redstart

526. Golden-crowned Warbler

527. Rufous-capped Warbler

528. Yellow-breasted Chat

529. Olive Warbler (AM)

530. Hepatic Tanager (AM)

531. Summer Tanager (AM)

532. Scarlet Tanager (AM/B)

533. Western Tanager (AM/B)

535. Northern Cardinal (AM)

536. Pyrrhuloxia (AM)

537. Rose-breasted Grosbeak (AM)

538. Black-headed Grosbeak (IM)

539. Blue Bunting (AM)

540. Blue Grosbeak (AM)

541. Lazuli Bunting (AM)

542. Indigo Bunting (AM)

543. Varied Bunting (AM)

544. Orange-breasted Bunting (AM)

545. Painted Bunting (AM)

546. Dickcissel (AM/B)

547. Olive Sparrow

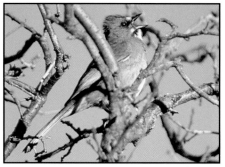

548. Green-tailed Towhee (B)

549. Rufous-sided Towhee (western race) (AM) 550. Canyon Towhee

551. Abert's Towhee 552. White-collared Seedeater (AM)

554. Bachman's Sparrow 555. Botteri's Sparrow

556. Cassin's Sparrow 557. Rufous-crowned Sparrow

558. American Tree Sparrow

559. Chipping Sparrow (B)

560. Clay-colored Sparrow

561. Brewer's Sparrow

562. Field Sparrow

563. Black-chinned Sparrow (AM)

564. Vesper Sparrow

565. Lark Sparrow

566. Black-throated Sparrow

567. Sage Sparrow

568. Lark Bunting (AM/B)

569. Savannah Sparrow

570. Baird's Sparrow

571. Grasshopper Sparrow

572. Henslow's Sparrow

573. LeConte's Sparrow

574. Sharp-tailed Sparrow

575. Seaside Sparrow

576. Fox Sparrow

577. Song Sparrow

578. Lincoln's Sparrow

579. Swamp Sparrow (B)

580. White-throated Sparrow

581. Golden-crowned Sparrow (B)

582. White-crowned Sparrow

583. Harris' Sparrow (W)

584. Dark-eyed Junco (slate-colored group) (M)

585. Yellow-eyed Junco (M)

586. McCown's Longspur (AM/B)

587. Lapland Longspur (AM/W)

588. Smith's Longspur (W)

589. Chestnut-collared Longspur (AM/W)

590. Snow Bunting (AM/B)

591. Bobolink (AF)

592. Red-winged Blackbird (AM/B)

593. Eastern Meadowlark

594. Western Meadowlark

595. Yellow-headed Blackbird (AM)

596. Rusty Blackbird (AM/B)

597. Brewer's Blackbird (AM)

598. Great-tailed Grackle (AM & AF)

599. Boat-tailed Grackle (AM)

600. Common Grackle (AM)

601. Bronzed Cowbird (AM)

602. Brown-headed Cowbird (AM)

604. Orchard Oriole (AM)

605. Hooded Oriole (AM)

606. Altamira Oriole

607. Audubon's Oriole

608. Northern Oriole (eastern form) (AM)

609. Scott's Oriole (AM)

610. Pine Grosbeak (AM)

611. Purple Finch (AM)

612. Cassin's Finch (AM)

613. House Finch (AM)

614. Red Crossbill (AM)

615. White-winged Crossbill (AM)

616. Common Redpoll (AF/W)

617. Pine Siskin

618. Lesser Goldfinch (AM)

619. Lawrence's Goldfinch (AM/B)

620. American Goldfinch (F/W)

621. Evening Grosbeak (AM)

622. House Sparrow (AM)

INDEX

(Latin names and page numbers that refer to illustrations are italicized)